AT THE OPEN MARGIN:

The NPS's Administration of Theodore Roosevelt National Park

by David Harmon

THEODORE ROOSEVELT NATURE & HISTORY ASSOCIATION

MEDORA, NORTH DAKOTA

The Theodore Roosevelt Nature and History Association is a
non-profit cooperating association whose purpose is to aid
the educational, scientific, and research programs of the
National Park System areas in North Dakota. Membership in
the association is open to the public.

Published by the Theodore Roosevelt Nature and History
Association, P.O. Box 167, Medora, North Dakota 58645.

International Standard Book Number 0-9601652-3-1

Printed in the United States of America.

It was a land of vast silent spaces, of lonely rivers,
and of plains where the wild game stared at the passing
horseman.
                    -- Theodore Roosevelt, An Autobiography

Contents

List of Figures and Tables

Preface

When the National Park Service sent the State of the Parks Report to Congress in 1980, it publicly acknowledged some of the most difficult problems currently facing the System. Internal threats to the parks have been known for many years,[1] but the value of the State of the Parks Report is in its account of the sheer extent of external threats to the System. In four of the seven "threat categories," external exceeded internal sources.[2]

Moreover, the National Park System is now undergoing considerable expansion: not of territory, but of its own agenda for action, constituency, and sense of purpose. This expansion is partly responsible for the lack of fundamental data and managerial expertise the Report so deplores.

I have made the expansion of national park responsibilities, roles, and problems the point of departure for this history. My analysis of Theodore Roosevelt National Park follows these premises:

1) The park doesn't stand alone; it is an active member of the local and regional community.

2) As a community member, the park increasingly depends upon outside entities that can help or hinder the fulfillment of its mission.

3) As this situation has become more and more apparent, the park's administration has changed accordingly.

4) The transition from National Memorial Park to National Park is a fitting backdrop to these management changes.

Theodore Roosevelt is not comparable in scale with the great wilderness parks of the West. It is not a pristine wild area. Even so, when the park was created in the 1940s it was a pristine rural area, one of only a few parks where continuing processes in nature and the imprint of human living were of equal interest. It remains a rural park today, somewhat civilized, but even in the pride of summer the beauty of its landforms is underlain with the same vein of menace that fascinated the dude Roosevelt. The park is rural, but never pastoral; still rural, but no longer pristine. Recollection of the perfectly rural setting the park enjoyed thirty-five years ago makes the recent physical and social dislocations associated with energy development in the northern Great Plains all the more bitter to the spiritual descendants of Roosevelt, those who still cherish "ranch life in the Far West."

Threats exist, then, not only to the physical resources of the park, but to the collective memory of a unique way of life. This bears upon one of the park's goals: to provide a setting which allows the motivated visitor to re-create the experience of Roosevelt himself. Such opportunities are more possible than one might think. For example, much of the oil development in the immediate vicinity of the park has taken place between the Elkhorn Unit, site of Roosevelt's home ranch, and the South Unit. As late as the early 1970s, the Elkhorn was only a little less isolated than in the open range days, and visitors travelling up from the South Unit could share Roosevelt's sense of adventure in going to his retreat. Now, oil roads have been cut and wells dug all through the intervening country, and the Elkhorn's isolation is gone. With it passed a chance for the visitor to empathize with Roosevelt. A potential linkage across time has been lost.[3]

A note on other histories

Two histories of the park have already been written. Dale Strand's account, completed in 1962 as a master's thesis for the University of North Dakota, is useful for events in the late 1920s and early 1930s. He also documents the Greater North Dakota Association's role in the park's development, but overstates its importance. Strand takes a narrow, commercial view of the value of the park.

Rather more balanced is Warren Petty's history completed during his tenure in Medora as park historian. There are two versions of this study: a draft of 1965 in the park library, and an abridged version which appeared in the Spring 1968 issue of North Dakota History. The draft manuscript is the more valuable. Petty is strongest on events up until 1947.[4]

Documentation in this paper

Keep in mind that whenever reference is made to "Theodore Roosevelt," the park is meant; "Roosevelt" refers to the man (except, of course, in some of the quoted matter).

Notes are usually in the forms recommended by the 13th edition of the Chicago Manual of Style. Numbers in parentheses are used instead of superscripts after single-spaced, indented quotations.

The following abbreviations are used in the notes:

BLM	Bureau of Land Management
DSC	Denver Service Center, National Park Service
MWRO	Midwest Regional Office, National Park Service
NDGS	North Dakota Geological Survey
NDSDH	North Dakota State Department of Health
NHP	National Historical Park
NHS	National Historic Site
NM	National Monument
NP	National Park
NPS	National Park Service
Reg. Dir.	Regional Director
RMRO	Rocky Mountain Regional Office, National Park Service
SHSND	State Historical Society of North Dakota
Supt.	Superintendent
THRO	Theodore Roosevelt National (Memorial) Park
USFS	United States Forest Service
USFWS	United States Fish and Wildlife Service
USGS	United States Geological Survey
WASO	Washington Office, National Park Service
WL	William Lemke

Unless otherwise indicated, all letters, memorandums, theses, and dissertations are unpublished. The following abbreviations are used for locations of unpublished material:

THRO-A	Theodore Roosevelt National Park administration building, Medora
THRO-L	Theodore Roosevelt National Park library, Medora
THRO-S	Theodore Roosevelt National Park storage building, Medora
WL Papers	William Lemke Papers, Chester Fritz Library, University of North Dakota, Grand Forks

Notes to the Preface

1. The much-quoted phrase "loving the parks to death" may even predate the National Park Service. See William C. Everhart, The National Park Service (Boulder, CO: Westview Press, 1983), 177.

2. "State of the Parks Report 1980," unpublished MS (Denver: RMRO, 1980), 7. Of the 4345 threats reported, 2391 were external and 1954 internal.

3. The local county government (Billings County) also plans to build a bridge across the Little Missouri River near the Elkhorn within the next ten years. Micki Hellickson (Chief Naturalist, THRO) to author, 14 May 1985. Note also that, as defined in the summary of the State of the Parks Report (p. 1), "threat" refers not only to activities damaging physical resources, but to those degrading park values or experiences.

4. Strand's thesis was apparently unknown to or ignored by Petty. See Dale J. Strand, "The History of the Theodore Roosevelt National Memorial Park" (master's thesis, University of North Dakota, Grand Forks, 1962); Warren J. Petty, "History of Theodore Roosevelt National Memorial Park (draft)," unpublished MS, ca. 1965 (THRO-L) (hereafter cited as "Draft History"); Warren James Petty, "History of Theodore Roosevelt National Memorial Park," North Dakota History: Journal of the Northern Plains 35:2 (Spring 1968), 385-441 (hereafter cited as "History").

Acknowledgments

This history is a record of hard work, of people working to preserve history, both human and natural. It is also the product of hard work, and not just my own.

Dale Blahna, Steve Brechin, and Mark Fly, three friends at the University of Michigan, helped me in many ways, not the least of which was passing along their knowledge of outdoor recreation and conservation.

The Theodore Roosevelt Nature and History Association was generous enough to support my research at the park. It is a model cooperative association whose endeavors deserve the highest praise.

Dan Rylance of the Department of Special Collections at the Chester Fritz Library of the University of North Dakota provided me with copies of William Lemke's correspondence in a timely fashion. The State Historical Society in Bismarck also assisted with archival research.

Edwin C. Bearss and Barry Mackintosh of the Washington Office of the National Park Service did me the favor of reading the entire manuscript. Jim Bennett, John P. Christiano, Don Henderson, Deborah Mangis, Mark Scruggs, and Chris Shaver of the Service's Ar Quality Division in Denver reviewed the portions relating to air quality. Their comments have been most helpful. Of course, the analysis and interpretation of events are mine alone, as is the responsibility for accuracy.

Whatever is good about this history is creditable to the staff at Theodore Roosevelt. It was my pleasure to work with them for a summer's time. Jeff Bradybaugh, Paula Cech, Robert Powell, Skip Snow, Susan Snow, Barry Sullivan, Patti Sullivan, and Harvey Wickware all offered useful suggestions, research assistance, or critiques of the text. I especially thank Micki Hellickson, the park's chief naturalist. She knows the North Dakota badlands as well as anyone and her knowledge, coupled with an unstinting interest in my research, have made this a demonstrably better history. To all the staff I extend my thanks. In their dedication they epitomize the finest qualities of the National Park Service; in their vigor and love of nature they epitomize the finest qualities of Roosevelt himself. Perhaps that is his best memorial.

Part 1:

The Intent of the Government

> One of the most troublesome of the park proposals
> of these years and later was for the Theodore
> Roosevelt Memorial National Park in North
> Dakota. . . .
>   -- John Ise

1) The Creation of the Park

For some in North Dakota, the national park idea was nothing more than a money idea.

"Twenty-five hundred miles of startling scenic beauty," blared the advertisement by the National Parks Highway Association of Jamestown, North Dakota. The year was 1927; the group, a collection of entrepreneurs looking to build tourism in a state with none to speak of; the advertisement, a pamphlet touting a motoring route which would link four of the finest parks then in existence. The Association's logo consisted of four medallions, one each for Yellowstone, Glacier, Crater Lake, and Mount Rainier, arrayed around a larger central one bearing the legend "Roosevelt National Park." But inscribed in tiny letters above that legend was the one-word rub: "proposed."[1]

The National Parks Highway Association's unabashed promotion of a national park for North Dakota, one that could stand alongside a Yellowstone, was a logical consequence of the attitude prevailing in the National Park Service during its first years. Stephen Tyng Mather, the agency's first director, wanted the Park Service (created in 1916) to cater to the devotees of the recently-born craze for automobile touring. No doubt sharing Mather's desire to build as broad a base of support as possible for the new agency, Secretary of the Interior Franklin K. Lane helped set the tone by proclaiming national parks "the people's playgrounds." It was admitted that, for most of these motorists, "the parks were merely the latest travel sensation, serving as objectives for the passion for the long road, which only then was finding its larger expression." Nevertheless, their motivations were of secondary concern to Mather, who had to put people in the parks if he were to demonstrate the need for a National Park Service. He invited the newly mobile public-at-leisure into the parks by endorsing schemes such as the National Park-to-Park Highway, a 3500-mile loop originating in Denver.[2] The National Parks Highway Association of North Dakota was simply following a respected example.

Yet almost as soon as he had begun, Mather was forced to back away from encouraging every park booster group which came along. He was quickly engulfed with park plans that did not come anywhere near the high standards he wanted for the System. Mather realized it would take a good portion of the agency's and his own personal time to sift out park proposals from profit proposals.[3] Unfortunately for the North Dakota park promoters, their efforts on behalf of a Roosevelt national park got underway in earnest just as the NPS retrenchment was taking place.

The retreat was not unnoticed by the most important of the park boosters, the Roosevelt Memorial National Park Association. As early as 1924 it discerned "a well-established policy in the western states to discourage the creation of more national parks" because existing ones were supposedly in dire need of improvement. In the sudden absence of encouragement, the Roosevelt Memorial National Park Association approached its own national park idea along a number of tacks.[4]

National parks, it thought, were devices to promote social equity:

> This policy [of discouragement] must be changed. Federal parks are for all the people, not alone for those who have the time and means to travel far. Some state must lead in the attempt to break down the restriction. Evidently that duty is to fall to North Dakota. (5)

Or scenic wonderlands:

> Evidently in the opinion of the Park Service authorities, the question of chief importance is whether or not this region possesses an adequate scenic asset. . . . A part of the [Association's] park plan is the construction of a state and national highway from Marmarth to Watford City following the edge of the [Little Missouri River] canyon with many observation points from which the beauty of the Bad Lands may be appreciated. (6)

Or public health facilities of a kind with sanitariums and hospitals:

> The people who most need such facilities cannot afford either the time or the means to visit them. . . . The state and nation must co-operate to provide health facilities adequate to the needs of the people. (7)

In these statements the Roosevelt Memorial National Park Association (later, the Greater North Dakota Association) fleshed out three themes which have recurred throughout the history of the park.

First, its social equity argument was less about making the fruits of federalism available to everyone than it was a statement of pique. The Association, which presumed to speak for all the people of North Dakota, felt the Park Service was slighting it because it represented a sparsely-populated farm state. Such feelings of inferiority are perhaps just now beginning to recede with the redesignation of Theodore Roosevelt as a National Park: when the state had only a National Memorial Park, it seemed to say something about where North Dakota stood, not only with the Park Service, but with the rest of the nation.

Second, disagreements over the scenic quality of the North Dakota badlands have persisted since Brigadier General Alfred Sully, marching through the region on a punitive expedition against Indians, reportedly called it "hell with the fires out." When the naturalist writer John Burroughs visited the badlands with President Roosevelt just after the turn of the century, his reaction was, surprisingly, just as simplistic. He found the region "utterly demoralized and gone to the bad--flayed, fantastic, treeless, a riot of naked clay slopes, chimney-like buttes and dry coulees." A century later these remarks still have to be lived down. Scenic value has always been an important and sometimes decisive criterion used in selecting new national parks.[8] But it is undeniably subjective, and decisions which rely upon it leave themselves open to endless debate.

Third, when the Roosevelt Memorial National Park Association placed national parks alongside hospitals and sanitariums, it was hinting at an understanding of the intangible benefits of national parks. When Theodore Roosevelt National Memorial Park was finally created in 1947 and 1948, most of its supporters still valued it solely as a marketable commodity. Yet a few of the more insightful saw it primarily as a necessity for health, a needed contrast to civilization, a refuge for the spirit.

But the primacy of the materialistic park idea has never been challenged. When thoughts of a national park for North Dakota first gained currency around 1920, the ranchers were the only local group that might reasonably have been expected to oppose the idea. Yet at first they were rather favorable, hoping that a park might draw enough dudes to their ranches to provide a supplementary income.[9] But as soon as they learned of the size of the first formal proposal, of the amount of grazing land that would be needed, they became dead set against it.

Without their support, even the "strong agitation" the park promoters used to advance the establishment of a reserve covering most of the watershed of the Little Missouri River could not turn the issue. One early plan called for a park of 1,300,000 acres, or 2030 square miles. If approved, it would have been the third largest national park then in existence. But such grandiose pro-posals included far, far too much good stock land for the liking of the ranchers. Once opposed, they stayed that way, and rejected another plan of 1927 that called for a much smaller park: a strip of land twelve to fourteen miles wide extending ninety miles along the Little

Missouri from Marmarth to the eastern swing of the river south of Watford City. The ultimate strength of the ranchers's political position is demonstrated by the fact that, once in 1927 and three times in 1929, the North Dakota Legislative Assembly went on record favoring a park, yet could not translate its sentiment into any effective action at all.[10]

The badlands New Deal

But economics, not politics, dictated the future to many ranchers as the agricultural depression of the 1920s became the Great Depression of the 1930s. In western North Dakota, many ranches were homesteads that had only recently been established. Between 1900 and 1910 the rural population, number of farms, and amount of land in agriculture increased fourfold in that part of the state. Growth continued until the farm price collapse of 1920. Things only got worse in the early 1930s. Average annual income for farms in North Dakota fell from $2775 to $804 in the space of two years,[11] and many homestead claims in the badlands were abandoned outright. A good number of other ranchers looked to sell out, and at just about any price. But there were no buyers in the private sector for this "submarginal" land.

It took the election of another Roosevelt to set in motion the events that led to the creation of the park. About a year into Franklin D. Roosevelt's first term, his new Resettlement Administration was given authority to buy land of little agricultural value. Under this program many of the homesteaders in western North Dakota were only too happy to get rid of acreage that was barely productive. There was no official pressure to sell, but one badlands rancher recalled that "some of the land buyers were kind of aggressive in maybe wanting to make a name for themselves on the basis of how much land they bought. . . ."[12]

In western North Dakota land was acquired mainly for setting up leased grazing and rehabilitation areas under the Department of Agriculture. Indeed, most of what was purchased under the auspices of the Resettlement Act is now part of the Little Missouri National Grasslands. Part of the new federal holdings was earmarked for a park, though.

This is not to say that the Roosevelt administration sought these reserved lands for the National Park System; far from it. It wanted to turn them into a state park by means of technical assistance from NPS. In the 1920s Mather had promoted the creation of more state parks (primarily as a way to deflect inferior national park proposals) but he did not allow the Service to take a direct role. Franklin Roosevelt's secretary of the interior, Harold L. Ickes, was far more of an activist than any Mather had worked with. Ickes was determined to expand the federal presence in conservation and used the newly-formed Civilian Conservation Corps to involve the

National Park Service in developing state park systems. So in 1934 a cooperative agreement to start a Roosevelt Regional Park Project was signed by the Resettlement Administration, the Civilian Conservation Corps, NPS, and the state of North Dakota.[13] Site development was begun immediately by the CCC.

It was always the intention of the Park Service that the project should lead to a state park.[14] Circumstances worked against this outcome, however. The magnitude of the submarginal purchase put the amount of land beyond the administrative capability of the State Historical Society, which was then responsible for North Dakota state parks. Even though the State Historical Society was nominally sponsoring the CCC camps, actual development of facilities was acknowledged to be a federal undertaking, just as NPS directed the buy-out from its Omaha office.[15] The federal government was alone in referring to the area as the "Roosevelt Regional State Park."[16]

Clearly, the administration was amenable to using federal funds and expertise for getting state park projects off the ground, and it made little sense to have the Park Service offer its help piecemeal, one state at a time. Perhaps instructed by the example of the Roosevelt project, early in 1935 it was decided to standardize NPS assistance through the Recreational Demonstration Area (RDA) program.

As it had in North Dakota, the Service would buy

certain lands around the country considered unsuitable to agriculture but with demonstrable recreation potential. The RDA program comprised four types of projects: highway rest areas, vacation and recreation areas near cities, state park system extensions, and areas eligible for and worthy of inclusion in the National Park System.[17] Roosevelt Recreational Demonstration Area was one of the earliest of the forty-six that were eventually created.[18] Still uncertain was how much land would be set aside for the Roosevelt RDA and whether the state would accept responsibility for its operation.

Lingering thoughts of a ninety-mile strip of parklands were quashed by local cattlemen. As one rather modestly recalled, "it was just be a stroke of luck"--and a timely visit to the Omaha acquisition office--"that we kept from buying all the land from Medora clear up to Watford City for a park."[19] Even so, something over 60,000 acres of submarginal land was purchased by the Service for the RDA, lying in two unconnected blocks roughly corresponding to today's North and South units.[20] Most of the land sold for about $2.00 an acre, making it by far the least expensive purchased under the RDA program.[21]

Although they were being run by the Park Service, the RDAs were not considered part of the National Park System. In June 1942 Congress cleared the way for the transfer of all RDAs from federal to state ownership, and it seemed that the Roosevelt Regional Park would finally become a state park. But only two months later President Roosevelt approved a list of RDAs reserved to further study for possible inclusion in the National Park System. Roosevelt RDA was on it.

Why did the administration grant this "special status" to an area in which its own park agency had never professed a certain interest? One reason was that the North Dakota state government had made it clear that it did not want the Roosevelt project as a state park. Russell Reid, the superintendent of the State Historical Society, had already publicly stated that North Dakota was in the project only "until plans for Federal land purchase programs are completed"; it was the Society's hope that the two units of the RDA would "eventually become part of the National Park System and be designated as national monuments."[22]

Another reason was that despite its general tone of discouragement, the Service had several times extended the possibility of including the North Dakota badlands somewhere in the System. According to John Ise, author of what is probably the most comprehensive history of the National Park System, in the late 1920s the Park Service "was fighting the Roosevelt project"--presumably, the 1927 plan put forward by the Roosevelt Memorial National Park Association. If true, this makes subsequent events all the more puzzling. For instance, the report of a fact-gathering tour of the area in 1928--attended by Mather,

11

among others--led to NPS cautiously, and tentatively, recommending national monument status. Four years later Mather's successor, Horace Albright, echoed this opinion in a speech, implying that becoming a national monument was the first step toward national park designation.[23]

But political considerations were undoubtedly at the core of the decision to grant special status to the Roosevelt RDA. The Service could not afford to antagonize Gerald P. Nye of North Dakota, who at the time the special status list came out was the ranking minority member on both the Public Lands and Surveys Committee (now known as the Interior and Insular Affairs Committee) and the Subcommittee on Interior Appropriations of the Senate. He was the first committed congressional supporter of a Theodore Roosevelt national park. Nye organized the 1928 fact-finding tour and influenced the congressmen who went along to report favorably for full national park status.[24] Nye was known as "a sound advisor to the Park Service on legislative matters"[25] and his opinions were well taken by the agency.

A newer champion of a national park for North Dakota was Representative William Lemke. Remembered today primarily for his association with the Non-Partisan League and his failed candidacy for president of the United States in 1936, Lemke has also been credited with single-handedly securing the enabling legislation for the national memorial park.[26] This is an overstatement, but only a slight one. Although less riveting than some of his more flamboyant exploits, his work for a park is certainly a large part of his political legacy. Oddly enough, Lemke was no admirer of Theodore Roosevelt.[27]

Lemke's first proposal

It is likely that the Park Service would have preferred to keep the Roosevelt RDA languishing in special status limbo until such time as it could make North Dakota see the wisdom of taking over. Newton Drury, who had been director of NPS since 1940, did not think the northern badlands could sustain national park status. In any case, as long as World War II lasted, Drury had no choice but to douse Roosevelt park proposals: he was busy enough trying to dole out a budget that had been cut eighty-five percent since the beginning of his tenure.[28]

For his part, Lemke hoped to get a park bill past the talking stage, to at least get it to a committee hearing. He laid the table for serious consideration when he persuaded the chairman of the House Public Lands Committee, J. Hardin Peterson of Florida, to inspect the badlands in July 1944. It had to be demonstrated to NPS and the rest of the government that this part of North Dakota was of national interest and not merely the subject of local firecracker-stand exaggeration. Peterson was convinced. After the trip he and Lemke drafted a resolution asking the Department of the Interior to support the creation of a national monument on the lands of the south part of the recreational demonstration area. Peterson's support on the committee ensured a hearing for North Dakota park legislation.

This pleased the Service not a bit. It had been unwilling to repudiate the local and congressional interests, but in truth it did not really seem to want the northern badlands in the National Park System in any capacity. With Lemke poised to introduce a national park bill in the next session of Congress, it was imperative for the Service to move quickly and bring about a final disposition of the Roosevelt project.

Having failed to make the area a state park, in September 1944 NPS suddenly revived an old possibility: turn it into a wildlife refuge. This was an idea that had been briefly considered in the late 1930s.[29] Indeed, 8500 acres of the north part of the RDA had been "set aside because of its especial fitness for a refuge in contrast to the rest of the park land,"[30] but it is unlikely that any active wildlife management ever took place as a result. Regardless, the Park Service seized the idea and by January 1945 came to an agreement in principle with the United States Fish and Wildlife Service to turn over the entire RDA. In June of that year President Harry S Truman released the RDA from its special status, clearing the way for a permanent transfer.[31]

A more direct rebuff to Lemke could not be imagined, but, undaunted, he introduced a national park enabling bill and brought it to hearings before the sympathetic

14

Peterson and his Committee on Public Lands in November 1945 and January 1946. The members were asked to consider making a national park out of 36,000 acres from the south part of the newly-proposed Theodore Roosevelt National Wildlife Refuge, and to release the rest of the old RDA acreage to grazing.[32]

Much of Lemke's persuasion at the November hearing went toward disabusing the committee members of the notion that the area under consideration contained Mount Rushmore.[33] After the two Dakotas and their respective badlands had been distinctly separated, testimony settled down to an examination of the process that was apparently leading to the creation of a national wildlife refuge. The highlight was Lemke's questioning of Fish and Wildlife's director, Ira Gabrielson, and NPS's Drury.

Gabrielson could not be drawn out regarding the behind-the-scenes negotiations over the area's status. He contended that FWS had targeted the North Dakota badlands for possible acquisition even before the start of the submarginal land purchases, and reminded the committee that the Department of the Interior's official position was in favor of making the Roosevelt RDA into a wildlife refuge.[34] Drury--apparently no great friend of Lemke's[35]--also steadfastly defended the proposed transfer. His argument, weakened somewhat by his admitted lack of firsthand knowledge about the northern badlands, was to the point: the area was simply not up to national park standards.[36]

Ignoring this, Lemke argued that not only were North Dakotans in general opposed to FWS taking over the recreational demonstration area, but that local ranchers were more amenable to NPS control because of the large amount of land excluded from his park plan. "The part we are leaving out is the best grazing land," went one of Lemke's pitches to the committee.[37]

Lemke was in fact telling half-truths. First of all, he had exaggerated the preferences of a few civic leaders into a phantom state-wide consensus favoring NPS over FWS control. In reality, the Medora Chamber of Commerce had gone on record in favor of any plan that would maintain federal administration of the south part of the RDA because they felt that such would best benefit the local economy. The Chamber's president informed Lemke that

> we have been warned that the present set-up [the RDA] is doomed to cancellation as it now stands and we do not want to see this come to pass, and are particularly desirous that some disposition be made of the area whereby it could and would be a source of entertainment and attraction to the public.
>
> In view of these facts, we ask that you use your efforts to bring about a creation of the Roosevelt Monument, Roosevelt Park, or else concur in our belief that the Wild Life proposal is the only thing left to save the area.

So while the first choice of the civic leaders was NPS control, they were not at all opposed in principle to the idea of a Theodore Roosevelt National Wildlife Refuge, as Lemke implied at the hearings.[38]

Second, his assertion about local rancher support was not quite accurate. The Medora Grazing Association, a small but influential group of ranchers in Billings County, wanted most of the south part of the RDA opened to grazing. In 1942 they sent a resolution to this effect to Secretary of the Interior Ickes, and re-affirmed it in letters to NPS in 1944 and to Lemke just before the park was authorized. They hoped that control of the RDA would be transferred to the Soil Conservation Service along with the authority to reserve a small portion for recreation, sell off other portions, and "allow the use of the rest by local resident users who have been using it"[39]--namely, themselves and other cattlemen who had been grazing stock semi-illegally within the RDA since the dismantlement of the Civilian Conservation Corps. Overall, then, local support for Lemke´s first park proposal was strong, especially among civic organizations and chambers of commerce, but by no means unanimous.[40]

At the hearings the Fish and Wildlife Service offered to sanction limited grazing within the pending refuge. Still, Lemke could not agree with Director Gabrielson´s claim that wildlife management was the highest and best use of the area. He tried to pin down Gabrielson on just how much fish and game already existed in the badlands:

> LEMKE: So whatever wildlife refuge is going to be there you will have to create, that is, get in there and get it started, isn´t that correct?

> GABRIELSON: There is seed stock in there. We can build it up.

17

This tepid response spurred Lemke to the wild assertion that the badlands "never had any great wildlife population" and therefore should be made into a national park on the basis of its scenic value.[41]

In making this argument against a national wildlife refuge, Lemke unwittingly ruined his chances for obtaining full national park designation. Contending that the badlands lacked a variety of natural resources was precisely the wrong image to convey when he was seeking designation as a natural area. If, on the other hand, Lemke wanted to leave open the possibility of a historical area designation, to exclude the two sites in the badlands most directly connected with Roosevelt would also be a grave error. But this is exactly what his bill did, leaving out the Elkhorn and Maltese Cross Ranches because they were "quite a distance away from any of the scenic beauties." More importantly to Lemke, they were also in the Little Missouri River bottoms, thus part of the "best grazing land" he wanted to exclude to appease the ranchers.[42]

Lemke gambled: by intentionally downplaying Roosevelt's association with the region, he hoped to enhance the chance for a national park designation by taking away from NPS the opportunity to suggest a national historical park classification. But in the hearings he had also seemed to de-emphasize the area's natural endowments in his careless exchange with Gabrielson. Lemke was left with nothing but scenic values to cite in support of his bill--enough to get the legislation through Congress, but not past President Truman, who pocket-vetoed it in August 1946. Three months later the Roosevelt Recreational Demonstration Area officially became the Theodore Roosevelt National Wildlife Refuge.[43] Lemke's tactics had assured the failure of his own proposal.

The Theodore Roosevelt National Memorial Compromise

Toward the end of the January 1946 hearings Lemke realized his mistake and at the last minute offered to make the bill more historically relevant by including the Elkhorn Ranch site and the Chateau de Morès in Medora, the home of the Marquis de Morès, an ill-starred financier and stockgrower who founded the town.[44] But it was too late for changes. So when the new Congress convened in January 1947, Lemke introduced House Resolution 731, a bill identical to the one Truman vetoed except that now the Elkhorn site was included from the start.[45]

Truman had refused to sign Lemke's first bill on the advice of not only the Service, but prominent conservationists ranging from Devereux Butcher, who relayed the National Parks Association's disapproval, to Horace Albright, who still saw the area as a national monument but not a national park. And in the last public comment on the bill, Oscar L. Chapman, the acting secretary of the interior, stated that the North Dakota badlands were best suited to a purpose of wildlife management.[46]

Lemke's chances of overcoming this formidable opposition were better than might be imagined, however. Now that he had established a favorable precedent within Congress, and had gotten some experience in dealing with NPS, he was much better able to exploit the ambiguity the agency had shown in its opinion of the area. Lemke took note of the several instances in which the Service had seemed to come out in favor of including the badlands in the System.

Without a doubt the confused front presented by the Service on this question was due partly to cases where an NPS official told a banquet of local citizens what they wanted to hear, and partly to genuine indecision over the quality of an area on the margin of national park worthiness as it was then understood. So it cannot have come as a total surprise when Drury, in response to the introduction of H. R. 731, reversed himself and called for a compromise in which a Theodore Roosevelt National Monument would be created.[47]

But the indefatigable Lemke held out for national park status, and when he secured House approval of H. R. 731 in early 1947, events appeared to be repeating themselves, for surely Truman would not have embarrassed Drury by approving an unchanged version of Lemke's second bill after the Service had gone to the considerable trouble of offering a compromise.

Faced with the same depressing scenario, in March the Park Service finally relented--partially. After clearing it with the Department of the Interior, Lemke was approached with a second offer: NPS would not oppose a Theodore Roosevelt National Historical or National Memorial Park. The idea of calling it a memorial park had been current since at least early 1945, but the origin of the title can be traced to the Roosevelt Memorial National Park Association of the 1920s. The rationale was that the Service would not have to begrudge another "inferior" national park, yet Lemke could have those two precious words in his title.

Most local residents had no objection, but "it was felt by some that since the word memorial would put [the new park] into a special class from other national parks it would serve to degrade it." Lemke, in accepting the title, declared, "I can see no great difference between the Theodore Roosevelt National Park and the Theodore Roosevelt National Memorial Park," and thought the designation, far from degrading the new park, would put it "in a class by itself" with the name suggesting "something more, not less, than a national park in the ordinary usage."[48] He assured his supporters that the memorial designation would mean no difference in the park's development.[49] As it turned out, he was wrong on both counts.

All the parties involved were as satisfied as they would ever be (the Fish and Wildlife Service, perhaps realizing their jurisdiction in the badlands was tenuous, gave in as well) and H. R. 731 sailed through Congress to

Truman's pen on April 25, 1947. One imagines that the signing was the occasion of much relief in the high echelons of the Service--relief tempered with resignation.

Yellowstone turned upside down

The National Park Service took over the South Unit of the Theodore Roosevelt National Wildlife Refuge on August 13, 1947, but the North Unit remained under FWS control.[50] Lemke had no intention of leaving it this way. Even before Truman signed the enabling act Lemke was telling people in Watford City that the North Unit would not be left behind. "May I suggest that you wait with this until we first get the Roosevelt Park established, then it would be easy to add the rest," he reassured one supporter, knowing full well that it would not be easy. The Service had told Lemke repeatedly that, as little as it wanted the South Unit, it wanted the North Unit even less.[51]

NPS's preferences did not unduly concern Lemke, so in 1948 he set about to finish the business he had begun by introducing legislation (H. R. 5587) to add most of the north part of the defunct RDA to the new national memorial park. A little later he proposed a second bill (H. R. 5816) to correct the enabling act's erroneous boundary description of the Elkhorn and to add to the South Unit the petrified forest formations northwest of the Little Missouri. H. R. 5816 also eliminated the provision in the enabling act requiring a statue of Roosevelt to be erected in Medora, with the funds saved going toward a park museum.[52]

At the House hearings on his North Unit bill Lemke presented a parade of local advocates, mostly civic leaders from the Watford City area. Some urged the committee to include the North Unit because of its beautiful scenery (one man called it "an inverted Yellowstone Park"); others, recalling the recreational demonstration area, told of the community pride created by the presence of a park; still others thought the North Unit addition would be a perfect tourist complement to the new Garrison Dam.[53]

But the civic leaders thought their most compelling argument was the land's lack of immediate economic utility: it wasn't good for anything else, so why not make it a national park? "The proposed park site is of rough terrain," declared one witness, "and of little practical use to mankind. . . ." Another supporter called the land in the North Unit "just about worthless." Lemke himself characterized the proposed addition as "lands with no commercial value." Although some local ranching interests opposed the addition precisely because it would put more land toward "non-productive purposes,"[54] the weight of sentiment in Watford City was on the side of Lemke.[55]

This was exactly what the committee wanted to hear, of course. The stockmen had already done their work, winnowing down the earliest park proposals and the RDA to the baddest of the badlands. But just to make sure of their support, Lemke included a perpetual easement in his

23

North Unit bill, forever reserving to local ranchers the right to drive stock through the park to railheads by using the Little Missouri River corridor.[56]

No doubt thoroughly sick of the matter, Undersecretary Chapman nevertheless voiced the Department of the Interior's opposition to the bill in a letter to the Senate. Two of his arguments had validity: it would indeed be hard to administer the North Unit from Medora, and the new area "would contribute no basic historical values" not already existing in the South Unit, at least in terms of commemorating Roosevelt, who was known to have been in the North Unit area only once in his life. A third, that the proposed addition would add "little to the natural values" of the park, was just plain wrong and reflected a lack of familiarity with the subtleties of the badlands landscape, not to mention its ecology.[57]

Lemke realized that the fate of the North Unit depended on how well he could counter Chapman's arguments. He could not refute the point about administrative difficulties, but in letters to supporters he outlined a strategy that he knew would appeal to the narrow conception of national parks held by most of his fellow congressmen. "I am going to introduce another bill [H. R. 5587], but we will have to support that bill with evidence, first that the people of North Dakota and Montana want it. Second, that its scenic beauty is equal to the south area. Also, that Theodore Roosevelt visited it several times from his ranch, and that it is connected with Theodore Roosevelt personally. I presume he hunted there." He wrote Russell Reid of the State Historical Society of North Dakota asking for a letter of support for the record. "Point out the scenic value as well as the historical value of [the North Unit], and that it is just as scenic as the Yellowstone Park only in a different way," he suggested, adding "I also need some good pictures showing the scenery of the area included in my bill."[58] Even in the 1940s, scenic value was still thought one of the most crucial of all national park criteria.

All this notwithstanding, the Department's opposition to the addition was pretty much a formality, with the House hearings having the air of a foregone conclusion about them. The Fish and Wildlife Service had not done much to consolidate its foothold in the badlands, and, after all, NPS had run the proposed park addition as an RDA for so long that despite all the official disavowals it seemed to the local people that the North Unit was a real part of the National Park System.

With the exception of Lemke every official involved was probably weary of the whole thing and wanted it over with. The House Committee on Public Lands, finding that "the so-called badlands of North Dakota have a distinct recreational, scenic, and historical value different from that to be found in any other national park" reported H. R. 5587 and H. R. 5816 favorably.[59] Both quickly passed Congress and were signed into law within days of each other in June 1948. The unique and troublesome geographic make-up of the park had been set.

Lemke´s role in the creation of the park

Why William Lemke should have devoted five years and more, late in a long political career, to a cause he had never before espoused and to the memory of a man whom he did not personally admire, is a question that may never yield to a wholly satisfying answer. In all his voluminous correspondence on the creation of the national memorial park he gives few hints at the reasons behind his diligence. His biographer, Edward C. Blackorby, is undoubtedly correct in stating that Lemke hoped to salvage his waning political reputation by orchestrating the park through Congress,[60] but this conclusion doesn´t lead to a real understanding of what drove him to work so hard to achieve success in this instance.

It would almost be too obvious to point to a mercenary ideology behind his efforts. Time and time again he wrote of the financial benefits which would accrue to North Dakota if the park were established, of the "millions" of dollars a national park would bring.[61] His view of the park cannot have been too dissimilar to that of the Greater North Dakota Association, confident as it was that "the entire state and eventually the nation will appreciate this great play-ground, which will give North Dakota a real touring objective."[62]

Lemke certainly had no inkling of the philosophical underpinnings of the national parks. Even after all his dealings with NPS he never mastered the agency's terminology, variously referring to his project as a "National Park," "National Monument," "Memorial Park," and even as a "Great Plains State Park."[63]

This is more than a case where a person's ideas outstrip his ability to express them. Lemke seemed to have no ideals at all for his proposed park, no way to fit it into the National Park System, until he latched onto Conrad Wirth's suggestion that a park in the badlands might be made representative of the natural and human history of all the Great Plains states. Thereafter Lemke referred to this as if it were part of a plan he had had for the park all along.[64] More damning was the fact that Lemke had little idea of what Roosevelt accomplished in the badlands and cared even less for its accurate commemoration. For example, the legal description of the Elkhorn Ranch site was given incorrectly in the park's enabling act of April 25, 1947. Lemke knew of this likelihood beforehand (he had been given three conflicting descriptions), but, as he peevishly wrote to a constituent, "I haven't time to wait and find out just where this ranch was located," and insisted upon including the dubious description in H. R. 731 "as it is." It was all right with him if NPS wanted to bother with properly locating the site after the park had been secured.[65] He did not seem to think it worth his while to actually visit the ranch site, even though the passage of H. R. 731 was contingent upon its inclusion.

Similarly, Lemke was perfectly willing to have the language of his legislation manipulated--and in some cases, dictated--by local interests if he thought it would make passage easier. A perfect example was his handling of H. R. 5816, the bill to correct the Elkhorn description and add the petrified forest to the South Unit. This bill appeared innocuous enough, but it ran into vehement opposition from the Medora Grazing Association. Despite its impressive name, the Medora Grazing Association was actually just a small cadre of well-organized ranchers who had taken advantage of the relaxation of grazing restrictions during World War II to run cattle in the south part of the Roosevelt RDA--a privilege they soon came to consider their right.[66] They objected to provisions in H. R. 5816 which changed the boundary of the newly-created national memorial park to include part of the Government Creek drainage just north of the South Unit.[67] Ignoring protestations from many sources characterizing the Grazing Association as a tiny faction who cared for nothing except themselves, Lemke chose expediency and caved in to their demands (it must be noted that NPS also acquiesced without much contest).[68] Although he got the petrified wood formations included in the final version of H. R. 5816, Lemke also inserted into his bill the boundary changes the Grazing Association wanted, almost to the letter.[69] He allowed a small group of ranchers to literally write part of the boundary of the park as it exists today.

William Lemke was a consummate politician, not a conservationist. Everything he did during the struggle to get the park established proves it. Yet why he should have chosen a project so unlike any of the others he had undertaken, and why he was so suffused with a fervor to see its accomplishment, remains a mystery. Perhaps the solution awaits another biographical study of this enigmatic man who was in many ways not only a representative of his state in Congress, but representative of the singular, and sometimes troubled, character of North Dakota.[70]

Theodore Roosevelt National Memorial Park was dedicated on June 4, 1949. A crowd estimated at as many as 40,000 (cars were parked for three miles on either side of U. S. Route 10) gathered in the natural amphitheater between Peck Hill and Painted Canyon, east of Medora. They ate and chatted. They saw an elaborate pageant of patriotic and historical vignettes. They listened to the usual oration, and heard Director Drury, in a complete about-face, say "the Congress established this area because of the striking form and color of the Badlands scene, the interesting geological story that helps to explain how these forms came to be, and the unusual fauna and flora." Not one word about the human history of an area that he, two years earlier, had suggested calling a national historical park.[71]

Everyone enjoyed the day. By all accounts, it was

the biggest social event that part of the country had seen
for fifty years.

Notes to Chapter 1

1. Bessie Tisdale Tracey, Campfire Songs of the Peaceful
    Valley Ranch (N.p., 1927), unpaginated. The National
    Parks Highway, as envisioned by the Association, would
    have generally followed the route of U. S. 10 (now
    Interstate 94) from Fargo to the Cascades. See Albert
    H. Yoder, "The Proposed Roosevelt Memorial Park," The
    Quarterly Journal of the University of North Dakota
    15:1 (November 1924), 47.

2. Quote from Joint Committee on Recreational Survey of
    Federal Lands, Recreation Resources of Federal Lands
    (Washington, DC: National Conference on Outdoor Rec-
    reation, 1928), 54. See also Robert Shankland, Steve
    Mather of the National Parks (New York: Alfred A.
    Knopf, 1970), 3-4, 145, 146-150 (originally published
    1951); John Ise, Our National Park Policy: A Critical
    History (Baltimore: Johns Hopkins Press, 1961), 195-
    199; Jenks Cameron, The National Park Service: Its
    History, Activities and Organization, Institute for
    Government Research, Service Monographs of the United
    States Government #11 (New York: D. Appleton and Co.,
    1922), 27-28; Donald C. Swain, "The Passage of the
    National Park Service Act of 1916," Wisconsin Magazine
    of History 50:1 (Autumn 1966), 4-17.

3. See Joint Committee on Recreational Survey, 51, 54-55;
    Shankland, 184-185; Ise, 296-300.

4. Quotation from Yoder, 44. For the RMNPA´s origins and
    activities, see Petty, "History," 397-403.

5. Yoder, 44-45.

6. Ibid., 46-47.

7. Ibid., 50-51. Compare the purposes of national parks
    as listed in a conference held during World War I
    (1916): "first, stimulating patriotism; second, fur-
    thering knowledge and health; and third, holding tra-
    vel in America." Quoted in Joint Committee on Recrea-
    tional Survey, 48.

8. In 1918, Secretary Lane charged Mather: "In studying
    new park projects, you should seek to find scenery of
    supreme and distinct quality. . . ." Nine years
    later, Mather reported on the System in the National
    Parks Bulletin. "As now constituted, it is made up of
    areas of incomparable scenic grandeur," he wrote, and
    while he went on to admit "the scenic supremacy of an
    area alone is not sufficient to gain its admission
    into the National Park System," the only other prere-
    quisite mentioned was that "it must also be suscept-
    ible of whatever development is necessary to make it

available for use by the millions of park visitors who
may care to use it, without in any way injuring [its]
extraordinary natural features. . . ." Quoted in
Joint Committee on Recreational Survey, 49, 52-53.

Burroughs´s quote is from his Camping and Tramping with
Roosevelt (New York: Houghton, Mifflin, 1916), 63-64; see
also p. 16. Huth´s curious speculation, apropos of
Burroughs´s comments, that "it could well be that the
members of the presidential party discussed the causes of
such utter destruction of a landscape, and that here [in
the North Dakota badlands] T. R. reconfirmed his determination that conservation was to be one of the major
achievements by which his term in office was to be remembered," is a misapprehension. Huth´s phrase "utter
destruction" leaves the impression that human misuse,
rather than natural processes, was the cause of the landscape Burroughs found so unappealing. Roosevelt well knew
the difference between the intrinsic nature of the badlands (which was, in fact, what Burroughs was describing)
and the degraded state of its pastures caused by stock
overgrazing since the mid-1880s. It is unlikely that this
1903 visit to the badlands he had known so long would have
triggered the reaction Huth posits. See Hans Huth, Nature
and the American: Three Centuries of Changing Attitudes
(Lincoln: University of Nebraska Press, 1972), 180-181.
Originally published 1957 by the University of California
Press, Berkeley and Los Angeles.

9. Minot Daily News, 26 October 1963.

10. Joint Committee on Recreational Survey, 21; see also
    7, 15, 22, and 23. As laid out in the 1927 proposal,
    the park would have been 60,000 acres in extent:
    Strand, 25. For the Assembly´s resolutions, see
    Russell Reid (Supt., SHSND) to WL, 2 June 1948 (WL
    Papers).

11. Howard W. Ottoson, Eleanor M. Birch, Philip A. Hen-
    derson, and A. H. Anderson, Land and People of the
    Northern Plains Transition Area (Lincoln: University
    of Nebraska Press, 1966), 49, 69.

12. "Congressman Don Short," text of interview appearing
    in North Dakota History 43:2 (Spring 1976), 65.

13. Kay Franklin and Norma Schaeffer, Duel for the Dunes:
    Land Use Conflict on the Shores of Lake Michigan
    (Urbana: University of Illinois Press, 1983), 186-
    187; Shankland, 185. All land acquired by the fed-
    eral government took place within "purchase boun-
    daries"; for the initial size of the project, see
    Petty, "History," 410.

14. Strand, 12, 30; Conrad L. Wirth, Parks, Politics, and

the People (Norman: University of Oklahoma Press, 1980), 343.

15. "Congressman Don Short," 65; Petty, "History," 409.

16. It did so even after the project was designated a Recreational Demonstration Area. A 1937 NPS-sponsored wildlife survey referred to the North Unit area as "North Roosevelt Regional State Park": Thomas L. G. Osmer, "A Report of Wildlife Study Made in North Roosevelt Regional State Park, Watford City, North Dakota, June 10 to September 15, 1937," unpublished MS, 1937 (THRO-L), 1. See also the description of the "Roosevelt Regional State Parks" published in 1938 as part of the American Guide Series of the Works Progress Administration: Federal Writer's Project, North Dakota: A Guide to the Northern Prairie State (Fargo: Knight Printing Co., 1938), 173-181. In a 1944 soil survey of Billings County there is a reference to a "Roosevelt State Park" of 3000 acres, separate from the Roosevelt RDA: M. J. Edwards and J. K. Ableiter, Soil Survey, Billings County, North Dakota, series 1934, #25 (Washington, DC: U. S. Department of Agriculture, 1944), 6.

17. Wirth, 177-178. At first the RDA program came under the Federal Emergency Relief Administration, but was turned over to NPS (except for funding requests) in November 1936.

18. Ibid., 184.

19. "Congressman Don Short," 65.

20. The exact figure is disagreed upon. Conrad Wirth, who was directly involved with the RDA program, put the acreage at 63,483. In the House of Representatives hearings on Lemke's first proposal, it was given as 66,376, with 61,000 federally owned (42,700 in the South and 18,300 in the North Unit). The 1944 soil survey (see n16 above) gave it as 63,635. Finally, an unpublished summary dating from around 1943 listed the RDA acreage as follows:

	South Area -- Billings Co.	North Area -- McKenzie Co.
total purchased RDA lands	44,356.90	18,836.56
public domain	2,549.02	6,051.49
total state school land (donated to federal gov't)	4,331.46	1,280.00
total purchased by state	680.00	173.30
total not purchased (private land)	3,182.27	1,878.65

```
total within primary
    purchase unit          55,099.65              28,220.00
```

Roosevelt was easily the largest of all the RDAs.

See, respectively: Wirth, 185; U. S. Congress, House, Committee on Public Lands, 79th Cong., 2d sess., 30 January 1946, Hearings on H. R. 4435, 5; Edwards and Ableiter; "Tabulation of Lands in Roosevelt Recreational Demonstration Area, Summarised as to Ownership Status and Taxable Value," unpublished MS, ca. 1943 (WL Papers), 1-2.

21. See Wirth's comment, 188; "Congressman Don Short," 65; and Robert Byrne, "Final Project Report, Roosevelt Regional Park, North Dakota R-1, Secondary Purchase Unit," unpublished MS, 1934-35 (Bismarck: Robert Byrne Papers, State Historical Society of North Dakota), unpaginated.

22. Russell Reid, "The North Dakota State Park System," North Dakota Historical Quarterly 8:1 (October 1940), 69. See also Roy W. Meyer, "Theodore Roosevelt Memorial Park" [sic], National Parks Magazine 39:212 (May 1965), 17-20.

23. Ise, 299; Petty, "History," 404-405. In 1928 Mather's only public objection to the area was that it was too full of private holdings to support a park: Shankland, 185.

24. Ise, 299. In his indispensable study Ise displays little familiarity with the North Dakota badlands, speaking of the Roosevelt project in the same breath with such obviously inferior parks as Sullys Hill. See 136-142, 299, and 343.

25. Wirth, 329.

26. Edward C. Blackorby, Prairie Rebel: The Public Life of William Lemke (Lincoln: University of Nebraska Press, 1963), 272; Strand, 33; Petty, "History," 425.

27. Nor was Roosevelt of Lemke, who had first come to statewide attention when he took a hiatus from his Fargo law practice to campaign for Wilson in 1912. Lemke then became nationally known in association with the Non-Partisan League, whose politics of neutrality during the Great War led Roosevelt, at the very end of his life, to brand it as anti-American. See Robert P. Wilkins, "Theodore Roosevelt and ´Dacotah´: A Mutual Disillusionment," North Dakota Quarterly 26:2 (Spring 1958), 58-62; and Blackorby, 271.

28. Wirth, 227.

29. Petty, "History," 416-417.

30. Osmer, 1. The refuge area was south and east of the Little Missouri River.

31. Petty, "History," 419.

32. Hearings, H. R. 4435, 3; Strand, 32-33.

33. Hearings, H. R. 4435, 3.

34. Ibid., 16-17.

35. In his book (p. 343), Wirth recalls that "Representative Lemke wanted it to become a national park, but Director Drury didn't think it qualified. . . . The difference of opinion between Drury and Lemke became very pronounced."

36. Hearings, H. R. 4435, 20. There are also indications that NPS thought the proposal a duplication of Badlands National Monument (now National Park), which had been proclaimed in 1929: Meyer, 19.

37. Hearings, H. R. 4435, 3.

38. Paul W. Lebo (President, Medora Chamber of Commerce) to WL, 17 August 1945 (WL Papers). See also A. T. Boyd (Secretary-Treasurer, Medora Grazing Association) to Weldon W. Gratton (Custodian, South Roosevelt RDA), 11 July 1944 (WL Papers).

39. "Resolution adopted at the Annual Meeting of the Medora Grazing Association held at Medora, North Dakota on June 25, 1942," memorandum accompanying letter of Boyd to Ickes, 29 June 1942; Boyd to Gratton, 11 July 1944. Quotation from letter of William P. O'Connell (Vice-President, Medora Grazing Association) to WL, 11 March 1947 (all WL Papers).

40. See the following letters of support to Lemke: R. Fay Brown (President, Bismarck Chamber of Commerce), 8 September 1945; C. T. Thompson (Belfield Chamber of Commerce), 24 December 1945; Carl Indergaard (Belfield American Legion), 26 December 1945; Ann M. Brown (Secretary-Treasurer, Medora Chamber of Commerce), 29 July 1946 (all WL Papers).

41. Hearings, H. R. 4435, 11-15.

42. Ibid., 5 (quote) and 16. When some local residents testified on behalf of Lemke before a Senate committee they framed their support of the park in terms of the land having little present commercial value.

U. S. Congress, Senate, Senate Report #1897, to Accompany H. R. 4435, 79th Cong., 2d sess., 29 July 1946, 2. Alfred Runte has pointed out the central importance of the "worthlessness" argument to the creation of the National Park System in his National Parks: The American Experience (Lincoln: University of Nebraska Press, 1979), esp. 48-64. For another indication of Runte´s thesis, see Franklin and Schaeffer, 5-6.

43. Petty, "History," 423, 421. The park area may have been known locally as a wildlife refuge somewhat earlier. See William P. O´Connell to WL, 11 March 1947 (WL Papers).

44. Hearings, H. R. 4435, 21-22.

45. It also called for erecting an expensive monument to Roosevelt in Medora in lieu of purchasing the Maltese Cross Ranch site.

46. Chapman to J. Hardin Peterson, quoted in Senate Report #1897, 2.

47. Petty, "History," 424.

48. Second quote: WL to R. Fay Brown, 10 March 1947; first and third quotes: Strand, 36-37. See also WL to Dickinson Chamber of Commerce, 3 November 1945, and telegram of J. J. Eaton and J. F. Tester to WL, 13 March 1947 (WL Papers). The compromise was reported in Senate Report #54, to Accompany H. R. 731, 80th Cong., 1st sess., 19 February 1947. Interestingly, Ise recounts (p. 299) the attempts Senator Joe Robinson of Arkansas made in the late 1920s to get another national park for his state: "The Park Service and conservation organizations were on guard and squashed every bill. There was a fear that Robinson might propose the park as a ´memorial,´ which would have made it harder to fight. . . ."

49. See B. E. Groom (ND Tax Equality Committee) to WL, 11 March 1947, and WL´s reply, 14 March 1947. In his correspondence on the matter, Lemke gave his supporters three reasons why NPS would not approve a Theodore Roosevelt National Park: it would not be big enough, not scenic enough, and would be named after a person (which was supposedly against agency policy). He also once wrote that Democrats in Congress had conspired against his bills because they would commemorate a Republican.

50. Strand, 38; Congressional Record, 80th Cong., 1st sess., 93:1624.

51. WL to Oliver Whitmer (McKenzie County Farmer's
    Union), 29 March 1947; see also WL to Fred Shipmen
    (Editor, McKenzie County Farmer), 21 December 1945;
    however, perhaps again NPS sent mixed signals about
    its intentions. Lemke reported to his supporters
    that only the highest echelon of NPS officials (pre-
    sumably under the influence of Drury--see n35
    above) were against the North Unit addition, while
    any NPS personnel who had actually visited the area
    were favorably disposed: WL to Roy P. Johnson (Fargo
    Forum), 26 May 1948. But Lemke seems to have told
    individual correspondents what each wanted to hear,
    and so contradicts himself on this point; cf. his
    letters to James Connolly (Manager, Dickinson Chamber
    of Commerce), 22 December 1947, and to Einar H. Dahl
    (Watford City, ND), 13 February 1948. Still, Conrad
    Wirth (who at the time was NPS's chief of lands) came
    away from a September 1947 inspection of the North
    Unit in favor of adding it to the national memorial
    park; see Arne Tollefson (Auditor, McKenzie County)
    to WL, 31 December 1947. Russell Reid of the State
    Historical Society thought the administrative costs
    of the North Unit addition, coupled with NPS's meager
    budget, was the source of any agency opposition (see
    text at n57 below): Reid to WL, 12 May 1948 (all WL
    Papers).

52. U. S. Congress, Senate, Senate Report #1419, to
    Accompany H. R. 5816, 80th Cong., 2d sess., 20 May
    1948.

53. U. S. Congress, House, Sucommittee on Public Lands,
    80th Cong., 2d sess., 9 April 1948, Hearings on H. R.
    5587, 1-6.

54. Ibid., 6, 12-13; Petty, "Draft History," 63.

55. The William Lemke Papers contain many letters from
    residents of northwestern North Dakota and eastern
    Montana in support of the North Unit addition.

56. The stock driveway easement (which also applied to
    the South Unit) was suggested to Lemke by Carl B.
    Olson, who had lived at Peaceful Valley Ranch. Lemke
    took the wording of the easement directly from Olson.
    See Olson to WL, 28 April 1948 (WL Papers).

57. Oscar L. Chapman to Richard J. Walsh (Chrmn., Senate
    Committee on Public Lands), 20 April 1948, quoted in
    U. S. Congress, Senate, Senate Report #1417, to
    Accompany H. R. 5587, 80th Cong., 2d sess., 20 May
    1948, 2.

58. WL to Einar H. Dahl (Watford City, ND), 13 February

1948; WL to Reid, 6 February 1947 (emphasis in the original). The North Unit supporters compared the cut of the Little Missouri to the Grand Canyon of the Colorado and the coloration of the Achenbach Hills and bentonitic clays to the landscape of Bryce Canyon National Park: L. M. Stenehjem (Watford City Assn. of Commerce) to WL, 14 February 1947 (all WL Papers).

59. U. S. Congress, House, House Report #1782, to Accompany H. R. 5587, 80th Cong., 2d sess., 22 April 1948, 2.

60. Blackorby, 271.

61. See for example his letters to M. J. Connolly (Asst. Secretary, Greater North Dakota Assn.), 5 May 1948, and to Erven M. Day (Secretary, Watford City Assn. of Commerce), 6 May 1948 (WL Papers).

62. M. J. Connolly to WL, 31 March 1948 (WL Papers).

63. WL to W. L. Gardner (New England, ND), 30 April 1948 (WL Papers).

64. Ibid., and WL to Harry Polk (Williston, ND), 20 August 1947 (WL Papers). See also his letters of 3 June 1948 to John Herner (Stanley, ND) and to Russell Reid (Supt., SHSND) (WL Papers).

65. WL to J. J. Eaton (Medora, ND), 2 and 5 April 1947. See also WL´s letters to Hugh Butler (Chrmn., Senate Public Lands Committee), 5 April 1947 and 22 April 1948 (all WL Papers).

66. Boyd to WL, 28 April 1948; WL to Boyd, 5 May 1948; and esp. Boyd to WL, 13 May 1948 (all WL Papers).

67. They also objected to the bill´s correction of the Elkhorn Unit boundary because NPS would gain control of the only well in Ellison Draw. Lemke responded that he had been told there were two wells, but had, in any case, "no objection to putting in a provision in the bill that the water from these two Artesian Wells shall be made available to the ranchers for their livestock." Boyd to WL, 1 May 1948; WL to Boyd, 1 May 1948, 2-3 (WL Papers).

68. For characterizations of the Medora Grazing Association, see the following letters to WL (all in the WL Papers): Leon Hellickson (Medora, ND) 11 November 1946; James B. Connolly (Manager, Dickinson Chamber of Commerce), 1 May 1948, and the extremely revealing pair of letters Connolly sent to WL on 15 May 1948; Hugh D. McGarvey (Belfield, ND), 16 May 1948; J. J. Eaton (Medora, ND), 19 May 1948; Russell Reid (Supt.,

SHSND), 2 June 1948. For NPS acquiescence, see WL to Reid, 3 June 1948.

69. In 1943 and 1944 NPS negotiated tentative boundaries with the Medora Grazing Association so that fences adjoining grazing lands would cost as little to maintain as possible. Boyd to WL, 1 May 1948. For the Grazing Association's influence on the final South Unit boundary, see Boyd to WL, 28 April, 1 May, 13 May, and 19 May 1948; WL to Boyd, 29 April, 5 May, and 17 May 1948; WL to James R. Connolly, 20 May 1948; and esp. WL to J. Harold Johnson (Auditor, Billings Co.), 21 May 1948 (all WL Papers).

70. For an approach to these problems, refer to Elwyn B. Robinson, "The Themes of North Dakota History," North Dakota History 26:1 (January 1959), 5-24; and Wynona H. Wilkins, "The Idea of North Dakota," North Dakota Quarterly 39:1 (Winter 1971), 5-28.

71. The dedication was delayed until 1949 at the request of Allyn Hanks, the park's first superintendent, who wanted basic organization, staff appointments, and the acquisition of the North Unit settled beforehand. See James B. Connolly to WL , 27 February 1948 (WL Papers). Drury's remarks are recorded in "Theodore Roosevelt National Memorial Park: Dedication, June 4, 1949," unpublished pamphlet (THRO-L), unpaginated.

2) From Memorial Park to National Park

To fully understand how Theodore Roosevelt has been managed in its first thirty-five years, one must recognize the political overtones of its establishment. The point cannot be emphasized too strongly: William Lemke's legacy was not just a park, but a National Memorial Park.

The memorial designation produced two lasting consequences. First, it made Theodore Roosevelt the "odd park out" in guidebooks and popular literature. Publicists tended to ignore it altogether because it wasn't a "full-fledged" national park and couldn't be easily classified anywhere else. This, combined with its remote location, meant that people usually lapsed when it came time to write about Theodore Roosevelt. Someone as well informed as John Ise, the eminent economist and historian, did not even get the name right.[1]

Perhaps they shouldn't be judged too harshly, for it cannot have been clear to outsiders why the Park Service classified Theodore Roosevelt as a historical area--the second, and for our purposes more important, consequence of the memorial designation. Until the Maltese Cross cabin was moved to Medora in 1959, the only historical resource directly connecting the park to the man it was memorializing was a detached 218-acre tract of badlands, thirty miles from any decent road and more than twenty from the main units of the park. It took a sharp eye to tell the difference between this, the site of Roosevelt's Elkhorn Ranch, and any other bit of the Little Missouri

River bottoms, for no buildings stood there nor had any since the turn of the century.[2] The rest of the park derived its historical qualities from intangible associations with Roosevelt or from being part of the 1880s cattle boom in Dakota Territory.

Much of the administrative history of Theodore Roosevelt has been shaped by the memorial designation and the ensuing management as a historical area, to which the park was ill-suited. Everything from formal planning to site development to the park's mission bore the stamp of the political compromise that brought into being a national memorial park.

Planning the park

Nowhere were the effects more evident than in the contents of the NPS planning documents for Theodore Roosevelt. Although there are any number which might be discussed specifically, three are considered here: master plans, statements for management, and the Basic Operations Declaration. A fourth, the interpretive prospectus, is treated in Chapter 12.

Until they were superseded by general management plans, master plans were the single most important element in the NPS planning process. They set forth the mission of the park, factors influencing its operation, and all future development projects. Theodore Roosevelt had three attempts at a completed master plan: in 1963, 1967, and

1973.[3] Although none ever received final, official approval, when taken together their contents give a good general indication of how the park's management practices evolved.

The 1963 plan was a "packaged master plan narrative" arranged, as the name implies, according to a predetermined format, rather like an environmental impact statement.[4] Its contents were anything but formulaic, however, broaching some ideas which were not realized until the 1970s. It in turn was replaced, at least nominally, by the 1967 Master Plan--nominally, because this version did not progress beyond the draft stage and was never officially approved, although it received a full-scale revision in 1970. Enactment of the National Environmental Policy Act (NEPA) that year changed the nature of park planning: the new law required a revision of the 1967 plan since the original did not follow procedures specified under it.[5]

Yet another draft master plan appeared in 1973. It was substantially similar to the 1967 plan and received tentative approval. But the 1973 plan was never finished because there was neither sufficient money nor staff to do the environmental impact statement required by NEPA.[6]

In the absence of an approved master plan, the controlling management document has been the park's statement for management. It recounts all factors affecting administration of the park, and is reviewed and updated frequently.[7] Theodore Roosevelt has had three statements for management, done in 1975, 1981, and the current version dating from 1985.[8] The staff is also guided by the Basic Operations Declaration, dating from 1982. It is a synopsis of park resources and present management programs.[9]

The end result of the post-NEPA planning process is the general management plan, which outlines all aspects of management for a period of ten to twenty years. General management plans replace the old master plans and differ from them in two ways: the process leading to the final GMP requires the Service to provide the opportunity for public participation by other agencies and private citizens; and anything in the GMP can be changed in mid-term with the approval of the regional director. Funds have recently become available to begin work on a general management plan for Theodore Roosevelt. The first public hearings were held in March 1984.[10]

The effect of the memorial designation on the park's mission

The most important thing to be gleaned from these plans is a sense of Theodore Roosevelt's mission as a national park unit. The rationale Lemke used to engineer the park's creation relied mostly upon the historical value of the area, but the unprecedented (and unrepeated) designation of Theodore Roosevelt as a national memorial park meant that the Service was not really bound to manage it in any particular way. Indeed, until the 1963 Master Plan was completed there was no broad directive on how the park should be managed, though the evidence that is available suggests that the park was managed as a historical area from the beginning.[11] Theodore Roosevelt was not officially classified as a historical area until 1964, when Secretary of the Interior Stewart L. Udall formally divided the National Park System into natural, historical, and recreational areas, but early on the staff did give the lion's share of attention to cultural resources. Only a handful of natural science monographs pertaining to the park date from before 1964, as compared with the reams of material churned out by archeologists and park historians (for which see Chapter 10).[12]

In the early years Service personnel were nevertheless confused about the purpose of the national memorial park. In 1961 a management inspection reported a "lack of clarity" among the staff as to the mission of NPS at Theodore Roosevelt. The inspecting official recommended that human and natural history each be given "its proper weight in the total picture" so as not to exclude the other.[13]

The 1963 Master Plan reflected this recommendation, couching the mission in rhapsodic language emphasizing the intangible benefits of national parks. "The purpose of Theodore Roosevelt National Memorial Park is to yield to the nation inspirational benefits through the experiences of visitors in this area of historic significance and scenic appeal," it stated. The park was also to be at the same time a kind of "natural research laboratory," a place where "those who seek relief from the pressures of urbanized civilization can enjoy the benefits derivable from places where nature's hand is still free."[14]

The 1963 Master Plan seemed to be leaning toward giving human and natural history equal stature, but the next year NPS published Udall's organizational plan. Entitled Road to the Future, it officially put Theodore Roosevelt in the historical category.[15] So when a new master plan was published in 1967, the "primary resource" of the park was identified as "Roosevelt's association with the Badlands and the open range cattle industry of the 1880s" and its mission became

> to memorialize Theodore Roosevelt by preserving, making accessible, and interpreting--for the benefit and the enjoyment of the people-- historic sites and features associated with him, as well as representative sections of the North Dakota Badlands that he loved so well, and where, as a young man, he hunted and ranched on one of America's last frontiers--an adventure which Roosevelt said prepared him for the Presidency.

This statement was repeated verbatim in the 1973 Master Plan.[16]

Not everyone was comfortable with the lopsided emphasis on human history. After a staffing study in 1968 found Theodore Roosevelt had the largest shortage of personnel in the entire System (eight management and protection people doing the work of twenty-two), Superintendent Arthur Sullivan was moved to write to the regional director:

The findings merely confirmed what we suspected
all along; that Theodore Roosevelt is the most
understaffed and overworked park in the National
Park System. . . . There is one other possible
explanation for the apparent understaffing,
although it is so remote we hate to even suggest
it. It is conceivable that, although categorized
a historical area, our operations are more akin
to natural areas. Just for the heck of it we
suggest this park be re-analyzed and compared
with other parks in Table II [which listed the
natural areas of the System]. (17)

Sullivan's intuition--that Theodore Roosevelt was
more a natural than a historical area--was echoed when the
park staff re-evaluated its management objectives in
1969,[18] and was expressed more explicitly as momentum for
redesignation began to build in the years following. The
1975 Statement for Management, discussing the paradoxical
position into which the memorial designation had placed
the park, admitted "it is now widely held that the primary
values of most of the park are natural rather than historic."[19]

Of course, when Theodore Roosevelt did finally become
a national park in 1978, the statement of mission shifted
to an overt emphasis on natural resources. Noting that
less than one percent of the park area is directly linked
to Roosevelt, the 1980 revision of the 1975 Statement for
Management declared:

The significance of the park's natural resources
was originally attributed to their role in
shaping the life of Theodore Roosevelt during
the era of the "open range" cattle industry,
which consequently influenced his role as a
conservationist during his Presidency of the
United States. Today the primary significance
of the park is that it affords individuals the
opportunity to experience and to reach an
understanding of it [the badlands], as Roosevelt

46

> once did. This significance is further magnified
> by the major impacts occurring on adjacent non-
> park lands. (20)

Because of the memorial designation the park was managed
as a historical area for its first thirty years, even
though it was far better suited to management as a natural
area.

The effect of the memorial designation on the park´s development

Similarly, until 1978 development priorities were
definitely weighted toward cultural rather than natural
resources. Every major planning document gave precedence
to the Elkhorn Unit´s development over that of the much
more heavily-used North and South units.[21] While this was
partly due to the desire to fulfill the provision in the
enabling act for the ranch´s reconstruction, basically the
series of ambitious plans for the Elkhorn were a way to
justify the historical area management approach that came
with the memorial designation.

The first Elkhorn development scheme did not appear
until the publication of the 1963 Master Plan because
necessary background research took most of the 1950s. It
was proposed at the height of MISSION 66 and with the hope
that a parkway would be built along the Little Missouri
connecting the three units (for which see Chapter 11).
The Elkhorn was to be a full-blown living history site,
with reproductions of all the buildings of Roosevelt´s
day, a working herd of longhorn cattle, and blacksmith

demonstrations. As the focal point of the parkway it would require additional land (some 1500 acres) on which to place a motel and service station, restaurants, saddle horse livery, 200-site campground, automobile pull-outs, and self-guiding trails, all to accomodate a projected 440,000 visitors each year.[22] A proposal very similar in scale was put forward in the 1967 Master Plan.[23]

Plans for the Elkhorn drawn up in the early 1970s were, by contrast, circumspect. Much more concern was shown for the effects of development upon nearby ranches and the natural environs, reflecting the beginnings of a shift in the park's management emphasis. For example, whereas in 1967 the connecting parkway had been called "not only desirable, but necessary to fulfill the Congressional mandate" to reconstruct the Elkhorn,[24] the 1973 Master Plan declared the parkway impracticable because "almost all the land involved would be private and a large number of private ranch properties would be disrupted" and because "a study has been proposed by the Forest Service to consider the Little Missouri River through the Badlands as a natural recreation riverway. To propose development of road improvements of parkway along the river would be preemptive and undesirable while such studies are being considered."[25]

New, streamlined plans for the Elkhorn appeared in the 1973 Master Plan and in an environmental impact assessment of 1976. They called for almost no development on the actual site, with perhaps only the ranch house being reconstructed. Infrastructure would be hidden away east of the river. There, visitors using the existing unimproved roads (the East River Road from the South Unit and the Blacktail Road coming in from U. S. Route 85) would find a terminal parking lot a half-mile from the site. Minimal facilities and four units of seasonal employee housing would be the only buildings, requiring the purchase of 40 acres instead of 1500. Scenic easements would be bought from adjacent landowners to preserve the historic ambience, with access to the ranch site by foot-bridge and walking path only.[26]

All these plans went toward making a tiny, remote plot of land which had averaged 200 visits a year into the centerpiece of the park. Most of the effort was motivated by the memorial designation, which, in effect, diverted attention from more pressing development needs--especially in the North Unit which is still without an adequate visitor center. In this respect, repercussions of the memorial designation continue to be felt today.

Re-creating the park: the omnibus bill of 1978

The movement to redesignate Theodore Roosevelt as a national park began as soon as President Truman signed the national memorial park into existence in 1947. In other words, sentiment for a national park was never extinguished. Many in North Dakota saw the memorial designation as simply an interim phase on the way to what was always referred to as "full" national park status, status which would confer prestige on the park and the state and make them both more attractive to visitors.[27] On occasion the State Assembly voiced this sentiment in appeals to NPS for a name change.[28]

Among the park staff, on the other hand, the desire was perhaps not so much for a national park designation as for any kind of change that would reclassify the park as a natural area; Superintendent Sullivan's comments, quoted earlier in this chapter, are an example. Toward the end of the 1960s they found their days occupied more and more by natural resource issues, while nominally following management plans that identified the development of the Elkhorn Unit as the park's first priority. New demands were being made of the staff, and they called into question the feasibility of continuing to manage Theodore Roosevelt for its historical qualities.

In the early 1970s a concerted effort to have the park renamed was started by tourism promoters and the state's politicians. Groups such as the Old West Trail Foundation, a travel marketing consortium covering five states, passed resolutions deploring the "undefined and meaningless" status of the national memorial park, and alleged a "lack of exposure" in both the Park Service's own promotional literature and commercially-produced guides. Because, they said, Theodore Roosevelt complemented "the other great Western parks" it deserved to be made "a fully qualified National Park under law."[29] Sentiment of local civic leaders was much the same. As the mayor of Medora put it, while a national memorial park has "the connotation of a graveyard plaque," the surrounding communities would benefit from increased tourism engendered by the prestige of having a national park nearby.[30]

North Dakota Senator Quentin Burdick assured that attention would be paid to these sentiments when he introduced legislation into the 92d Congress to have the park redesignated. It was the first of four such bills he sponsored in the 1970s.[31]

Until the summer of 1978, the NPS Washington Office (WASO) and the Department of the Interior opposed Burdick's legislation. Questioning whether Theodore Roosevelt satisfied the qualitative criteria for national parks, and citing various administrative precedents against redesignation, the central authorities argued instead for changing the land-use zoning within the park so that it could be managed as a natural area.

In general, the Service requires national parks to be areas large enough for three purposes: to encompass a "number of outstanding natural features," to allow for management of comprehensive biotic communities, and to provide for a wide range of public use.[32] In 1973 the Midwest regional director wrote WASO in reference to Burdick's first bill and the mounting support for redesignation within North Dakota: "We are aware that the Old West Trails Association [sic] and tourism interests within the

State of North Dakota are interested in seeing this name change. However, by applying the NPS criteria for parklands, we can see no way in which to support this designation change that would imply this area is a natural area of the park system."[33]

This statement became one of the precedents WASO used to argue against later versions of Burdick's redesignation bill. For instance, after Theodore Roosevelt became part of the Rocky Mountain Region in 1974, that regional office came out in favor of redesignation "since the park contains the best example of Badlands topography with related plant and wildlife associations to be found in North America," but its recommendation was countermanded by WASO partly on the grounds of the previous position of the Midwest Regional Office.[34]

Another important precedent involving national park criteria was Truman's veto of the first park bill in 1946. The president had rejected Lemke's initial legislation because he had been advised that "the area to be established by this bill as the Theodore Roosevelt National Park does not possess those outstanding natural features or scenic qualities that would justify its establishment as a national park." The Department of the Interior and WASO were reluctant to disregard this precedent in the absence of "the strongest possible justification" of national park criteria.[35]

Moreover, WASO argued that "Congress created this national memorial park in recognition of its historical association with Theodore Roosevelt," and since "the designation ´Theodore Roosevelt National Park´ connotes important natural significance rather than historical significance . . . the proposed title does not represent the purpose for which the area was authorized--specifically, to perpetuate the memory of Theodore Roosevelt."[36] However, WASO elsewhere admitted "the establishment history of this park leaves the significance of its resources to some degree unresolved," since the 1947 Senate report on the proposed park depicted conservation of natural resources as its principal objective. Still,

> when the park was authorized as a national memorial park, the significance of its natural resources was attributed primarily to their role in shaping the life of Theodore Roosevelt rather than to any intrinsic properties of the resources themselves. The validity of this evaluation remains a subject of controversy, particularly in view of the fact that the historic structures related to Theodore Roosevelt and the associated natural resources necessary to preserve the historic scene include a relatively small part of the park, the remainder of which is related to Roosevelt in only a symbolic or distant way. (37)

If any name change were to occur, the Department and WASO did not want it to be to "National Park." In a report to the Senate Committee on Interior and Insular Affairs, they noted that "this area is the only one in the National Park System which carries the designation ´Memorial Park. Inasmuch as it does contain values historically associated with President Theodore Roosevelt, we believe a more appropriate designation, and one which the Congress has adopted in numerous other areas, would be

'Historical Park.' We therefore would have no objection to . . . the redesignation of the area to a 'National Historical Park'."[38] The Department offered to support the redesignation bills Burdick offered in the 93d and 94th Congresses if they were amended to provide for a "Theodore Roosevelt National Historical Park,"[39] but the senator did not give in.

The Service's final argument against redesignation was that the park could for all intents and purposes be made into a natural area simply by re-zoning its internal land management classifications.[40] A WASO review of the park's 1975 Statement for Management sums up the complexity of the situation, and its preferred solution:

> Theodore Roosevelt National Memorial Park presents unusual problems with respect to the park's purpose, the significance of its resources, and the classification of its lands. When the park was classified as an historical area, it was automatically listed on the National Register of Historic Places. Until National Register forms have been submitted to delimit specific areas of the park as the historically significant resources, the whole park will remain on the Register and must be classified as an Historic Zone.
>
> It is now widely held that the primary values of most of the park are natural rather than historic. Although even natural resources not directly associated with Roosevelt may be said to commemorate his relationship with the Badlands, we understand that they are being managed to perpetuate an undisturbed prairie ecosystem rather than to preserve the prairie in the disturbed condition that prevailed during the Roosevelt years. It therefore is logical to eventually reclassify these lands as Natural Zones, restricting Historic Zones to areas directly linked to Roosevelt and intentionally managed to retain their historic aspect. . . . If these actions are taken, reclassification of the park as a natural area would be logical since only

a relatively small area would retain an Historic Zone designation. (41)

All this without having to go to Congress for a name change.

North Dakota politicians and business interests did not want to settle for anything other than "full park status," though. In 1975, Governor Arthur Link convened a meeting of prominent business people, the state's congressional delegation, NPS personnel, and members of the national park advisory board of the Rocky Mountain Region to see what could be done about moving redesignation along. This ad hoc group persuaded the entire Rocky Mountain advisory board to make a trip to the park in June 1977. As a result, it passed a resolution calling on the Service and the Department to consent to national park designation.[42] At the same time the state legislature passed a resolution of its own asking for the same change of name because, in the first place, "political compromise rather than common sense determined that the area be designated a National Memorial Park rather than a national park," and, more to the point, "status as a national park would bring appropriate status and recognition" to Theodore Roosevelt.[43] Local and regional leaders were thus united on the issue.

The final phase of the redesignation effort began in October 1977 when House Resolutions 9601, 9630, and 9631 were introduced into Congress. These bills provided for, among other things, increases in park development ceilings, changes in boundaries, and designation of wilderness areas (including those in Theodore Roosevelt--see Chapter 7).[44] They were collated and reintroduced in May 1978 as the nucleus of Representative Phillip Burton's parks and recreation omnibus bill, H. R. 12536.

As originally written, H. R. 12536 provided for a Theodore Roosevelt wilderness but not for the boundary and name changes which eventually formed part of the final version in law.[45] The format of the omnibus bill encouraged emendation, however: it began as a potpourri of proposals, and in the late spring and early summer many more were added. On July 10, 1978, a block of seventy amendments was introduced for inclusion. Among them was Section 616, which read in its entirety, "The area formerly known as the 'Theodore Roosevelt National Memorial Park,' established by the Act of April 25, 1947 (61 Stat. 52), shall henceforth be known as the 'Theodore Roosevelt National Park.'"[46]

The Service had withdrawn its opposition.[47] Section 616 was made a permanent part of the omnibus bill. During the floor debate in the House, not a single word was said about this section prior to its approval, although the next day Representative Larry Pressler of South Dakota used it to bolster his argument for a similar amendment pertaining to Badlands National Monument.[48] When the Senate held its hearings in July and August the situation was much the same, with almost nothing said about the Theodore Roosevelt redesignation. The only substantive

56

comment was a letter for the record from Burdick, who approved the name change as "the culmination of a thirty-year legislative effort to have this beautiful and historic site put on an equal basis with the other parks in the U. S. National Park System. . . . Currently the park has the dubious distinction of being the only national memorial park in the country, a classification which is elusive in its definition and its application."[49]

By October 1978, last-minute amendments put the omnibus bill into its final pre-passage form as S. 791. On November 10 President Jimmy Carter signed it into law as the National Parks and Recreation Act of 1978 (P. L. 95-625; 92 Stat. 3467). He thought it "the most significant conservation legislation to pass the 95th Congress."[50] Although the parts pertaining to Theodore Roosevelt made up but a tiny fraction of the whole,[51] that fraction was important to the people of North Dakota out of all proportion to its size.

Notes to Chapter 2

1. As in the epigraph to Part 1 of this history.

2. Still, to a receptive mind this scene was anything but unexceptional. In an unpublished manuscript (probably written soon after his visit to the park--see text at n5, Chapter 9), Olaus Murie, the wildlife biologist, described his first visit to the Elkhorn site--a place that he had read about as a boy:

> . . . its very simplicity was elegant. There at one time had stood a significant log cabin. By recognizing this humble spot on the bank of the Little Missouri we do more than establish a reminder of a prominent national political figure. It pleased me that this was not a mountain spire, a figure carved in a cliff, or some other obtruding feature. By selecting this spot where had once stood a cabin, representative of the bigger scene, a spot no different from the rest of it up and down the river (rather less striking, in fact, than most of it), we effectively recognize an adventurous era, a significant experience of mankind, a stretch of country that is capable of instilling in us something that can hardly be named in ordinary prose, but may only be guessed by the poet.

3. In Theodore Roosevelt's storage building there is a file which includes a map of the park's first road system, dated 1949. It bears the legend "part of the Master Plan for Theodore Roosevelt National Memorial Park." It is the only reference to an early master plan in any of the documents at the park. I have not been able to locate the full text of any such plan, but it is possible that one was written to guide the park's initial development.

4. Packaged Master Plan Narrative, Theodore Roosevelt National Memorial Park, unpublished MS, 1963 (THRO-A), unpaginated. Hereafter cited as 1963 Master Plan.

5. The Master Plan for Theodore Roosevelt National Memorial Park (Preliminary Working Draft) (Washington, DC: NPS, 1967). Hereafter cited as 1967 Master Plan. See also William J. Bruggle (Deputy Director, NPS) to Reg. Dir. (RMRO), memorandum, 4 May 1977 (THRO-S); and Theodore Roosevelt National Memorial Park Master Plan (Washington, DC: NPS, 1973). Hereafter cited as 1973 Master Plan.

6. Wayne W. Gardner (Div. of Park Planning, RMRO), to Reg. Dir. (RMRO), memorandum, 4 April 1983 (THRO-A).

7. David Harmon, "NPS Planning Documents and the Interpreter," Valley Forge Brief #5, December 1983 (Valley Forge, PA: Valley Forge NHP), 2.

. "Statement for Management: Theodore Roosevelt National Memorial Park," unpublished MS, November 1975, fourth revision, June 1980 (THRO-A); "Statement for Management: Theodore Roosevelt National Park," memorandum, 7 December 1981 (THRO-A). Hereafter cited as "1975 SFM" and "1981 SFM." The newest revision was not available to the author before this was written.

. "Basic Operations Declaration, Theodore Roosevelt National Park," unpublished MS, 1982 (THRO-A).

0. Harmon, 3; letter of Micki Hellickson (Chief Naturalist, THRO) to author, 14 May 1985. A draft Land Protection Plan has also recently been prepared by the park's staff. Land Protection Plans are one way the Service is now responding to the large increase in the number and severity of external threats to units of the System. They often propose solutions such as the purchase of scenic or preservation easements instead of fee-simple acquisition of adjacent lands from which incompatible uses originate. Refer to Janet L. Madden, "Tax Incentives for Land Conservation: The Charitable Deduction for Gifts of Conservation Easements" (Boston College Environmental Affairs Law Review 11:1 (1983), 105-148) for the legal background of this new protection technique.

1. See text at n14, Chapter 11.

2. Some of the early scientific research: Wheeler's work on amphibians and reptiles, Berg and Brophy's on fossilized wood, and Koford's on prairie dogs. For more detail on these studies, see respectively n49, Chapter 9; n34, Chapter 8; and n44, Chapter 9. For the 1964 reorganization, see Franklin and Schaeffer, 189; and n15 below.

3. George F. Baggley, "Management Inspection, Theodore Roosevelt National Memorial Park," unpublished MS, 15 December 1961 (THRO-S), 1.

4. 1963 Master Plan. This statement was promulgated a year earlier in order to get the staff thinking about "one centralized goal": "Statement of Mission and Purpose for TRNMP: Draft," unpublished MS attached to memorandum of Wallace O. McCaw (Supt., THRO) to Reg. Dir., 27 February 1962 (THRO-S).

5. See Stewart L. Udall (Secretary of the Interior) to George B. Hartzog, Jr. (Director, NPS), memorandum, 10 July 1964, published as Appendix A in Compilation of the Administrative Policies for Historical Areas of the National Park System, September 1968 version (Washington, DC: NPS, 1968), 72-73. See also "Superintendent's Monthly Narrative Report," memorandum, 12

October 1964 (THRO-S).

Later, when historical areas of the System came to be classified by theme, the park (along with Sagamore Hill NHS, Oyster Bay, NY; Theodore Roosevelt Birthplace NHS, New York City; and Theodore Roosevelt Inaugural NHS, Buffalo, NY) was assigned to the "Theodore Roosevelt" facet of "The American Presidency" subtheme of "Political and Military Affairs." The national memorial park was supplementally given the prime theme of "Westward Expansion," subtheme "The Cattleman's Empire," facet "Ranches of the Northern Plains." Part One of the National Park System Plan: History (Washington, DC: NPS, 1972), 39, 90.

16. 1967 Master Plan, 3, 6; 1973 Master Plan, 1, 3. The quotations can also be found in "Theodore Roosevelt National Memorial Park: Management Objectives," unpublished MS, 24 June 1969 (THRO-S), 1.

17. Arthur L. Sullivan (Supt., THRO) to Reg. Dir. (MWRO), memorandum 17 May 1968 (THRO-S). The staffing study cited is entitled "Analysis of management at historic and natural areas," memorandum from the Asst. Reg. Dir. of Administration (WASO) to all Reg. Dirs., 19 March 1968 (THRO-S).

18. "Although it was generally recognized that the park area possessed significant natural and scientific values, these [made] were subordinate and secondary to the intangible value of Roosevelt's historical association with the badlands region": "Management Objectives, Theodore Roosevelt National Memorial Park," memorandum, March 1969 (THRO-S).

19. "1975 SFM," 4.

20. "1975 SFM (1980 revision)," 1.

21. 1963 Master Plan, unpaginated; 1967 Master Plan, 4-5; 1973 Master Plan, 1-3; "Management Objectives," unpaginated; "1975 SFM," 6.

22. 1963 Master Plan, unpaginated.

23. 1967 Master Plan, 33-37.

24. Ibid.

25. 1973 Master Plan, 26-27.

26. Ibid., and "Environmental Assessment, Elkhorn Unit Development, Theodore Roosevelt National Memorial Park, North Dakota (Working Draft)," unpublished MS, 1976 (THRO-A), 1-18.

27. See Horace Albright's similar comments in text at n23, Chapter 1, and North Dakota Senator Quentin Burdick's, quoted in "State Coordinator's Monthly Report: October 1972," 26 October 1972 (THRO-A), 2. The feeling persisted among North Dakotans that they were being shortchanged by not having a national park. See also "State Coordinator's Monthly Report," 30 April 1975 (THRO-A).

28. "Staff Meeting Minutes," 20 June 1966, 1.

29. "State Coordinator's Monthly Report," October 1972, 1-2.

30. Rod Tjaden, *Dickinson Press*, August 1977. His thoughts were echoed elsewhere in the state: "For countless tourists the idea of a 'Memorial Park' must have conjured up images of plaques, a statue and a few acres of mani-cured turf. That special designation excluded the park from nearly all park service publications that featured national parks, monuments or historic parks. Those same publications in turn became source materials for private firms publishing atlases, guidebooks and directories." See "Theodore Roosevelt National Park--A dream come true," *Ransom County Gazette and Enterprise*, 28 December 1978. See also *McKenzie County Farmer*, 10 August 1978.

31. The bills were: S. 4072 (92d Cong., 2d sess., 1972), S. 1467 (93d Cong., 1st sess., 1973), S. 1609 (94th Cong., 1st sess., 1975), and S. 2062 (95th Cong., 1st sess., 1977). Representative Mark Andrews also introduced legislation in the the 95th Congress (H. R. 8637) that would have redesignated Theodore Roose-velt.

32. Acting Deputy Director (NPS) to Rep. Larry Pressler (SD), 6 July 1978, quoted in U. S. House, Subcommit-tee on National Parks and Insular Affairs, *Legisla-tive History of the National Parks and Recreation Act of 1978 (Public Law 95-625)*, 95th Cong., 2d sess., Committee Print #11 (December 1978), 514; J. Leonard Volz (Reg. Dir., MWRO), memorandum, 6 June 1973, quoted in Richard C. Curry (Assoc. Director for Legi-slation, WASO) to Reg. Dir. (RMRO), memorandum, 31 March 1976 (THRO-A), 2.

33. Curry to Reg. Dir., 1.

34. Quote from Lynn H. Thompson (Reg. Dir., RMRO) to Assoc. Director for Legislation (WASO), memorandum, ca. 1975 (THRO-A), 1-2.

35. Curry to Reg. Dir. (RMRO), 31 March 1976, 3 (Truman quote on p. 1).

36. First quote: Gary Everhardt (Director, NPS) to Secretary of the Interior, memorandum, 9 March 1976 (THRO-A). Second quote: Acting Asst. Secretary of the Interior to Senator Henry M. Jackson (Chrmn., Committee on Interior and Insular Affairs), memorandum, 23 August 1974 (THRO-A).

37. John E. Cook (Deputy Director, NPS) to Reg. Dir. (RMRO), memorandum, 3 February 1976 (THRO-A), 1, 2.

38. Acting Asst. Secretary of the Interior to Jackson, 23 August 1974, 1; repeated verbatim in Asst. Secretary of the Interior to Jackson, memorandum, 3 March 1976 (THRO-A), 1.

39. Ibid., and Everhardt to Secretary of the Interior, 9 March 1976, 1, 2.

40. Everhardt to Secretary of the Interior, 9 March 1976, 1; Curry to Reg. Dir. (RMRO), 31 March 1976, 2.

41. Cook to Reg. Dir. (RMRO), 3 February 1976, 3.

42. McKenzie County Farmer, 10 August 1978.

43. North Dakota State Senate Concurrent Resolution #4034, 45th Legislative Assembly, April 1977.

44. Legislative History of the National Parks and Recreation Act of 1978, 1-113, esp. 80.

45. Ibid., 117-120.

46. Ibid., 464. For a discussion of Burton's tactics and the background of the National Parks and Recreation Act of 1978, see Everhart, 146-147; and Ronald A. Foresta, America's National Parks and Their Keepers (Washington, DC: Resources for the Future, 1984), 80-82.

47. Perhaps because of the political climate prevailing under the Carter administration. Refer to Franklin and Schaeffer, 191-206, Everhart, 141-155, and Foresta, 85-86. See also U. S. Senate, Subcommittee on Parks and Recreation, 95th Cong., 2d sess., Hearings on S. 2706, S. 2848, and H. R. 12536, July-August 1978 (Publication 95-160), 208; and letter of Senator Quentin Burdick (ND) to Senator James Abourezk (Chrmn., Subcommittee on Parks and Recreation), 20 July 1978, attached to the above hearings report, 339.

48. Legislative History of the National Parks and Recreation Act of 1978, 514.

49. Burdick to Abourezk, 20 July 1978.

50. Legislative History of the National Parks and Recreation Act of 1978, 977.

51. The pertinent sections (the numbers refer to S. 791 and not H. R. 12536): Section 301 (16), which deleted 160 acres from and added 146 acres along the boundary of the North Unit; Section 401 (8), which designated 29,920 acres in the park as statutory wilderness (see Chapter 7); and Section 610, which changed the park's name. Ibid., 901, 916, and 947, respectively.`

Part 2:

A New Plains Economics: Energy Development and the Park

MR. ROCKWELL: May I ask one question? Is there
    anybody who is opposing this addition to the
    park?
MR. PRICE: No. I think that can be brought out a
    little later by one of our witnesses who has
    lived there a long time. He is a rancher near
    the park.
MR. ROCKWELL: There are only two groups I thought
    might possibly question it. One would be the
    livestock group that would want the land for
    grazing, if any, and the other would be the
    people who might want to go underground and look
    for oil and gold. We had a little difficulty
    with another park. After we had almost passed
    the bill, they came in here and wanted an
    extension of time during which they might want
    to drill for oil. I wondered if there was
    anything like that.
MR. LEMKE: There is not. The grazing people are
    satisfied with the submarginal lands they have
    outside.
MR. ROCKWELL: What about subsurface rights?
MR. LEMKE: There is no mineral in North Dakota
    outside of the freak, a little manganese around
    the spring in the Indian reservation near
    Rolette. We have so much lignite coal nobody
    is interested in any that might be in this area.
MR. ROCKWELL: There is no chance of oil?
MR. LEMKE: No chance of oil. . . .
                    -- Hearings to add the North Unit,
                       House of Representatives, 1948

3)   The Background of Energy Development

What happens outside a national park affects what happens inside it.   This premise, simple enough, is not necessarily obvious.   Indeed, for years there was a popular notion that, once created, national parks became islands of pristine nature set in a sea of development, saved forever, beyond the reach of the despoilers.[1]   It is a notion that has not yet been completely abandoned.

Aficionados of the parks have long been aware of the effects outside entities can produce.   John Muir at the turn of the century:

> The forty million acres of these [national park and forest] reserves are in the main unspoiled as yet, though sadly wasted and threatened on their more open margins by the axe and fire of the lumberman and prospector, and by the hoofed locusts [i.e., grazing sheep], which, like the winged ones, devour every leaf within reach. . . .

Fifty years later Freeman Tilden was still optimistic:

> I think it would be wrong to overemphasize here the attacks that are constantly being attempted on the integrity of the parks by private self-interest.   But they are very real, very annoying, always lurking in the background, and consequently they must be grasped by the owners of the property--the whole people.   As a rule they do not get very far.   The Service has the backing of hundreds of thousands of organized and ardent conservationists, who swarm forth like wasps when someone throws stones at the nest. (2)

Muir and Tilden were describing what are now called "external threats" to the parks.

A great revelation in park management in the last twenty years has been the expansion of the concept of external threats.   Managers have come to realize that external threats can also be indirect, originating not only immediately adjacent to the park but hundreds of miles away. They know now that more than trees and animals and artifacts can be threatened, but high-quality visitor experiences as well.

The best evidence is contained in the State of the Parks Report of 1980. This study, circulated widely upon publication, brought to light the magnitude of the threats to the parks: the great number of internal and external threats to resources, the lack of knowledge about the threats, the absence of baseline information about the resources threatened.[3] In short, the Report outlined some of the most acute problems currently facing the National Park System.

As for the general public, those with an interest in the parks are by now likely familiar with internal threats, or at least one in particular: the problem of overcrowding, of "loving the parks to death." It has been the subject of a slew of newspaper accounts, feature articles, and television reports.[4] But external threats have received far less popular attention. This is to be expected, because much of the debate on external threats takes place on a highly technical, esoteric plane and does not lend itself to short journalistic treatment. A second reason derives from the first: the problem of external threats is so complicated that the Service itself is just now beginning to grasp its extent. The State of the Parks Report was the first Service-wide assessment of how pervasive they are.[5]

Energy development is the archetypal external threat. It can cause physical deterioration of resources. It can change the social milieu in which the parks operate, and alter the surrounding political economy. It can even deny visitors important direct sensory experiences. But like most external threats, energy development cuts both ways: it can provide a great deal of money to individuals and governments, contributing to an increase in the material standard of living. Beyond this, the energy produced allows people mobility, mobility to visit remote places-- like national parks.

Thereby hangs a tale. Threats are only threats according to one's point of view. Even the most dire external threats carry some ancillary benefits, diffuse and delayed perhaps, but benefits nonetheless. It must be remembered that the Park Service has never set itself up as an intransigent opponent of the extraction and processing of oil, natural gas, and coal in the Northern Plains, despite portrayals to the contrary. The role it has wisely adopted is that of advocate, arguing not against development, but for balance: balanced land uses, economies, and choices open to the public. Still, NPS recognizes that it is its duty to make sure external threats do not become "a sacrifice by a public that, for the most part, is unaware that such a price is being paid."[6]

The rest of this chapter recounts the history of

Northern Plains energy development vis-a-vis the park. Chapter Four looks at Theodore Roosevelt's unique position as the only oil-producing national park. Aesthetic management is analyzed in Chapter Five, and possibly the gravest threats of all, those to the park's air quality, are discussed in Chapter Six.

The Williston Basin

Theodore Roosevelt is situated in the middle of the Williston Basin, one of the richest hydrocarbon regions on the continent. So-called because the city of Williston, North Dakota, is at its center, the "Basin" refers to a saucer-like depression in the crust of the earth, its bottom a Precambrian layer of granite. Long ago North Dakota was covered by shallow seas which advanced and receded, depositing layers of sediment. In the western part of the state the weight of the sediment was great enough to depress the earth's crust into a basin shape. This Williston Basin covers 130,000 square miles from northwest South Dakota into Manitoba and Saskatchewan, and from east-central North Dakota into northeast Montana. At the "Watford Deep" under the Killdeer Mountains the granite bottom layer lies 16,000 feet beneath the earth's surface.[7]

The porosity of the sediments filling the Basin made two things possible: the carving of the northern badlands by the ancestral Little Missouri River, and the creation of hydrocarbons. Over centuries the Basin became layered with organic material trapped in sandstone and sediments; slowly decaying, it formed oil, natural gas, and coal. These pockets then became topped with impermeable material, forcing the pools of oil and gas to filter through the porous sediment until they became permanently trapped against harder anomalies in the subsurface layers. There are two kinds of traps: structural and stratigraphic. Oil can be structurally trapped where domes of hard rock (called "anticlines") rise from the otherwise level granite bottom of the Basin, or, alternatively, in places where accumulation against a fractured impermeable layer is possible (a "fault trap"). Stratigraphic traps are porous areas containing pools of oil, surrounded by impenetrable rock.[8]

Finding oil in the Williston Basin, then, is a matter of finding these underground anomalies. Commercial exploration usually begins with a seismic survey. Seismography operates on the same principle as radar. Waves are generated from a fixed point at a constant speed, moving forward through some stable medium (in this case, earth) until they strike a denser object (the anomaly) and rebound to the starting point. The return time is measured and the distance to the anomaly calculated. In petroleum seismography, shock waves emanating from an explosive charge set at the bottom of a drill-hole are used.[9]

The labyrinth of leasing

Once oil is found, its ownership must be determined and, if it is to be extracted, a lease on the owner's rights obtained. In North Dakota there is a distinction made between "surface rights" and "mineral rights" to any parcel of land. The former confer the right to develop the surface for any number of purposes, including agriculture; the latter, the right to exploit any underlying mineral resources. Usually a single party owns both the surface and mineral rights to a tract, but sometimes not. If not, the tract is said to have "severed mineral rights." Obviously, complications arise if the owner of one set of rights wants to do something not to the liking of the other. In general, mineral rights are given precedence (the "dominant estate" doctrine); that is, in cases of disagreement the holder of the mineral estate has the right to use as much of the surface as is reasonably necessary for exploration and production.[10]

Ownership of petroleum reserves may also come into dispute. Oil often collects in underground reservoirs which cross the subsurface extension of property boundaries. If a well begins to produce from such a reservoir, the driller often tries to enhance its flowage by injecting gas or water, thus forcing more oil out. As a secondary effect some oil might be pushed across property lines. If this happens adjacent owners of mineral rights suddenly gain an interest in the producing well, for they have become part owners of the newly expanded pool. Dis-

70

agreements on the extent of ownership and amount of royalties follow. In order to protect the interests of everyone involved, the reservoir is "unitized." An engineering study is conducted to find out how much oil is present and how much lies beneath the various tracts; it is followed by a plan of unitization in which royalties and production rights are divided up.[11] A similar situation involving Theodore Roosevelt will be discussed in the next chapter.

The background of coal development

Coal leasing is rather different in that most of the lignite in the Williston Basin is strippable. Therefore, coal production requires ownership of both surface and mineral rights, since strip mining is a surface use of the land. At this writing coal leasing near the park is stalled by a fight over the federal government's plan to lease twenty-four tracts of public land within the Fort Union coal region. All federal leasing since 1976 has been done through competitive bidding. If the Fort Union lease sale takes place and recent trends hold, the successful bidders will likely be large multi-interest corporations--a far cry from the days when federal coal leases were bought by prospectors and individual land speculators.[12]

Private citizens were in fact the first to mine lignite in western North Dakota. Early ranchers fed their coal-burning stoves directly from the many coal veins which crop out in the badlands. While there is no evidence of commercial extraction within what is now the park, some small-scale mining may well have occurred since McKenzie County is underlain by twenty layers of workable coal. Seams are exposed all along the Little Missouri. And in fact there were four coal mines in Medora as of 1925: the High Grade and Demorès in the village, and the Red Trail and Little Missouri near the site of the cantonment, just west of the river.[13]

For decades it was thought that coal would be the mainstay of the state's energy production, but since the mid-1970s it has been eclipsed by oil and gas.[14] Yet North Dakota lignite is sought by utilities despite its poor heating value: compared with other classes of coal it is low in sulfur and ash and burns relatively cleanly.[15]

The background of oil and natural gas development

The state has known two oil booms, one in the 1950s and another in the 1970s. The first viable commercial drilling in the Williston Basin began in 1950. By 1953 the talk of western North Dakota was the opening of the Fryburg-Scoria oil field adjacent to the south boundary of the South Unit. It was the first discovery in the Basin outside of the Nesson Anticline and the first to have been found through seismography.[16] Within weeks of the discovery seismic surveys were being conducted around all sides of the South Unit, and near the North Unit too. Not an issue of the local newspapers appeared that did not

carry a hopeful story on oil.[17] As the accompanying charts show, while oil production
has seldom faltered after an impressive start, the number of new wells--a better indicator of boom conditions--went into the doldrums in the 1960s.

The second boom began after the oil embargo of 1973. Perhaps the best way to convey its amplitude is to recite some statewide statistics. In 1972 fewer than 100 new wells were drilled and only 4 new reservoirs discovered; net oil and gas revenue to the state was $3.2 million. During 1981, producers put in 848 new wells and found 83 new reservoirs; the state's revenue had increased 50 times, to $163.3 million. All this activity has wrought profound social changes in the state, changes that are only hinted at by the estimated twenty-six percent increase in North Dakota's population between 1970 and 1982.[18]

Although drilling slackened in 1982 because of a glut of oil on the world market, the Williston Basin is still exceptionally productive, with twenty-five to thirty-three percent of all drillings ending in positive strikes of oil; the national average is five to seven percent. In North Dakota the rate of successful wildcat wells (those drilled outside of established fields) has in the past few years run at twice the national average.[19] The western counties are now covered with producing fields
and the number of known oil-producing geological

structures has increased markedly. For example, in 1978 a large north-south structural trend called the "Billings Nose" was discovered along an imaginary line connecting the three units of the park. In 1974 there was only one oil field between the North and South units; by 1979 four more had been opened along the Billings Nose in the immediate vicinity of the Elkhorn Unit, making Billings County the leading oil producer in the state.[20]

Other mineral development

At the height of the national atomic development program in the 1950s, the small quantities of uranium known to exist in some North Dakota lignite deposits became an attractive object for prospectors. Fervor reached the point where several people asked to explore inside the park (all were turned down). Mining did take place to the east of the South Unit in what were known as the North and South Belfield Areas. Some 300 claims were filed, and ore-grade uraniferous lignite was mined there from 1956 to 1967. Low market prices have since brought an end to commercial production.[21]

No one can say what the future of the Basin's uranium will be. The same is true regarding leonardite, bentonitic clay, halite, and potash, all of which exist in viable amounts. Some analysts have ventured to predict that potash reserves will one day be considered more valuable than those of coal.[22] What is certain is that at least some of these minerals will be mined one day, becoming

74

part of the new plains economics.

Notes to Chapter 3

1. The transformation was considered immediate, almost
    automatic: "There are many more wilderness areas use-
    ful principally for their inspirational and stabili-
    zing effect on mankind, which should be brought into
    the parks, where they will be safe from the pressure
    of commercial exploitation." Harlean James, Romance of
    the National Parks (New York: Macmillan, 1939), 110.
    See also "NPCA Adjacent Lands Survey: No Park is an
    Island," National Parks & Conservation Magazine 53
    (March-April, 1979).

2. John Muir, Our National Parks (Boston: Houghton,
    Mifflin, 1901), 13; Freeman Tilden, The National
    Parks: What They Mean to You and Me (New York: Alfred
    A. Knopf, 1951), 21.

3. See "State of the Parks Report 1980," passim; Gary
    Gregory, "State of the Parks 1980: Problems and
    Plans," and T. Destry Jarvis, "Adjacent lands and
    Intermingled Ownership Problems," both in National
    Parks in Crisis, Eugenia Horstman Connally, ed. (Wash-
    ington, DC: National Parks & Conservation Assn.,
    1982).

4. For example, Robert Cahn's fifteen-part series in the
    Christian Science Monitor, "Will Success Spoil the
    National Parks?" (May-August 1968). See also Ever-
    hart, 61-74.

5. At Theodore Roosevelt there is some evidence of a
    relatively early shift away from the "park-as-an-
    island" viewpoint. In the 1967 Master Plan the image
    of an "oasis in the desert" was invoked twice: to
    contrast the topography of the badlands with the
    prairie's, and, more significantly, as a comparison
    between the land use and management of the park and
    that of the surrounding region. But in the 1973
    Master Plan, these references were deleted from an
    otherwise identically-worded passage. Cf. 1967 Master
    Plan, 7; and 1973 Master Plan, 4. See also n1 above.

6. "State of the Parks Report 1980" (executive summary),
    3.

7. Melvin E. Kazeck, North Dakota: A Human and Economic
    Geography (Fargo: North Dakota Institute for Regional
    Studies, 1956), 164-165; Robinson, History of North
    Dakota, 2; Lee C. Gerhard, Sidney B. Anderson, Julie
    A. Lefever, and Clarence G. Carlson, "Geological De-
    velopment, Origins, and Energy Mineral Reserves of
    Williston Basin, North Dakota," American Association of
    Petroleum Geologists Bulletin 66:8 (August 1982), 990;
    Erling A. Brostuen, Petroleum--A Primer for North

Dakota, NDGS Educational Series #13 (Grand Forks: NDGS, 1981), 1.

8. Kazeck, 164-165.

9. Brostuen, 8-11; letter of Micki Hellickson (Chief Naturalist, THRO) to author, 14 May 1985. So-called "thumper trucks" are also used.

10. Ron Anderson, North Dakota Oil and Gas Leasing Considerations, bulletin #29 (Fargo: North Dakota State University Co-operative Extension Service, 1981), 7-8. A case of severed mineral rights was enough to temporarily alter the make-up of the South Unit wilderness proposal (see Chapter 7).

11. Brostuen, 22. The unitization plan must also be approved by the North Dakota Industrial Commission, the state regulatory body overseeing such matters.

12. Before the passage of the Federal Coal Leasing Amendments Act of 1976, tracts could be let through non-competitive preference-right leasing. Patterns and Trends in Federal Coal Ownership 1950-1980: A Technical Memorandum (Washington, DC: Office of Technology Assessment, 1981), 3, 14-15.

13. Arthur G. Leonard, Earle J. Babcock, and Leonard P. Dove, The Lignite Deposits of North Dakota, NDGS bulletin #4 (Grand Forks: NDGS, 1925), 38, 98-103; and Kazeck, 157.

14. For a late example, see Coal Age (Western Coal Edition), mid-April 1973, 136-142.

15. E. R. Landis, "Economic Geology," in U. S. Congress, Senate, Mineral and Water Resources of North Dakota, report to the Committee on Interior and Insular Affairs, 93d Cong., 1st sess., 1973, 47-49.

16. Kazeck, 161-163; Albert Jacobsen, "Address [by the] President of Amerada Petroleum Corporation at the Oil Dedication Banquet Held at Williston, North Dakota on October 24, 1953," North Dakota History 20:4 (October 1953), 184-185.

17. Petty, "Draft History," 70. See also the issues of the McKenzie County Farmer for 1953.

18. Oil and Gas Activity in 1981," North Dakota Geological Survey Newsletter, June 1982, 25-27.

19. Randy Bradbury, "North Dakota: the oil boom is on," High Country News, 19 March 1982, 7; "Oil and Gas Activity in 1981," 17-30; Gerhard et al., 989.

20. Sidney B. Anderson and John P. Bleumle, Oil Exploration and Development in the North Dakota Williston Basin: 1981 Update, NDGS Miscellaneous Series #62 (Grand Forks: NDGS, 1982), 3.

21. See E. T. Frydenlund (Minot, ND) to John W. Jay, Jr., (Supt., THRO), 17 May 1955, and Jay's reply of 20 May 1955 (THRO-S); Petty, "Draft History," 74-75; and E. A. Noble, "Uranium in Coal," in Mineral and Water Resources of North Dakota, 83-85.

22. Gerhard et al., 990, 1008-1009.

4) Slant Drilling for Oil Under the Park

Unquestionably, many national parks are underlain with commercially exploitable petroleum reserves, for oil is no respecter of boundaries. Theodore Roosevelt is only one of many NPS areas (numbering fifty-nine in the late 1970s) encumbered by non-federal oil and gas rights.[1] With just a few exceptions extraction is forbidden in the parks, so the point may at first seem academic. It is not, as is evident from recent events at Theodore Roosevelt--events unprecedented in the history of the National Park System. Yet what has happened is nothing more than a variation on the reservoir unitization problem discussed in the last chapter.

When the Fryburg-Scoria oil field went into production in 1953 just outside the South Unit, it was of no particluar concern to the park staff.[2] Over the next twelve years the field produced thousands of barrels of crude oil without anything being thought amiss. But in 1966 a private company, Tenneco Oil, proposed to expand the effective area of the Fryburg-Scoria field by drilling into a number of adjacent tracts of parkland in Painted Canyon. These tracts had severed mineral rights, with the government owning the surface but not the minerals underneath. Tenneco possessed the mineral estate and wanted to open these tracts to production.

The company knew surface occupancy of the parkland was out of the question, regardless of the dominant estate doctrine. Tenneco's solution was to apply to the North

Dakota Industrial Commission, the state agency regulating oil and gas matters, for permission to use "directional drilling" to get at the oil. In other words, the well head would be outside the park in the already-developed Fryburg-Scoria field, but instead of going straight down the drilling would proceed obliquely, at a slant, to points within Tenneco's mineral estate underneath the park. Although twice as costly to put in as a regular well, slant wells would allow the company to extract oil and gas from beneath the park without disturbing the surface inside the boundary.

The Industrial Commission approved the Tenneco plan.[3]

Its decision must have been unexpected, for only after the fact did the government call in the U. S. Geological Survey to evaluate the reservoir Tenneco wanted to drill into. The Survey's report was startling. It turned out that the oil reservoir which had already been supporting the Fryburg-Scoria field extended underneath the park to areas where the United States held the mineral rights. USGS estimated that conventional straight wells operating entirely outside the park had been draining federally-owned oil from this reservoir since 1958, and dramatically so since 1962. The agency placed the public's loss for the period 1962-1966 at over $10,000--at a time when crude oil sold for $2.10 a barrel. And USGS calculated that further drainage of adjacent federally-owned oil would increase to a cost of $19,000 per well per year if the new Tenneco plan were carried out.[4]

Tenneco clearly had a legal right to exploit its mineral estate. It was up to the government to unitize the reservoir and stop the uncompensated drainage.

In its report USGS came out in favor of "protective leasing" of the federally-owned oil. Protective leases are nothing more than standard leases issued in cases where leasing is normally not allowed. They are authorized under the United States Code when oil and gas reserves are being drained from federal lands not subject to the Mineral Leasing Act.

Today, protective leases involving national parks require the producer "to minimize adverse effects that might result from oil and gas activities in proximity to parklands."[5] But in 1966 the Service had no regulations to guide them. The Midwest Regional Office knew that issuing protective leases might open a Pandora's box:

> With the limited information at our disposal . . .
> we are reluctant to accept the proposal that
> protective leasing is the most desirable
> procedure. Certainly if this were undertaken
> in the Memorial Park there would be considerable
> pressure to apply the same principle to other
> areas in the System where we have consistently
> resisted any such proposals.

Yet the NPS Solicitor's Office concluded that protective leasing was the only option that would ensure payment for the public's oil reserves.[6] The Regional Office unenthusiastically agreed:

> Protective leasing would, we realize, set a
> precedent with far-reaching consequences;
> however, if oil is being removed from under
> Federally-owned lands at Theodore Roosevelt,

> without compensation, it would appear that
> the public interest dictates some corrective
> action. We cannot simply ignore the situation.
> Criticism would inevitably result if we permit
> depletion of this valuable underground resource
> without compensation to the Government. (7)

Debate on the issue continued for the rest of the year and into 1967. By March it looked as though the Department of the Interior was ready to lease,[8] but a few months later the project was postponed indefinitely because of last-minute doubts about the legality of the title to some of the land.[9] Also, the passage of the National Historic Preservation Act in 1966 had further complicated matters. The law placed all of Theodore Roosevelt, as a historical area of the National Park System, on the National Register of Historic Places. Section 106 of the new law mandated protection for National Register properties and it was unclear whether slant drilling would be a violation.[10]

The project was delayed six years in all,[11] during which the Department of the Interior moved no closer to a Systemwide policy on slant drilling. Nor did it devise any alternatives to protective leasing. So when the Amerada Hess Corporation, which had acquired Tenneco's mineral rights, decided in 1972 to press the slant drilling plan, the government had no choice but to allow it and hold a protective lease sale.

On November 18, 1974, bids were opened on leases for the mineral rights to nine parcels covering 1288 surface acres. Amerada Hess was the only serious bidder, paying anywhere from $2729.83 per acre (parcel #8) to $51.60 per acre (parcel #5). The government realized $1,276,816.35 from the sale.[12] The leases were drawn up for the Department by the Montana office of the Bureau of Land Management. All were standard leases with an attached page of special stipulations (Figure 4.1). The production royalty to be paid to the government depended upon the number of barrels of oil and natural gas produced per well per day.[13]

As stipulated in the lease, before the company could begin drilling, an environmental assessment of the well area had to be conducted. In December the superintendent and chief ranger of Theodore Roosevelt, as well as representatives of the U. S. Geological Survey, the Medora District of the Forest Service, and Amerada Hess, inspected the drilling site. They concluded that the new wells would have "a minor impact on the environment" with the only potential adverse effect being a small loss of grazing land. After Amerada Hess filed a plan for controlling well blowouts and signed a standard surface reclamation agreement, they began drilling.[14]

Five slant wells were successfully completed in 1975[15] and are still producing today. For Amerada Hess the risk of doing the expensive directional drilling has paid off: in their first five years, the slant wells produced nearly 830,000 barrels. "These wells have extended northward the known parameters of the long-producing Fryburg field," wrote one industry analyst, "and have seemingly justified the company's paying of such a large amount for leasehold acreage."[16]

By their willingness to meet the special conditions of the lease, Amerada Hess gratified the park. Because Interstate 94 interposes between the park and the site of the slant wells the added aesthetic intrusion was considered negligible.[17] So, in a letter thanking the company "for their fine cooperation during the location and drilling of the five directional wells," Superintendent John Lancaster waived the stipulation requiring above-ground fixtures to be either screened from view or painted earth tones "because of the relatively unobtrusive location of the wells." He praised the helpful attitude of Amerada Hess "under this rather unique lease and development agreement."[18]

The decision to enter into this agreement had been a difficult one, made "at the highest Departmental level."[19] The opinions of two of the NPS principals involved fell on the side of keeping Theodore Roosevelt's situation unique. Calling protective leasing "contrary to and incompatible with the overall pronouncements of broad policy by Congress for areas within the National Park System," the Midwest Regional Office asked that such leasing be discontinued because "the operations authorized under protective oil and gas leasing have a significant adverse impact on maximum public enjoyment of the affected and surrounding park lands."[20] And despite the cooperation extended by

Amerada Hess, Superintendent Lancaster sensed that his park's relative good fortune could not be replicated elsewhere. He hoped that the Service would "immediately set a policy on future slant drilling activities. Slant drilling under the majority of this area and other National Park Service areas would be quite detrimental."[21]

A Servicewide minerals management policy review eventually appeared in 1978. It recommended thorough documentation, monitoring, and reclamation of oil and gas projects affecting non-federal parts of the parks, but could not rule out slant drilling and protective leasing until the complete mineral rights to all the parks were acquired.[22]

Although Theodore Roosevelt is still the only national park encumbered by slant wells, the petroleum industry has not failed to take notice of the box lid opening a crack. An article in the trade magazine _Montana Oil Journal_ confirmed the fear voiced by the Midwest Regional Office in 1966 when the Tenneco plan was first conceived. Entitled "Will National Park lands be developed for oil and gas exploration?," the article expressed the hope that Theodore Roosevelt "could be used in the future as the precedent for establishing exploration activity on or close to national park and monument lands." Declaring that "Amerada Hess has proved that oil companies can develop necessary domestic reserves on Federal lands without harming the environment," the author saw no reason why slant drilling could not be adapted to other parks. Dinosaur, Glacier, and Grand Teton were three which came immediately to his mind.[23]

The problems of slant drilling and protective leasing may well confront other NPS units soon. If so, decisions will ride not only on the merits of the case at hand, but on what has happened at Theodore Roosevelt.

Notes to Chapter 4

1. As of 1978, 303.95 acres out of the whole park acreage (given as 70,408.64) were considered encumbered. National Park Service Minerals Management Regulations for Nonfederal Oil and Gas Rights: Environmental Assessment (Denver: DSC, 1978), I-2. A good example of what can happen on encumbered land is the seismographic testing conducted in 1954 by Amerada Petroleum on the Olsen inholding at Theodore Roosevelt. See John S. McLaughlin (Asst. Reg. Dir., Region II) to Reg. Dir. (Region II), memorandum, 24 May 1954 (THRO-S).

2. See John W. Jay, Jr. (Supt., THRO) to Reg. Dir. (Region II), memorandums, 13 January and 26 July 1954 (THRO-S).

3. Fred C. Fagergren (Reg. Dir., MWRO) to J. S. Collins (Vice-President, Tenneco), 26 July 1966 (THRO-A); Hillary A. Oden (District Engineer, USGS) to Regional Oil and Gas Supervisor (USGS), memorandum, 23 June 1966 (THRO-A).

4. Ibid.

5. National Park Service Minerals Management Regulations, I-3 -- I-4.

6. Fagergren to Arthur L. Sullivan (Supt., THRO), memorandum, 5 July 1966 (THRO-A).

7. George F. Baggley (Acting Reg. Dir., MWRO) to Director (NPS), memorandum, 21 July 1966 (THRO-A). See also Eugene F. Lyttle to Chief of Office of Land and Water Rights (NPS), memorandum, 16 January 1967 (THRO-S).

8. See USGS to BLM (no other information given), memorandum, 21 March 1967 (THRO-S).

9. Harold Fysk (Montana State Director, BLM) to Director (USGS), memorandum, 7 July 1967 (THRO-A); Roland Lee (BLM) to USGS Office (Casper, WY), memorandum, 2 May 1972 (THRO-A). The land in question was that involved in the 1963 highway realignment preceding the construction of Interstate 94 along the right-of-way of U. S. Route 10 through Billings County.

10. For a related concern, see Ken Tapman (Compliance Officer, Advisory Council on Historic Preservation) to Edward H. Stone (Chief Landscape Architect, USFS), 17 April 1973 (THRO-A).

11. Lee to USGS, 2 May 1972.

12. Two private citizens also put in bids, but they were not competitive. C. Keith Miller (Chief, Division of Mining and Minerals, RMRO) to Supt. (THRO), memorandum, November 1974 (THRO-A).

13. Protective Oil Lease (Standard Form 3120-1, May 1968 version) between the United States (by BLM) and Amerada Hess Corporation, file L2427, leases M30613(ND) through M30620(ND), inclusive (THRO-A).

14. "Environmental Review," memorandum, 12 December 1974 (THRO-A); Amerada Hess Corporation, "Procedures for Blow Out Prevention and Control," unpublished MS, February 1975 (THRO-A); "Surface Restoration Requirements for Plugging & Abandonment Procedures on Oil and Gas Leases," memorandum, n.d. (Billings, MT: USGS).

15. "1975 Superintendent's Annual Report," 15; Robert D. Powell (Acting Supt., THRO) to Toni Ristau (DSC), 25 October 1977 (THRO-A).

16. A. J. Maslowski, "Will National Park lands be developed for oil and gas exploration?" Montana Oil Journal, 9 October 1980, 4.

17. See John O. Lancaster (Supt., THRO) to Reg. Dir. (MWRO), memorandum, 8 August 1973 (THRO-A).

18. Lancaster to L. A. Stricklin (Vice-President, Amerada Hess), 13 May 1976 (THRO-A). See also "Chief Ranger's Monthly Report," 18 June 1976.

19. John R. Vosburgh (Office of Public Affairs, WASO) to A. J. Maslowski, 8 August 1979 (THRO-A). See also Harvey D. Wickware (Supt., THRO) to Maslowski, 2 April 1980 (THRO-A).

20. "Criteria for Protective Oil and Gas Leasing of National Park Service Areas (draft)," memorandum, 1975 (THRO-A).

21. "1974 Superintendent's Annual report," 12.

22. National Park Service Minerals Management Regulations, III-3, III-11 -- III-14.

23. Maslowski, "Will National Park lands be developed for oil and gas exploration?", 4.

5) Aesthetic Management and the Quality of the Visitor Experience

One of the most important resources of the park is its rural ambience. Even though the essence of the badlands is its natural resources, protecting the character of that land can almost be considered the realm of cultural resources management, for by protecting the rural character of the badlands the Service also protects the scene Roosevelt knew. This is important because the integrity of both the natural and historical ambience is a prerequisite to the exercise of one's imagination, and with a little imagination (and a little more physical effort) visitors can empathize, rather than merely sympathize, with what Roosevelt did during his time in Dakota Territory.

The protection of the character of the badlands is achieved by means of aesthetic management. In its broadest sense, aesthetic management is concerned with the preservation of possibilities: as more and more of the country becomes industrialized and cultivated, national parks take on a correspondingly greater importance as places offering a different sensory experience. Theodore Roosevelt provides two such alternatives to visitors. The first is the chance to find solitude in natural surroundings. It has always been available in the park, but was greatly facilitated by the designation of wilderness areas in the North and South units in 1978. The second is the possibility of approximating Roosevelt's total sensory experience of a hundred years ago: to see what he saw, smell what he smelled, hear what he heard. This total sensory experience can be referred to as "the natural and historical scene."

The reader will note that these two alternative sensory experiences are not entirely exclusive of each other, for one's sense of solitude can be disrupted by the sight of an object which also degrades the natural and historical scene (such as a battery of oil tanks just outside the boundary of the park). The preconditions for the two overlap considerably. Nevertheless, for the purposes of discussion, they will be taken in turn.[1]

Solitude

Being by one's self has long been recognized as a desire of many who visit natural areas.[2] The solitude they seek is an avoidance, of two things: other people, and extraneous human-caused intrusions. For a variety of reasons backcountry use at Theodore Roosevelt has not been heavy (see Chapter 11), so without undue trouble a visitor can be alone. But today even a hike into the deepest badlands doesn't assure one of escaping the sounds, sights, and smells of the industrialized world.

The worst sensory impingement on solitude is noise, an insidious reminder that one is not far from civilization. Propane-powered oil pump engines and traffic along the Burlington Northern Railroad, U. S. Route 85, and Interstate 94 are the main sources of noise in the park.

Under the right meteorological conditions the thump of pumps, the clatter of fast-moving freight trains, and the meshing of semi-trailer truck gears can be heard at just about any point in Theodore Roosevelt.[3]

Seismic blasting and low-flying aircraft during exploration are only two of the potential sources of noise pollution associated with the search for energy in the Williston Basin. Cooperation with other agencies and private companies is essential if the Service hopes to minimize these intrusions; in fact, park personnel have occasionally met with the Forest Service (which controls most of the surface area in the Basin) to discuss common interests.[4] After one such meeting the Forest Service agreed to require seismic test crews to stay back a half-mile from the boundary of the North Unit.[5] The Service has also conferred with oil companies to reduce overflight noise, especially during the surge in exploration of 1978 to 1980 when "the number of low-flying helicopters and airplanes . . . multiplied to the point of detracting from the park's wild quality."[6]

Recent plans to improve the airstrip at Medora also jeopardize the park's ability to provide solitude. The present runway, just south of Interstate 94, receives light use. It is supposed to lie entirely on USFS land by virtue of a special use permit, but because of an error actually encroaches about three hundred feet onto park land. The Service has allowed this "only because there was good faith effort to find another location."[7]

In 1982 Medora officials and business leaders, with the support of the State Aeronautics Commission, revived an old proposal to extend the runway to a length that would accommodate private jets. They have since refused to consider a shorter rebuilt runway lying entirely outside the park; instead, they want NPS to provide land for their project.[8] The proponents of a longer airstrip include the Gold Seal Company of Bismarck, which has refurbished Medora and turned it into the top tourist attraction in the state. The company and its allies hope, naturally, to increase business by making the village more accessible to conventions and wealthy vacationers.[9]

The position of the Service is that the current encroachment is a misuse of park lands that would only be worsened by lengthening the runway. More important, the orientation of the runway (southeast to northwest), combined with the prevailing west-northwest winds, places the most prevalent takeoff pattern directly over the South Unit.[10] Since 1958 NPS has tried to have the airstrip moved elsewhere, but the Gold Seal proposal has "a fair amount of support from various levels of state and local government," and "to stand against it is viewed as the classic stand against 'progress'." The power of the "various levels" was shown in late 1984 whne the Forest Service announced its intention to cancel the permit for the airstrip on its land and to turn over the entire parcel (seventy to eighty acres) to NPS. After a public comment period, the village of Medora appealed the decision and won a reversal. The Forest Service then announced that it would neither cancel the permit nor transfer the land, but would instead take part in an environmental impact statement (though not as the lead agency) for an expansion of the airstrip.[11]

The natural and historical scene

Today, the Park Service recognizes that the primary significance of the park depends upon keeping the natural and historical scene of Roosevelt's time, so that people are afforded "the opportunity to experience the land and its resources and to reach an understanding of them, as Roosevelt once did."[12] It is hoped that visitors, by virtue of coming to the park, will gain an appreciation of the badlands similar to Roosevelt's own. For this to happen, the rural ambience of the park must be protected.

Maintenance of the visual scene is a first priority. Scenic degradation at Theodore Roosevelt has been caused by actual impairment of visibility and by the intrusion into park vistas of man-made structures not historically befitting the area.

A clear, sharp view of the badlands was important to Roosevelt when he ranched in Dakota Territory (see his description at the beginning of Chapter 9). The only sources of visibility impairment he experienced were smoke from wildfires and burning coal seams, blowing dust, and perhaps small plumes emanating from the Marquis de Morès's short-lived beef packing plant in Medora.[13]

In 1947 the park's air was considered virtually pristine. Visibility was so good that Congress cited the "truly rugged, scenic territory where the imagination may perceive most any shape or semblance" in support of the park's creation.[14] On the whole, air quality and visibility are still good, but recent energy development outside the park (and not just from sources immediately outside, but from those in the northern Plains as a whole and even beyond) has posed the possibility of degrading visibility within. The last decade has brought a sharp increase in particulate pollution, prompting one park report to declare that controlling visual degradation is essential if management objectives are to be met.[15]

But by 1977 energy exploration in the Williston Basin was beginning to boom, so the staff prepared the first documentation of overall air quality in the park, including gathering historical references to visibility and identifying important scenic vistas.[16] In that same year the Clean Air Act Amendments were passed. This law has had a profound effect. It made the park a "Class I" area; now, the most stringent rules to prevent significant deterioration of Theodore Roosevelt's air quality are in force.[17]

Class I designation led the staff to prepare a completely new assessment of visibility. It listed anthropogenic and natural sources of impairment, areas and features of Theodore Roosevelt most subject to degradation, distances of threats from the park, and management practices affecting visibility. External sources of impairment included agricultural cultivation and increased oil company traffic along scoria-dirt roads, causing "fugitive dust"; flash burning of sludge from pits next to oil wells, creating heavy columns of black smoke which can be seen for miles; automotive emissions from traffic on Interstate 94; and suspended particulate matter carried aloft to the park from electrical generating and coal gasification plants a long distance away, both of which cause decreased ambient air quality. Still, the staff reported that "at present manmade impairments appear to be very limited and only infrequently impair visibility," and that natural elements disrupt visibility five days or fewer during the summer visitor season. They resolved to preserve this excellence against deterioration by taking "appropriate positive action in those instances in which present air quality is affected or threatened."[18]

Visibility monitoring has increased. TSP (total suspended particulates) levels have been measured in the South Unit since September 1974 and in the North Unit since December 1978 by the North Dakota State Department of Health. The park staff itself measures visibility with a teleradiometer, with rangers taking readings from Skyline Vista on Johnson's Plateau or from Painted Canyon.[19] Daily measurements are taken by aiming the teleradiometer at fixed points on Bullion and Sentinel buttes south and west of Medora. From these readings, the NPS Air and Water Quality Division has begun to issue seasonal summaries of visibility which graph the results of the teleradiometer readings in terms of "standard visual range."[20]

Activities such as the teleradiometer measurements, and the general heightened interest in aesthetic management, helped the staff to make a final identification of the most important vistas in the park. After Theodore Roosevelt was designated a Class I area in 1977, the Environmental Protection Agency came out with regulations (40 Code of Federal Regulations 51.300 ff.) that gave the "federal land manager" (who, with respect to NPS, is the secretary of the interior) the opportunity to identify these prospects as "integral vistas." An integral vista is a view, originating within a Class I area but encompassing a specific landmark or panorama outside, which is deemed important to the experience of visitors. These EPA regulations would not have assured the protection of air quality within integral vistas; what they would have done was require state governments to include the vistas in their air quality implementation plans. The states would have then been compelled to weigh the costs and benefits of preventing visibility degradation within integral vistas as part of deciding whether to allow a new source of pollution whose output might affect them.

Using draft guidelines developed by NPS, the park's list of integral vistas (Table 5.1) was completed in 1980 and approved by the Rocky Mountain Regional Office and the Washington Office. In January and April 1981 it was published in the Federal Register for public comment and presented to the state of North Dakota.[21]

However, despite an internal "regulatory impact analysis" which showed that the benefits of officially publishing final lists of integral vistas would exceed the costs, in October 1985 the Department of the Interior announced that it would not make a final regulation designating such vistas. In declining to take up the extraterritorial responsibility that integral vistas would have conferred on the National Park System, Secretary of the Interior Hodel cited the possibility of incurring the resentment of state governments and the likelihood of "prolonged litigation" over the final regulation. The Department emphasized that the scenic views contained within the integral vistas should be protected from degradation, but using existing regulatory programs to resolve any conflicts.[22]

Inappropriate man-made structures near the borders of the park are a second way visual debasement of the natural and historical scene can occur. At Theodore Roosevelt such intrusions are again largely attributable to recent energy exploration: drilling rigs, tank batteries, and pumps can be seen from any high ground. The damage their presence does to the visitor experience is subtle, but real.[23]

Hopes of controlling such intrusions have been based on creating a scenic buffer zone just outside the boundary in which no new surface industrial development would be allowed. NPS first negotiated for it with the Forest Service in 1974, the year the master plan for the Little Missouri National Grasslands was published. A great deal of confusion followed about whether a buffer zone had or had not been created.

The intent of USFS as evidenced in its plan seemed clear: it promised to map out a buffer zone where "no activity which will detract from the values within the adjoining National Park, except for occupancy under [existing] oil and gas leases" would be allowed.[24] Maps contained in the final environmental impact statement to the National Grasslands plan showed a scenic control zone, which in turn was treated as a fait accompli by the park's 1975 Statement for Management.[25] Later correspondence between the local district of the Custer National Forest and Theodore Roosevelt referred to the buffer zone as having been definitely established.[26] Nevertheless, even though no new surface occupancy was allowed within the buffer zone, USFS permitted seismic testing to continue and issued new oil and gas leases as long as companies agreed to slant-drill into their parcels from outside the buffer zone.[27]

This is where the matter stood until 1982 when the Forest Service, responding to the surging interest in oil and gas leasing, published the Wannagan Roadless Area Oil and Gas Plan for its land abutting the Petrified Forest Plateau along the northwest boundary of the South Unit. The new plan indicated that surface occupancy for energy exploration and production would be allowed on land previously identified as part of the scenic buffer zone.

Commenting on the Wannagan plan in a letter to the Forest Service, Superintendent Harvey Wickware recalled to the USFS District Ranger's attention the language of the Little Missouri National Grasslands management plan, the maps showing a buffer zone, and the references in letters to a buffer zone and to a "no surface occupancy" rule. "We had thought that the Forest Service's 1974 Management Prescription for the Badlands Planning Unit [of the National Grasslands] afforded more protection to the zone of influence around Theodore Roosevelt National Park than is apparent from our review of the Wannagan (Roadless) Area Oil and Gas Plan," wrote Wickware.

> We had assumed that we would have little concern
> about adverse development off the [northwest]
> corner of the South Unit since the area was
> designated essentially roadless, and Item D,
> page 42 of the Prescription did "not allow new
> surface occupancy beyond the latest date of
> expiration for existing leases". . . .
>
> As you are aware, in 1978 Congress designated
> most of that area in the South Unit that lies
> west of the Little Missouri River as National
> Wilderness. The boundaries of this Wilderness
> adjoin the Wannagan Area for a distance of some
> 3.5 miles. . . . Our experience with oil and
> gas development at other locations in the
> vicinity of the park leads us to believe that
> development of the Wannagan Area to any degree
> can not but adversely affect the value of
> adjacent park lands that the National Park
> Service is pledged to protect. Any surface

development within a mile or so of the [north-
west] corner of the South Unit will distract
from the visual experience of visitors in the
Wilderness. . . .

The Plan you have prepared appears to be well
conceived and well done with due consideration
for the resource values that your agency and
its policies call for. If the Plan were for
an area some distance from the boundaries of
Theodore Roosevelt National Park, we would most
likely not be obliged to fault it. However,
the proposed development area's close proximity
to the park makes the Plan for development
unacceptable to the National Park Service.

"Therefore," he concluded, "unless we are misinterpreting

the Wannagan Plan, there has been a reversal of the sur-

face occupancy policy and the buffer zone referred to in

other U. S. Forest Service planning documents no longer

exists."[28]

The park staff does not now consider the USFS buffer

zone to be valid. The draft version of the Natural Re-

sources Management Plan recommends a formal agreement

between the Park Service, Forest Service, and Bureau of

Land Management to restrict new surface development, and

perhaps even to gradually remove non-producing oil equip-

ment, from publicly-held lands adjacent to Theodore Roose-

velt. Establishing a meaningful buffer zone is a vital

part of the park's proposed aesthetic management pro-

gram.[29]

Conducting similar negotiations with owners of adjoin-

ing private land is more problematical, but the Service

has had some success in persuading oil companies to camou-

flage their storage tanks by painting them earth tones or

hiding them behind ridges.[30]

The visual effects of adjacent wells have even been felt at night. At the height of exploration in the badlands many producers were burning off excess natural gas at the well head. There was so much of this flaring that many nights the horizon was much brighter than its usual inky black. Light pollution has abated somewhat in the past few years as more wells have been connected to natural gas pipelines, but the park staff is still concerned about the problem.[31]

A far more serious consequence of flaring is the fouling of the park's fresh air by the odor of released hydrogen sulfide gas. Olfactory pollution is harder to document than most because it cannot be objectively measured and may persist only briefly. An overnight stay in a campground pervaded by a smell like rotten eggs would, however, be enough to convince anyone of the importance of olfaction to a pleasant visitor experience.[32]

The release of this "sour gas" so that it enters the park in concentrations noticeable by humans[33] is a violation of North Dakota's ambient air standards, intentionally set low enough to prevent "nuisance odors" associated with energy development.[34] But since the hydrogen sulfide is suspected to be a product of an aggregate of wells, control of its flaring falls outside the Class I PSD permit process--unless the current joint study by NPS and the North Dakota Department of Health can show that the aggregate is emitting enough to be considered a separate "point source." If that can be proven, these wells would have to find a place in the Class I PSD increment.[35]

One last component of the Rooseveltian scene is the remoteness of the badlands--arguably the main enticement Dakota Territory held for the young New Yorker, even greater than the prospect of bagging a buffalo. Of all the aesthetic qualities associated with the natural world, remoteness is perhaps the most difficult to assess. Whereas solitude is an individual experience, remoteness is an overarching quality making solitude possible. Remoteness still exists in the park, but the various encroachments discussed in this chapter have, collectively, diminished it. Inevitably, drilling for oil and gas has made the badlands as a whole less remote, and industrialization along the borders of the North and South units has, in effect, shrunken the size of the park in terms of the physical space in which visitors may now experience nature in an unimpaired state.[36]

As an example, until a few years ago the Elkhorn Ranch site was quite as remote as when Roosevelt made it his home ranch, his retreat where he could write and think and escape the incessant visitors to the Maltese Cross. Its remoteness was exactly the quality he most prized. Latter-day visitors to the Elkhorn were offered a rare chance not to merely sympathize with Roosevelt in the abstract, but to empathize with him by experiencing first-hand the feelings he felt. As late as 1974, only one oil field existed between the North and South units, so the basic integrity of a trip to the Elkhorn was unchanged. But over the last decade heavy development in the immediate vicinity of the ranch site has destroyed the Elkhorn's remoteness as surely as if the connecting parkway (see Chapter 11) had been built.[37]

So, although the resources aesthetic management seeks to protect are often intangible or obscure, their loss can have a remarkable effect on the visitor experience.

Notes to Chapter 5

1. Strictly speaking, the natural and historical scenes themselves are separate, because the park now manages natural resources to perpetuate the ecosystem which is thought to have prevailed before the beginning of European settlement in western Dakota Territory-- hence, before Roosevelt's arrival in 1883. "Basic Operations Declaration," unpaginated.

2. See, for example: John C. Hendee, George H. Stankey, and Robert C. Lucas, Wilderness Management, Miscellaneous Publication #1365 (Washington, DC: USFS, 1978), 176-186.

3. "Natural Resources Management Plan and Environmental Assessment, Theodore Roosevelt National Park (draft)," unpublished MS, 1983 (THRO-A), 34-35 (hereafter cited as "NRM Plan"). It notes that, unlike the others, noise from the railroad is part of the historical scene, since Medora grew up because of the Northern Pacific Railroad in the 1880s.

4. Bradbury, 6-7; "Chief Ranger's Monthly Report," 14 June 1977.

5. "Chief Ranger's Monthly Report," 2 December 1982.

6. Bradbury, 7.

7. Harvey Wickware (Supt., THRO), quoted in Bismarck Tribune, 11 June 1983; "Chief Ranger's Monthly Report," 8 September 1977.

8. "State Coordinator's Monthly Report," 31 August 1982; Bismarck Tribune, 11 June 1983; "NRM Plan," 34.

9. Indeed, Gold Seal offered to donate some of its own land to facilitate the longer runway. Dickinson Press, 12 June 1983.

10. Ibid.; "NRM Plan," 34.

11. Quotation from "North Dakota and the National Park Service," unpublished MS, 9 November 1982 (THRO-S), 5; Hellickson to author, 14 May 1985. The Park Service has indicated that it too would participate in an airstrip EIS, if prepared by qualified individuals.

12. "Basic Operations Declaration," unpaginated.

13. "NRM Plan," 14; "Preliminary National Assessment of Class I Related Values: Visibility Report, Theodore Roosevelt National Memorial Park," unpublished MS, August 1978 (THRO-A), unpaginated.

14. "Visibility References in the Legislative History: Theodore Roosevelt National Park," unpublished MS, ca. 1978 (THRO-A), 2.

15. "Preliminary National Assessment of Class I Related Values," unpaginated.

16. "NRM Plan," 14.

17. North Dakota´s other Class I area is the wilderness portion of Lostwood National Wildlife Refuge in Burke and Mountrail counties.

18. "Preliminary National Assessment of Class I Related Values," passim.

19. "NRM Plan," 14; "Researchers and Visitors Monitor Park Air Quality," Frontier Fragments 5 (1985-86), unpaginated.

20. For example, the "1981 Seasonal Visibility Summary Report for Theodore Roosevelt National Park," attached to memorandum of James Littlejohn (Monitoring Specialist, NPS Air and Water Quality Division, Denver) to Supt. (THRO), 15 March 1982 (THRO-A).

21. 46 Federal Register 3646; 46 Federal Register 23389; 40 Code of Federal Regulations 51.300 ff.

22. Loretta Tofani, "U. S. Won´t List Most Beautiful Views," Washington Post, 26 October 1985.

23. Acknowledged in the survey the park staff filled out for the "State of the Parks Report 1980." See "Questionnaire: Threats to the Parks," unpublished MS, May 1980 (THRO-A), 3, 10.

24. Management Prescription for the Badlands Planning Unit, Little Missouri National Grasslands (Billings, MT: Custer National Forest, USFS, 1974), 50. The restrictions around the Elkhorn Unit were tougher: no off-road vehicle use, crop irrigation, or seismic prospecting--all of which were permissable in the buffer zones around the North and South units. Ibid., 43, 54, 56, 62, and 225; "Environmental Assessment: Elkhorn Unit Development," 14.

25. Management Prescription for the Badlands Planning Unit, 68; "1975 SFM," attached constraint maps. For the Department of the Interior´s reaction to the buffer zone, see Stanley D. Doremus (Deputy Asst. Secretary of the Interior) to D. C. MacIntyre (Supervisor, Custer National Forest), memorandum, 12 August 1974, 1, in Addendum to the Management Prescription

for the Badlands Planning Unit, Little Missouri National Grasslands (Billings, MT: Custer National
Forest, USFS, n.d.).

26. See Robert W. Hamner (District Ranger, Medora Ranger
District, USFS) to Harvey D. Wickware (Supt., THRO),
3 August 1979 (THRO-A). Attached to this letter is
another map showing a buffer zone around the park.

27. Ibid.

28. Wickware to Jerry B. Reese (District Ranger, Medora
Ranger District, USFS), 26 May 1982 (THRO-A).

29. "NRM Plan," 35-36.

30. Wickware to Hamner, 12 May 1980 (THRO-S).

31. See "Star Light, Star Bright. . . . Night Sky
Delights Park Visitors," Frontier Fragments 5 (1985-
86), unpaginated.

32. Cf. Wickware's comments published in the Dickinson
Press, 24 February 1983, with the letter of Lowell J.
Ridgeway (ND Petroleum Council) to Sen. Mark Andrews
(ND), 21 March 1983 (THRO-A). The park keeps a log
in which visitors can note instances of hydrogen
sulfide odor: "Researchers and Visitors Monitor Park
Air Quality," unpaginated.

33. Hydrogen sulfide is first noticeable at concentra-
tions of 150 g/m^3 and decidedly noticeable at 500
g/m^3: NPS Air and Water Quality Division, "Fact
Sheet: Hydrogen Sulfide (H_2S) at Theodore Roosevelt
National Park (THRO)," unpublished MS, 1983 (THRO-A),
unpaginated.

34. Robert T. Angelo and Kurt W. Anderson, Western North
Dakota Air Quality Study (Bismarck: NDSDH, 1981), 36-
37.

35. "State Coordinator's Monthly Report," 30 March 1983.
See also Dickinson Press, 24 February 1983; Wickware
to the ND State Industrial Commission, 2 June 1980
(THRO-A); Lee C. Gerhard and Sidney B. Anderson, Oil
Exploration and Development in the North Dakota
Williston Basin, NDGS Miscellaneous Series #57 (Bis-
marck: NDGS, 1979), 16-17; "State Coordinator's
Monthly Report," 2 February and 6 May 1983.

36. When the Forest Service drew up its master plan for
the Little Missouri National Grasslands, it explicitly stated that energy development would mean the loss
of some of the badlands's remoteness. See Management
Prescription for the Badlands Planning Unit, 85.

37. Ibid., 131. See also "State Coordinator's Monthly Report," 5 September 1979.

6) Air Quality Management

> Degradation of the air quality over the park
> is the most significant threat to park resources.

One does not often find such a sweeping declaration in the park management literature, but there it is, in a prominent place in the draft of Theodore Roosevelt's Natural Resources Management Plan. Nor are any punches pulled when it comes to identifying the cause: "The air quality within the park is being threatened by increasing development outside."

A more straightforward assessment of the predicament could not be given. Declining air quality, says the plan, is the park's "number one resource management problem" because air "is the most important, yet the most difficult to manage" natural resource.[1]

As we have seen, air pollution has decidedly affected the aesthetic quality of the park. This chapter will discuss its effects on ambient (i.e., overall) air quality, whose degradation is a physical threat to resources ranging from vegetation to historic structures. The many and subtle consequences of air pollution are what make it so hard to mitigate and why it rightly heads the list of Theodore Roosevelt's priorities.

Monitoring

The most remarkable aspect of the air quality problem is how suddenly it arose. Before the mid-1970s the park's air was "uncompromised," substantially the same as it was during the life of Roosevelt. When the Clean Air Act of 1970 created nationwide ambient air quality standards, it had no immediate effect on the park--all the standards were already being easily met.[2]

The park began monitoring air quality just at the start of North Dakota's latest oil boom. In 1974 a total suspended particulates (TSP) collector was installed in the mixpit maintenance yard of the South Unit, near Peaceful Valley Ranch. A private company working under an Environmental Protection Agency contract ran the unit for the first year; it has since been operated by the state. Monitoring did not really hit stride, though, until the height of the boom in 1979; indeed, the staff believes that any data gathered before then did not register the influence of all the new gas and oil wells.[3] By 1982 air quality monitoring was one of the park's major resource management activities. Aside from sampling particulates, Service personnel now analyze the acidity of atmospheric deposition and take teleradiometer readings. NPS also cooperates with the State Department of Health in its operation of monitoring equipment in the park (including measuring ozone levels in the North Unit). Also, as a result of a temporary cooperative venture between NPS and the Bureau of Land Management, Forest Service, and Fish and Wildlife Service, the state of North Dakota now keeps track of hydrogen sulfide (H_2S) levels using a permanent station located in the Lone Butte Oil Field east of the

North Unit. Finally, under the auspices of the Theodore Roosevelt Nature and History Association, the Park Service ha sponsored a study of lichens as indicators of changes in air quality. They are the plant species most sensitive to sulfur dioxide and should, therefore, be the first to exhibit adverse effects.[4]

The Service does not yet have enough information about recent changes to be able to predict future trends in air quality. Each monitoring project is currently at a different stage, producing a like effect in terms of the staff's knowledge of each pollutant.

Since they were the first to be studied, more is known about trends in particulates than the others. Even so, the park now has only ten years of data from the South Unit and five from the North Unit, since a TSP unit was not installed there until 1979. In that same year the University of California at Davis received a contract from the EPA to put in a fine particulate sampler at the South Unit mixpit and two high volume samplers (one each in the North and South units) to obtain a breakdown of TSP. These aerosol samplers are part of the Western Fine Particle Monitoring Network. Particles trapped in them are laboratory-tested for suspended sulfate, nitrite, and fine sulfur.[5]

During the boom years of 1979 to 1981 the park's overall TSP level stayed below legal standards (refer to Appendix E) but rose each year. Still, individual pollutants, such as suspended sulfates and nitrites, exceeded or very nearly approached their state-set limits.[6] Scientists studying these findings for the State Department of Health theorized that the cause might have been abnormally dry weather, but "industrial emissions . . . associated with the 1,500 megawatt expansion of coal-fired electrical generating capacity in west-central North Dakota from 1979 to 1981 also may have contributed to these recent concentrations."[7] Yet at the same time, sulfur dioxide, nitrogen dioxide, and nitric oxide levels "were generally less than the detection limits of the analysis instruments."[8]

If the information on TSP can be said to indicate no general trend in ambient air quality, the same also seems to be true of what is known about changes in the acidity of air over the park. Theodore Roosevelt´s acid deposition monitoring equipment, situated in the North Unit, is part of the National Atmospheric Deposition Program, which is designed to chart changes in the acidity of air over all the United States by means of a rigorous, systematic sampling and analysis procedure. (The first annual summary of NADP data--for the year 1982--only became available in 1985.) All NADP sites operate in the same way. Wet- and dry-fall are monitored using separate catchments, a recorder of discrete instances of precipitation, conductivity and pH meters, and a weight scale. Deposition is collected at regular intervals and sent to a central laboratory for analysis. Results are returned to the park and to NPS´s Water Resources Field Support Laboratory so that baseline "normal" levels of acidity can be determined.[9]

No such baseline has yet been postulated, but preliminary indications from other sources have recently become available. In 1982, Clifford M. Wetmore, a scientist with the University of Minnesota, was engaged to do a lichen flora of all three units of the park and to make some tentative judgments on how the Park Service could use natural sources to monitor air quality. Wetmore, who had done a similar study for Voyageurs National Park, completed his research at Theodore Roosevelt in 1983. The next year, permanent photographic plots of the rarest lichen species were established to monitor their status annually, and a year later permanent plots of aspens were made to keep track of the park's ozone levels, since these trees are sensitive to ozone. Also in 1985, the United States Geological Survey completed a baseline study of toxic heavy metals in the park's soil and vegetation. In all three of these projects encouraging results were returned: Wetmore reported that in the course of his work he noticed little deterioration in the physical condition of the lichens, even though he found many species which are known to be particularly sensitive to acid deposition; no foliar injury to the aspen trees was found in 1985, indicating low ozone levels; and baseline amounts for toxic heavy metals were all within normal ranges, with no elevated sulfur levels.[10]

Acid deposition and TSP are but two of NPS's concerns

at Theodore Roosevelt. In the absence of a "normal" baseline it cannot be said with certainty how much of a problem they have been or will be. However, an impartial observer would concede that overall air quality in the park has worsened over the past decade. The question for policy makers, though, is not merely how much of a decline has occurred, but how much of a decline is acceptable. For this a legal baseline has been established: the Class I Prevention of Significant Deterioration standards of 1977.

Prevention of Significant Deterioration: PSD

The Clean Air Act Amendments of 1977 introduced a system to classify the nation's lands which was designed to help maintain the air quality associated with different locales. This Prevention of Significant Deterioration program divided up those areas of the United States already meeting both the national secondary ambient standards (standards set at a level thought adequate to prevent detrimental effects to property, the environment, or other components of the public welfare) and the stricter primary ambient standards (which are meant to protect public health) into three groups: classes I, II, and III. Each class represents a different level of acceptable deterioration of ambient air quality. Class I areas have the strictest PSD standards; in other words, the quality of the air over these areas is allowed to deteriorate the least of the three.

It must be understood that the PSD classes are not, strictly speaking, indicative of an area's current air quality. The classification is merely intended to assist in preventing deterioration of existing air quality, whatever its current state might be. Improvement of existing air quality is addressed by individual state implementation plans and not by PSD. However, because of the nature of the classification system it is true that many Class I areas already have good ambient air quality as compared with most of the country. This is certainly true of Theodore Roosevelt, which, like many other sizable NPS units outside of urban areas, was designated Class I.[11]

PSD standards are important because they provide, at least in theory, a means by which the Park Service can protect air quality (and values related to air quality) in units of the System. To help regional offices and individual parks in pursuit of this goal, NPS set up an Air and Water Quality Division in Washington, D. C. The division is involved not only in PSD matters, but in every aspect of the subject as it pertains to national parks.[12]

Each Class I area has a "base level" of air quality and an "increment." The base level is variously interpreted as the ambient quality of the air at the time of the first PSD application, or as the quality prevailing under perfectly "natural" conditions.[13] Obviously the two are radically different and the interpretation greatly affects how much overall pollution will be allowed in a

Class I area. The increment is simpler and written right into the law: it is the amount of allowable deterioration to the base level air quality. Increments can be exhausted by new sources of pollution. For example, if a new power plant opens near a Class I area and puts out sulfur dioxide in quantities equal to the increment, the PSD increment for sulfur dioxide is said to be "consumed" and no other sources emitting sulfur dioxide would be allowed to locate near the Class I area unless they obtained a special certification from the federal government (for which see below).

Two things should be noted. First, the Environmental Protection Agency has defined increments only for sulfur dioxide and particulates. Second, the PSD regulations apply only to "new sources" of pollution--that is, to emissions from facilities for which construction started after January 6, 1975.

The federal government does not always handle the entire PSD process. Some states have been given charge of implementing the law, but only if they have developed programs which are both acceptable to the Environmental Protection Agency and are at least as stringent as the federal PSD regulations. North Dakota is such a state, with the Department of Health responsible for enforcing PSD regulations. It performs the computer modeling estimation of the amount of new pollution, estimates which decide whether the increment has been consumed. It also evaluates privately-done analyses.[14]

Variances

In the jargon of the Clean Air Act, the Secretary of the Interior is referred to by the generic term "federal land manager." According to the law, the federal land manager (whose responsibilities in the Theodore Roosevelt case were assumed by Interior's assistant secretary for fish, wildlife, and parks) "has an affirmative responsibility to protect the air quality related values . . . of a Class I area and to consider . . . whether a proposed major emitting facility will have an adverse impact on such values."[15] As this statement implies, there is a way for a PSD increment to be legally exceeded. If the company proposing a new facility near a Class I area can demonstrate to the satisfaction of the federal land manager that the pollution produced in excess of the amount allowed by the increment will have no unacceptable adverse impact on air quality related values in the park, a "notice of certification" will be issued to the state. If the state accepts this certification of no unacceptable adverse impact, it may in turn issue a "variance," a waiver of the Class I PSD regulations so that the company can go ahead and build the facility. Even should the federal land manager find that a new facility would produce an unacceptably adverse effect, it is possible for the company to obtain a variance by convincing the state governor--or, if the federal land manager still objects, the president--to overrule. If the decision reaches the chief executive, the president's decision is final and cannot be reviewed in court.[16]

Variances are a major loophole in the PSD regulations. It is possible for the Service's recommendations on new polluting sources to be overridden on any of three levels: by the Department of the Interior, the state, or the chief executive. Theodore Roosevelt has been involved in controversy over variances from the time it was named a Class I area. Much of the park's struggle to maintain its ambient air quality turns on this crucial process.

The variance controversy arose quickly because the Class I PSD increment for sulfur dioxide was consumed quickly. In 1977 five pending new-source energy facilities were evaluated for their effect on sulfur dioxide levels in Theodore Roosevelt. The increment for sulfur dioxide, as measured in 24-hour concentrations, is five micrograms per cubic meter. Therefore, the combined daily output of sulfur dioxide from these five facilities could not exceed five micrograms per cubic meter. Each assigned a place in the increment in the order in which its permit application was received. The UPA/CPA coal conversion plant was the first to submit its application to the state, so its contribution of 1.4 micrograms per cubic meter found a place in the increment. The results for all five facilities are summarized in Table 6.1.

The entire sulfur dioxide increment was immediately

consumed by these new sources.[17] This did not sit well with energy developers wanting to process the coal, oil, and natural gas of the state, for unless the existing point sources relocated or cut back their emissions so others could find a place in the increment, or variances were granted, no new facilities could be built. The former being most unlikely, developers devoted their efforts to obtaining variances.

The consumption of the increment soon had the attention of the state's journalists. Any proposed energy plants which were to be located within an imaginary triangle linking the North and South units and the Coal Creek plant near Underwood (Figure 6.1) were considered subject to the PSD new source increment. Determined by an approximation of the path pollutants would take if the wind blew steadily from Coal Creek to the park, the triangle was considered part of Theodore Roosevelt's airshed. It was dubbed the "Smokestack Triangle" by journalists, and became to the general public a readily understandable, if somewhat inaccurate, symbol of the PSD variance process.[18]

Being in the middle of a situation portrayed as a battle between economic development and the environment was not a pleasing prospect to the park staff. By 1979 they were noting with dismay the number of editorials appearing in the region's small newspapers urging a "balance" between the use of mineral resources and preservation of air quality. "There will be a confrontation sometime soon about the Class I air over the park," wrote

Superintendent Harvey Wickware the next year. "We will deepen our ´bad guy´ image because of our mandated position [to protect Theodore Roosevelt´s ambient air quality]. There will be hard times for us in North Dakota in this regard."[19]

He was only too right. By the end of 1980, eight construction applications for the Smokestack Triangle had been received. The applicants all contended that the computer models the State Department of Health had used in 1977 to predict sulfur dioxide emissions from the original permittees were outdated and should be replaced by their own, newer models. The state´s response was encouraging: "If the newer long-range models can provide a more realistic prediction of changes in air quality and can show that increment is available beyond the 1977 prediction, then some energy development will be allowed."[20] Of the eight projects announced for the Smokestack Triangle, six went all the way through the variance process.

Models and meteorology

The models referred to are computer simulations of pollutant dispersion; PSD decision-making depends on being able to predict where airborne pollutants will go, and in what concentrations, after they leave a given smokestack. Models are necessary because the numerical increments are too small to be reliably measured in the field. But modeling is imprecise because of the assumptions necessitated by complicated atmospheric processes. That fact contributed to the controversy in North Dakota, for the way the computer analysis was performed--what data were chosen, which formulas were used, what assumptions were made--profoundly influenced the results. Models were developed for each of the six facilities, and each was somewhat blighted by technical inadequacies.

In 1980, soon after their applications were filed, the six companies submitted their own models to the State Department of Health.[21] The results were difficult to judge because of the variety of models used. The Department reviewed them, held a public hearing to assess the adequacy of the proposed techniques, and after a thorough survey chose from the applicants´s models the ones it thought best suited for making uniform estimates. The Environmental Protection Agency, while not approving for general use the state´s choice of models, found its basic approach sound and legally defensible, and mostly concurred in its findings of fact.[22]

The Department of Health´s re-evaluation of its 1977 methodology originally was to have used a generalized screening model to select "critical scenarios," with these then being run through a more refined model. However, the Department revised the screening model so much (partly in response to comments made at the public hearing) that it never got to the refined-model stage. Park Service officials attended the assessment hearing and met with the Department to review the estimates of air quality produced by the revised screening model. For the most part NPS also could not fault the state's modeling approach.[23]

Most computer models are based on Gaussian plume dispersion theory, which combines engineering and climatic data to produce results. The importance of accurate weather statistics to the efficacy of these models cannot be overstated.[24] The Department of Health was criticized for using only one year of meteorological data gathered in 1964 from a station at Bismarck, well over a hundred miles from the park. The state justified the chosen data base by asserting that the weather for Bismarck and the badlands was generally the same; they also pointed out that 1964 was the last year in which hour-by-hour readings were taken.[25] But one analyst argued that the state's models could be run using every third hour of surface readings, thus enabling the use of a broader data base--the years 1971 to 1975--to better ascertain the frequency of occurrence of meteorological conditions.[26]

Another problem with the computer models was their applicability. Through 1979 estimates of pollution effects on Theodore Roosevelt were prepared using Gaussian steady-state models. The EPA recommends their use only to a radius of fifty kilometers from the emitting source, but the park was farther away than that from some of the six proposed facilities. The Department of Health knew this when it did its original analyses, but had no choice: the Clean Air Act Amendments of 1977 required that the amount of consumption of the PSD increments be determined as soon as possible, and at the time no larger-scale models had been adequately tested.[27] It was an unusual instance of legislation outdistancing theory.

By 1980 so-called "mesoscale" (medium- to long-range) models had been developed, so the companies had a point when they demanded that the analyses be redone. Still, the new mesoscale models did not account for ruggedness of terrain any better than the steady-state ones. Computer models assume that the land between the polluting source and the receptor is perfectly flat. Introducing variations in terrain alters both the predicted dispersion and concentration of the pollutants. One would think that, of all places, North Dakota would fit the models's assumption best. But the terrain of Theodore Roosevelt National Park is certainly not flat, and this fact could not be compensated for in the mesoscale modeling.[28]

Once the data was inserted into the models, it could be analyzed in any number of ways, with the results subject to varying interpretations and reasonable differences of opinion. At one point the Environmental Defense Fund charged the Park Service, whose Air and Water Quality Division did the technical review of the computer models, with making a mathematical error in the equations used to predict deterioration of visibility. Using higher coefficients, the Environmental Defense Fund maintained that if the variances were granted to all the applicants, the new sources of pollution would reduce visibility seventeen to thirty-four days a year rather than the six predicted by NPS.[29] Other discrepancies and questionable computations can be found.[30]

Finally, the expense of doing the computer simulations prevented them from being as complete as they perhaps should have been. For example, the Department of Health did not always perform a comprehensive examination of particulate levels because of "the relatively low TSP emission rates of the sources involved, and the somewhat less restrictive Class I increments for TSP. Further," it added, "the computer costs of modeling would substantially increase with a detailed TSP analysis."[31] Instead, it modeled a worst-case TSP episode for the North Unit, and found it to be well within the increment for 24-hour concentrations. The Department did not analyze average annual TSP concentrations.[32]

The technical review and waiver

The Department of Health's mesoscale modeling indicated that, if all six plants were built, sulfur dioxide concentrations higher than the 3-hour increment in the North and South units and much higher than the 24-hour increment in all three units would occur. So in 1982 the state informed five of the companies that they would have to apply to the federal land manager for a variance. The sixth, Phillips Petroleum, did not need a variance because its predicted emissions were below the "significance level" as subsequently set forth in state government regulations implementing the Clean Air Act Amendments of 1977. But in the technical review of the variance applications and the state's modeling procedures, NPS's Air and Water Quality Division (acting as proxy for the federal land manager) went ahead and evaluated all six of the projects.[33]

The technical review took four parts: A BACT (best available control technology) analysis; an evaluation of the state's air quality modeling; a study of the new source's effects on values associated with air quality; and a summary of findings.

Each company had to demonstrate that it would use the best available combinations of equipment to control emissions. One of the applicants, Warren Petroleum, had to redo its initial BACT because the Air and Water Quality Division found alternative sets of equipment that would bring better sulfur recovery.[34]

The evaluation of the Department of Health's findings on air quality focused on three individual pollutants and visibility. NPS concurred with the state and found that, if anything, it had overestimated sulfur dioxide concentrations. The Service also agreed with the state's decision not to estimate average annual concentrations of TSP because "it is obvious from the results of the 24-hour screening analysis that the annual average Class I increment for particulate matter (5 micrograms per cubic meter) will not be exceeded with the introduction of the new sources. Also, concentration estimates for Elkhorn Ranch were not made because of the extremely low estimates for the other units and because there is no reason (based on the SO_2 analysis) to expect higher particulate matter concentrations at Elkhorn Ranch." Even though expected concentrations of fluoride, the third pollutant considered in the technical review, were below the government's significance level and so not subject to PSD regulations, the Air and Water Quality Division made an estimate since fluoride is so toxic to vegetation.[35]

Each applicant met the Environmental Protection Agency's criteria for plume perceptibility; that is, considered separately, none of the sources were expected to cause a smoke plume visible from Theodore Roosevelt. Still, NPS decided that a study of the cumulative effect of these new sources on visibility should be made. The division estimated the reduction in visibility with the help of the teleradiometer and fine particulate data gathered from the South and North units. They predicted that permitting the new sources would cause less than a two percent reduction in the park's standard visual range.[36]

The Air and Water Quality Division also evaluated the effects of the proposed projects on "air quality related values"--species of flora and fauna, cultural resources, soil types, and surface waters sensitive to air pollution. Five out of the six applications contained no discussion of these effects and the sixth's was inadequate.

Of the park's flora, lichens were the species thought most at risk. In the North Unit, sulfur dioxide had already reached concentrations which elsewhere had been detrimental to lichens. In early June 1982, NPS personnel made a field trip to the park to look for symptoms of injury to sensitive vegetation. No sulfur dioxide damage to lichens was found, nor was ozone damage seen in five indicator species: ponderosa pine, clematis, globemallow, alfalfa, and milkweed. They were examined because the presence of sulfur dioxide lowers the ozone concentration threshold for injuring some plants.

The Air and Water Quality Division's fluoride concentration estimates were not high enough to ascribe an adverse effect to vegetation or insects. But the technical review did note that fluoride cannot be metabolized and accumulates until toxic levels are reached; therefore, perennial plants and herbivores who feed on them would be at risk from long periods of exposure to low levels of it. The division's review could not predict what effect increased TSP levels might have on birds at Theodore Roosevelt, nor could it do more than remark on the possibility that fish and amphibians might be hurt by increased acid deposition.[37]

The technical review admitted to "considerable uncertainty" in its determination of the effects of the new polluting sources, enumerating a long list of cautions.[38] After all was said and done, though, the Air and Water

Quality Division strongly implied that even if all the permits were denied, concentrations of the three pollutants were already high enough to produce some ill effects in the park's ecosystem, although none had been observed. "In fact," the reviewers wrote, "the five applicants contribute relatively small percentages of the maximum predicted concentrations" and "none of the probable effects are expected to occur on a scale large enough to irreversibly change ecosystems functions and structures or to affect visitor use and enjoyment." With this finding of no unacceptable adverse impact, the division, acting for the federal land manager, recommended that the state approve all the applications for PSD variances.[39]

The NPS technical review did not go uncriticized. The National Parks and Conservation Association thought the visibility and vegetation analyses were not good enough.[40] During the public comment period, many substantial criticisms (fifty pages in all) were made by the Dacotah Chapter of the Sierra Club, the Dakota Resource Council, the Technical Information Project, and the Environmental Defense Fund. Some of them were effectively rebutted by the Service; others, less so.[41]

Many of these criticisms were specifically prompted by the preliminary finding of no unacceptable adverse impact, which had been announced on July 12, 1982. In late August the public comment period was reopened briefly upon the receipt of regional air quality statistics showing a sharp increase in wintertime sulfur dioxide levels over the first six months of 1982. The Air and Water Quality Division subsequently issued a supplementary technical review (with an expanded discussion of visibility); in it the Service found no reason to change its preliminary finding.[42] On September 20, a final determination of no unacceptable adverse impact was published in the Federal Register. The way was cleared for the state to grant variances to the projects.[43]

The real effects of Theodore Roosevelt's PSD experience will probably not be felt for a few years. "At the current time the State and the Service are on the same wavelength on this issue," noted an in-park report in late 1982. "With the Service certifying no adverse impact from the six major sources most of the weight of the decision is now on the State Health Department. The day of reckoning is not far off, however. The first and subsequent denial of such certification on the part of the 'Federal Land Manager' will bring great weight to bear upon the Service by state officials and the leadership of the major industries involved. Major litigation is all but a foregone conclusion."[44]

Coal leasing in the Fort Union Region

The "day of reckoning" may come if and when the Bureau of Land Management completes the long-delayed leasing of federally-owned coal in the Fort Union Coal Region, an administrative appellation encompassing eastern

Montana and western North Dakota. BLM estimates that about 1.6 billion tons of accessible coal underlie the Region. Originally, BLM planned to offer twenty-four tracts for lease (Figure 6.2).

While most of the Fort Union coal would be shipped out for burning, some would probably remain to fuel existing and proposed power plants in the Northern Plains.[45] This presents a problem to NPS because some of these facilities would be west of Theodore Roosevelt, with the prevailing winds bringing their pollutants directly to the park. All the new sources involved in the variance process discussed above are east of Theodore Roosevelt--still within its airshed, but likely to produce only episodic degradation of the park's ambient air quality. Hence, the federal land manager's certification of no unacceptable adverse impact was, in their cases, a relatively straightforward decision. Granting variances to new sources west of the park would be quite another matter.

BLM's own Fort Union regional environmental impact statement predicted that, no matter which leasing alternative was approved, TSP concentrations would go beyond state and federal standards, the sulfur dioxide increment for Theodore Roosevelt would be considerably exceeded, and visibility within the park would decline. BLM anticipated that companies interested in leasing would voluntarily comply with the Class I PSD regulations to gain access to the federal tracts.[46]

In early 1983, as the Fort Union leasing date neared (it has since been delayed), environmentalists charged that the Park Service, given its recent recommendation of a no unacceptable adverse impact certification, was preparing to make Theodore Roosevelt a "sacrifice area" by not opposing the BLM leasing program. This the Service denied, and reported to the newspapers its official concern about the BLM plan.[47] NPS was particularly worried about three tracts close to the park. Perhaps responding to that concern, in June 1983 the secretary of the interior withdrew two of them (North Wibaux-Beach and Zenith) from the lease sale and made leasing of the third (South Wibaux-Beach) subject to special stipulations requiring the lessor to protect Theodore Roosevelt's air quality.[48]

The most difficult resource to manage

Air quality management is the most complicated, and the most important, resource management question facing the park. The air over Theodore Roosevelt is still relatively clean but how much it will be allowed to deteriorate is the essence of the controversy.

As we have seen, the PSD regulations, which are meant to limit deterioration, are imperfect. Variances are not the only loophole. The park staff suspects that most of the hydrogen sulfide sour gas coming into the park comes from aggregate oil well flaring, from individual wells which are not yet considered "point sources" and therefore not subject to PSD regulations. They also put out considerable amounts of other pollutants: a study of 235 wells near the park showed that from July 1981 through June 1982 they emitted about 20,000 tons of sulfur dioxide.[49] Yet these data only suggest another complication: the variance process can actually work to the betterment of the park's ambient air quality. Three of the six applicants-- Phillips, Warren, and Amoco--wanted to build treatment plants to process natural gas which otherwise would be flared or vented into the atmosphere from individual wells. Even though gas treatment plants themselves produce pollution, their construction could cause an overall reduction in hydrogen sulfide and sulfur dioxide emissions from non-point sources around Theodore Roosevelt as more and more wells hook up with pipelines connected to the treatment plants.[50]

The oil boom of the 1970s and early 1980s is now over, and as the rush to develop new fields slackens there are indications that some citizens in North Dakota are beginning to share the park staff's concern about ambient air quality.[51] Public support for the park's position is of course essential if NPS is to keep air quality degradation to a minimum. Gaining that support requires demonstrating to the public how quickly the problem has arisen and how severe it can just as quickly become. After all, as recently as 1976 the park's own superintendent could rather nonchalantly report that, while state-sponsored air quality research "is not directly related to the park, some information, valuable to the park, will be derived."[52]

Then again, the park's air was considerably cleaner in 1976 than it is today.

Notes to Chapter 6

1. The quotations can be found on pp. 9, 14, and 16 of the "NRM Plan." See also "1982 Superintendent's Annual Report," 12.

2. "NRM Plan," 14.

3. Ibid., 14, 15; "Chief Ranger's Monthly Report," 8 August 1974.

4. "1982 Superintendent's Annual Report," 12; Ray Snow, "One Piece of the Research Action: Theodore Roosevelt NP," Park Science 2:3 (Spring 1982), 11.

5. "NRM Plan," 14; R.G. Flocchini et al., "Characterization of Particles in the Arid West," Atmospheric Environment 15:10/11 (1981), 2017-2030; R.G. Flocchini, "A Synoptic Scale Fine Particle Monitoring Network in the Western U.S.," unpublished MS, ca. 1980 (THRO-L), unpaginated.

6. Angelo and Anderson, Western North Dakota Air Quality Study, 12, 27, and 33; Robert T. Angelo and Kurt W. Anderson, The Chemistry of Atmospheric Precipitation in North Dakota: A Preliminary Report With Comments on the Ambient Air Quality and Meteorological Characteristics of Western North Dakota in 1981 (Bismarck: NDSDH, 1982), 86, 88. TSP have exceeded the legal limits in a couple of instances, but only under extraordinary conditions such as a prolonged east wind or after the eruption of the Mount St. Helens volcano in May 1980. See Flocchini et al., 2020-2021.

7. Angelo and Anderson, Chemistry of Atmospheric Precipitation, 86.

8. Angelo and Anderson, Western North Dakota Air Quality Study, 33-35.

9. "NRM Plan," 31.

10. Ibid., 32; Clifford Wetmore, "Lichens and Air Quality in Theodore Roosevelt National Park," unpublished MS, 1983 (THRO-A); L.P. Gough, J.L. Peard, R.C. Severson, L.L. Jackson, B.F. Arbogast, J.M. Motooka, S.W. Snow, E.E. Engleman, and J.P. Bennett, "Baseline Elemental Composition of Selected Plants and Soils, and Assessment of Airborne Element Contamination, Theodore Roosevelt National Park, North Dakota," USGS Open-File Report 85-251, 1985 (THRO-A); John P. Christiano (Chief, NPS Air Quality Division) to Harvey Wickware (Supt., THRO), memorandum, 16 December 1985 (THRO-A), 2-3.

11. As of 1983, North Dakota was the only state in complete compliance with federal clean air standards.

Fargo Forum, 8 May 1983.

12. Myron F. Uman, "The PSD Program of the National Park
     Service," unpublished MS, 1980 (THRO-A), 4.

13. Ibid., 6. See also 40 CFR (a)(13)(i) -- (14)(i).
     For a valuable explanation of the background and
     effect of the Clean Air Act Amendments of 1977 on the
     parks, refer to Robert Maynard, "The Clean Air Act
     Amendments and the National Parklands," University of
     Michigan Journal of Law Reform 11:2 (Winter 1978),
     290-316, and esp. 295 (for baselines).

14. Martin R. Shock, The Selection of a Complete Modeling
     Procedure for the Simulation of Mesoscale Ground
     Level Air Quality Considerations (Bismarck: NDSDH,
     1981), 6. North Dakota was one of the first states
     to adopt PSD regulations (in January 1976). In May
     1977, EPA delegated PSD enforcement responsibility to
     the state; see Final West-Central North Dakota Re-
     gional Environmental Impact Study on Energy Develop-
     ment (N.p., BLM and State of North Dakota, 1978), 12.
     See also Maynard, 296.

15. Uman, 2, quoting the Clean Air Act Amendments of
     1977, Section 165 (d)(2)(b). Maynard (p. 303) has
     this to say about the Federal Land Manager's role in
     carrying out the Act:

          The federal land manager, who is given an
          "affirmative responsibility to protect the
          air quality related values" of federal Class
          I areas under his jurisdiction, is crucial
          to [the PSD] scheme. Legislative history
          characterizes this duty as that of a diligent,
          aggressive advocate for protection of air
          quality over these lands. The manager is to
          resolve all doubts about the air quality
          impacts of new development in favor of
          continued protection. He is expected to
          initiate the new source permit review process
          by notifying the state of expected threats to
          the air quality related values of Class I
          lands, as well as reviewing the pollution
          effects of proposed new sources within the
          administrative process. . . . Clearly, the
          federal land management agencies must perform
          their adversary function if the amendments
          are to protect national parklands effectively.

16. Air Pollution Control Regulations of the State of
     North Dakota (ND Administrative Code), Article 33-15,
     Chapter 33-15-15, paragraphs 4-6 (pp. 13-14); Final
     West-Central North Dakota EIS, 17. For a full
     discussion, see Maynard, 306-307.

17. Final West-Central North Dakota EIS, 21-23; Air Quality Effects Analysis and Permit Application of Western Natural Gas Processors, Ltd., Natural Gas Processing and Sulfur Recovery Plant, Billings County, North Dakota (Bismarck: NDSDH, 1979), 48.

18. See for example the Bismarck Tribune, 22 September 1979, 1.

19. "State Coordinator's Monthly Report," 2 October 1979; quotation from Annual Management Review, Theodore Roosevelt National Park, North Dakota: 1980 (Medora: NPS, 1980), unpaginated.

20. Natural Resources Interim Plan (Bismarck: Natural Resources Council, State of North Dakota, 1980), 10.

21. The six projects for which variances were originally sought: Basin Electric Power Cooperative's 500 megawatt addition (AVS #3) to its Antelope Valley electric generating plant; Warren Petroleum's expansion of its Little Knife natural gas processing plant; Nokota's coal-to-methanol plant; a 500 megawatt generating station of Minnesota Power and Light; and gas processing plants of Amoco and Phillips Petroleum. See NPS Air and Water Quality Division's "Technical Review of Six PSD Permit Applications Potentially Affecting Theodore Roosevelt National Park and Lostwood National Wildlife Refuge," unpublished MS, 17 June 1982 (THRO-A), Table 2 (contained in unpaginated appendix).

22. "Technical Review," 4.

23. Ibid.

24. Maynard, 303-305; and Richard A. Dobbins, Atmospheric Motion and Air Pollution (New York: John Wiley & Sons, 1979), 219-249, esp. 243. Shock (p. 4) writes: "The choice of input data, particularly the wind field, is a critical aspect of the air quality modeling process."

25. Air Quality Effects Analysis of Warren Petroleum Natural Gas Processing Plant, Billings County, North Dakota (Bismarck: Division of Environmental Engineering, NDSDH, 1978), 44, 46, and 39.

26. Shock, 67.

27. Ibid., 4.

28. Ibid., 58; Maynard, 305; Air Quality Effects Analysis of Basin Electric Power Cooperative Antelope Valley

Station Unit 3, Mercer County, North Dakota (Bismarck: Division of Environmental Engineering, NDSDH,
1982), 144-145. See also "State Coordinator's Monthly Report," 4 March 1980.

29. Dickinson Press, 15 September 1982. "This is not a
clear-cut science," said NPS Air Quality Division
liaison John Christiano in reference to the difference of opinion.

30. In a later study, the state admitted to the "post-
processing of hourly output . . . in order to remove
calm wind bias from calculated 3-hour and 24-hour
concentrations. . . ." See Air Quality Effects
Analysis of Cities Service Company Lignite Gas Plant,
Burke County, North Dakota (Bismarck: Division of
Environmental Engineering, NDSDH, 1983), 38.

31. Air Quality Effects Analysis, Antelope Valley Unit 3,
171.

32. Ibid., 173. This TSP format is also used in the Air
Quality Effects Analysis and Permit Application of
Amoco Production Company, Whitetail Gas Processing
Plant, Billings County, North Dakota (Bismarck: Divi-
sion of Environmental Engineering, NDSDH, 1982), and
Air Quality Effects Analysis of Warren Petroleum
Natural Gas Processing Plant (Expansion), Billings
County, North Dakota (Division of Environmental Engi-
neering, NDSDH, 1982).

33. "Technical Review," 1. For significance levels, see
40 CFR (b)(23)(i) and 40 CFR (i)(8)(i), and Air
Quality Effects Analysis and Permit Application of
Koch Hydrocarbon Company Gas Processing and Sulfur
Recovery Plant, McKenzie County, North Dakota (Bismarck: Division of Environmental Engineering, NDSDH,
1980), 59.

34. "Technical Review," 2-4.

35. Ibid., 4-7. Quotations from pp. 5 and 6, respectively.

36. Ibid., 7.

37. Ibid., 11-12. None of the cultural resources in the
park were thought susceptible to deterioration caused
by acid deposition (but cf. "Questionnaire: Threats
to the Parks").

38. "Technical Review," 11.

39. Ibid., 13-14. Quotation from p. 14.

40. "Attack on Clean Air at Teddy Roosevelt NP," National

Parks Magazine 56:11/12 (November-December 1982), 30.

41. "Response to Public Comments on the Federal Land Manager's Determination of No Adverse Impact on Theodore Roosevelt National Park and Lostwood National Wildlife Refuge Under Section 165(d)(2)(c)(iii) of the Clean Air Act," unpublished MS, September 1982 (THRO-A), passim.; Duane Sebastian (Chairperson, Dakota Resource Council) to Gene Christianson (Division of Environmental Engineering, NDSDH), 5 June 1982 (THRO-A).

42. "Supplemental Information to the July 1982 Technical Review of Six PSD Permit Applications Potentially Affecting Theodore Roosevelt National Park and the Wilderness Portion of Lostwood National Wildlife Refuge," unpublished MS, August 1982 (THRO-A), 1, 7. The state believed the high sulfur dioxide figures were a temporary increase caused by flaring from a new oil field.

43. "Theodore Roosevelt National Park and Lostwood National Wildlife Refuge; Final Certification of No Adverse Impact," *Federal Register* 47 FR 41480 (20 September 1982). The certification was made effective as of 15 September 1982. See also Greg Turosak, "Park Service OKs Energy Projects," *Bismarck Tribune*, 20 September 1982.

44. "North Dakota and the National Park Service," 2.

45. "NRM Plan," 23.

46. *Fort Union Coal Regional Environmental Impact Statement; Air Quality Information Supplemental to the Fort Union Coal Region Draft Environmental Impact Statement* (Billings: MT State Office, BLM, 1982), S-11--S-35; Dan Gorham, "Roosevelt Park Air Threatened," *High Country News*, 13 May 1983.

47. *Dickinson Press*, 24 February 1983.

48. Ibid., 10 June 1983.

49. "State Coordinator's Monthly Report," 30 March 1983; NDSDH, "Final Report: Sulfur Dioxide Emission Inventory for Sources Near the Theodore Roosevelt National Park (draft)," unpublished MS, February 1983 (THRO-A), 19.

50. "Fact Sheet: Hydrogen Sulfide (H_2S) at Theodore Roosevelt National Park (THRO)," 2.

51. "State Coordinator's Monthly Report," 7 June and 8 August 1983.

52.   "1976 Superintendent's Annual Report," 10.

Part 3:

Resource Management

> By what way is the light parted,
> Or the east wind scattered upon the earth?
> Who hath cleft a channel for the waterflood,
> Or a way for the lightning of the thunder;
> To cause it to rain on a land where no man is;
> On the wilderness, wherein there is no man;
> To satisfy the waste and desolate ground;
> And to cause the tender grass to spring forth?
> -- Job 38: 24-27

7) Wilderness Designation

As in so much else, when it comes to wilderness the northern badlands offer little in the way of clear-cut answers. To some, like Brigadier General Sully, the region was a wilderness of the spirit, an area darkly considered, populated only by raw wind. For Roosevelt, it was the kind of wild country that exhilarates, for the wind breathed there as he himself never could.

The issue of exactly what constitutes wilderness is likewise subjective. Although some would argue that wilderness is delimited by identifiable natural parameters which make it fundamentally different than other land uses, at its heart wilderness is a social concept. It varies across time, place, and people.

If the most stringent definition of wilderness were applied to Theodore Roosevelt, the park would have none. No one has maintained that any part of the park is absolutely pristine--even the remote Achenbach Hills of the North Unit were subjected to scattered cattle grazing before the 1940s.[1] It would be perverse, however, to contend that such marginal uses by semi-permanent human populations have negated the land's essentially wild character. In fact, precisely because they were "the farthest away from the state highway, the park road, park improvements, and other interventions by man," the Achenbachs were recognized as a de facto wilderness by NPS as early as 1937.[2]

Since it is also so difficult of access, much of the

other land in the park has, by default, been managed as wilderness. Even though it was prepared at the height of MISSION 66, the 1963 Master Plan recommended keeping most of the park in a wild state. All the South Unit west of the Little Missouri and north of a power line in section 16 was internally zoned as wilderness, as was everything south of the river and more than a half-mile north of the scenic drive in the North Unit.[3] What were lacking were legal safeguards against future development of these areas.

A first wilderness plan

Purposeful consideration of wilderness management in the park awaited the Wilderness Act of 1964. It defined wilderness as "country where natural conditions are still dominant, to be kept free of roads, structures, and mechanical equipment,"[4] and required the Park Service to evaluate the feasibility of statutory wilderness in its areas. Members of the Wilderness Society joined NPS personnel for the first organized field studies of Theodore Roosevelt in the late summer and early fall of 1966. The Society's avowed purpose was to preclude further road development.[5] The resulting proposal, timed to coincide with the 1967 Master Plan, called for 23,400 acres to be designated under the terms of the Act. In the South Unit, this consisted of everything west of the river and north of the power line, except for the petrified forest formations (which were subject to a privately-owned surface mineral claim) and a thin corridor along a buckboard trail which was proposed to bisect the area.   In the North Unit, practically all land south of the Little Missouri was included.[6]

This working plan soon became entangled in minutiae, such as whether the North Unit should be disqualified because of Project Skywater, a Bureau of Reclamation rain making program begun in McKenzie County in 1964.[7] Worse yet was the arcane logic the park staff was forced to use to keep historical values paramount in a park better suited to management as a natural area.   Witness the discomfort of Superintendent Arthur Sullivan over the fate of the North Unit's herd of longhorn cattle:

> We contend that the safeguarding of the histori-
> cal integrity of the park and the presentation
> and interpretation of park historical values
> should take precedence over any wilderness
> values which are incidental to the area.   If the
> North Unit wilderness proposal becomes law, we
> will forever have closed the door to a freedom
> of choice in the matter of the longhorn story
> interpretation.   We are loathe to tie the hands
> of future administrations in this matter and for
> this reason recommend the North Unit wilderness
> proposal be withdrawn. (8)

This argument taxes credulousness and it is hard to believe that Sullivan made it entirely in earnest.   If anything, the values represented by the longhorns are incidental to the park since they are an allusion to the general conditions prevailing in the badlands open range cattle industry during the 1880s and do not even represent the breeds Roosevelt raised (see Chapter 10).

Thus the informal working plan became bogged down. It was abandoned outright after the enactment in 1970 of the National Environmental Policy Act. Wilderness designation was sure to be a "major" and "controversial" federal undertaking as defined in NEPA, so any plan now had to be able to withstand public comment and an environmental impact assessment. With this in mind, the park staff decided to start anew with a revised, official proposal.

How best to leave the land alone

The new proposal mirrored the philosophy of the 1970 revision of the 1967 Master Plan. It deviated substantially from the informal working plan that prompted Sullivan's comments--in fact, it turned his suggestions upside down, calling for wilderness in the North but not the South Unit. Apparently the presence of the unresolved surface mineral claim and the proposed buckboard trail was thought to put all the area west of the Little Missouri out-of-bounds for wilderness consideration. In contrast, the North Unit proposed wilderness was far greater in extent than that originally planned, including large areas north as well as south of the river.

In addition, the new plan brought up some management concerns sure to be contested during the environmental review. Some thought that dish tanks, the man-made catchments attached to flowing water wells throughout the backcountry, had no place in a wilderness area. Also, the legality of designating river bottom lands was brought into question because of the perpetual stock driveway easement conceded to local ranchers at the park's creation. Finally, despite its fickle flowage the Little Missouri was officially considered a navigable stream. Legally, then, the ownership of the watercourse was vested in the state of North Dakota.[9] This anomaly held potentially disastrous possibilities for wilderness management in the river corridor. Such distractions threatened to turn the whole process as slow and muddy as the river itself in summer.

The disparate treatments planned for the North and South units contributed to a division of public opinion on the proposal. Response meetings were scheduled for December 1970 in Watford City and Medora. They were the first opportunity ever for lay people to formally comment on the management of the national memorial park.

Northwestern North Dakota businesses and civic organizations arrayed themselves against the official proposal as soon as it became known that most of the North Unit might be made a wilderness area. The Watford City Association of Commerce headed the opposition. At its November 1970 meeting, Superintendent James Thompson presented the Service's views on the matter, sparking some "heated discussion."[10] The Association of Commerce then outlined its case in a position paper appearing in the McKenzie County Farmer about a week before the hearings. It is worth examining in detail, not only as a reaction to a specific management proposal but also because it reveals how completely the contradictions inherent in the NPS Organic Act had been internalized by one community. The ten points paraphrased below show that the civic leaders of Watford City were just as equivocal about the purpose of a national park as the theoreticians of the Park Service had been in 1916.

The wilderness plan for the North Unit was opposed because the Association of Commerce thought

1) it would virtually close the park to motoring;
2) the North Unit "should not be limited to the special group who have the physical ability to challenge the wilderness, but should be open to the aged, the children, the physically handicapped, and the motorized tourist. Complete isolation of any part of the north unit is not in keeping with the concept of public use";
3) the rugged topography of the badlands would always preclude full development of the area, and so developable areas near the present park road should not be included in the proposal;
4) even though the Park Service was to be commended for its "preservation of natural resources, guidance in assisting America to seek the beauty of our country, and development in making the tourist comfortable in his leisure," no future restrictive legislation should be passed;
5) the North Unit's role as a tourist attraction was all the more important in the light of North Dakota's declining population, since the North Unit had "unlimited potential for development";
6) wilderness designation would destroy the economic value of the North Unit to the surrounding area;
7) the label "wilderness area" discourages tourism;
8) since Forest Service multiple-use management had been successful in the area, "it is reasonable to assume that the natural beauty of the Park will not be damaged by wild animals, buffalo, long-horned cattle, or humans";

9) wildfires in the wilderness area might "endanger or engulf surrounding farm and ranch land";
10) the national memorial park belonged, first and foremost, to the citizens of North Dakota: "It is their creation; their contributions in time, effort and determination making this reservation of historic and scenic area possible. It appears illogical for Congress to make any pertinent decision without the consent of the residents of the surrounding areas, and the State of North Dakota." (11)

Here we see a national park conceived as a crass money maker (points one, three, five, six, and seven), as a useful but secondary economic entity of the region (points five and nine), as a democratic institution (point two), and as a touchstone of community (point ten). Points three and five contradict each other and point four nearly contradicts itself. Point eight illustrates how poorly the citizens distinguished between the objectives of the Park and Forest services.

Howsoever confused a mandate, the Association of Commerce position received the support of fifty-three Watford City businesses in a full-page advertisement in the _Farmer_. As an alternative to the NPS plan, the Association called for enlarging Squaw Creek campground, paving the road from the campground to Oxbow Overlook, building a visitor center at Squaw Creek, and installing a new campground south of the river.[12]

Meanwhile, those who thought the NPS wilderness plan did not go far enough were also preparing for the public hearings--principally, the Wilderness Society, which was the most constant champion of badlands wilderness. Yet its arguments turned less on the park's intrinsic wilderness qualifications than on using the plan to tie up future development. In a leaflet announcing the hearings to its membership, the Society called for extensive designation in the South Unit as well as the North. It maintained that "three fully suitable wild areas which are in need of special protection against further development pressures" existed in the South Unit. The NPS decision to propose no wilderness there partly because of the presence of management roadways was not reason enough "to sacrifice a major wilderness opportunity to these insubstantial and temporary features of man's impact." As for the exposed power line running across the South Unit, it "should not be there in any case and can be treated as a temporary non-conforming use to be removed later." The Society saw indulgence at work in the elimination of the wilderness area proposed for the Big and Petrified Forest plateaus as part of the original working plan. "While the Park Service does not recommend this area as wilderness, it has recently come up with the idea of a horse-drawn wagon or buckboard route stabbing directly into the heart of this wild area," it wrote. "Conservationists recommend the Little Missouri Wilderness [the Society's name for all land west of the river] as a certain means of forestalling just this kind of development within valued wild parklands."[13]

The Wilderness Society, it must be said, was willing

to adopt a rather loose interpretation of wilderness to meet its anti-development goals. It called for a "Badlands Basin Wilderness" east of the loop drive in the South Unit, including "the magnificent Painted Canyon, a wild area viewed by thousands from an overlook along the Interstate Highway."[14] Apparently this was a wilderness to be easily peered into. The incongruity of asserting that people standing not fifty yards from a highway rest area would be able to experience wilderness seems to have been lost on the Society. One is reminded of Joseph L. Sax's comments on the plan to give visitors a "wilderness threshold experience" by putting in a tramway to the top of Guadalupe Peak in Guadalupe Mountains National Park:

> Peering at a wilderness from a tramway station . . . is not a wilderness experience; the sense of wilderness is not achieved by standing at its threshold, but by engaging it from within. Not everyone will seize the chance to experience wilderness, even in the modest dose that Guadalupe Park presents. The opportunity can and should be offered as a choice, to be accepted or rejected, but it should not be falsified or domesticated. (15)

The public hearings

Predictably, the Watford City public hearing was dominated by anti-wilderness sentiment. One of the few who spoke in favor was a Sierra Club representative who accused the opposition of harboring "a narrow commercial attitude." Superintendent Thompson also defended the NPS plan, saying that the developed sections of the North Unit could support five times the current visitor use.[16]

145

The Watford City session was most notable, though, for the glimpse it gave of the relationship between the people of the northwestern North Dakota (and eastern Montana) and the North Unit. More so than in Medora, the people around Watford City considered the North Unit "their" park, the scene of family reunions, Sunday picnics, and the spring clean-up. They saw the Park Service agenda of ecosystem monitoring, resource management, and extended recreational use as at best irrelevant, and at worst antithetical, to local desires and needs.

The comments of the residents at this hearing leave the striking impression that they believed an implied compact existed between themselves and the National Park Service regarding the establishment and subsequent operation of the North Unit. "The residents of McKenzie County have been very generous in making available their land for the use of the general public," said one Watford City civic leader.[17] This revealing remark suggests that resentment of the federal government still lingered over the submarginal land purchase program of the Depression years. Even though most of the land ended up as national grasslands, to the benefit of local stockmen, the fact that the government had acquired title while everyone was down and out on their luck still struck some as unfair.[18]

When the North Unit was established in 1948 the local people seem to have also established a unilateral, unwritten compact with the Park Service: manage and develop the park for tourism, provide an economic return to make up for the land grab, and you will be supported. For a long time NPS acted as if it had agreed to such a bargain. But now, with the wilderness proposal, it must have seemed to local residents that the Service was reneging. In calling the NPS plan "ill-advised," State Senator J. Garvin Jacobson voiced the thoughts of many when he characterized it as a betrayal of the economic benefits which had been implicitly promised to area residents.[19]

Even more infuriating to the local citizens was the advocacy of out-of-state environmentalists from the Wilderness Society and the Sierra Club, people who understood little of the historical basis of the North Unit and nothing of the generation of expectations that arose from it. In summing up for the opposition, Lee M. Stenehjem, representing the Association of Commerce, spoke as the archetypal self-reliant North Dakotan:

> We fail to see that North Dakota needs an outside man from Washington [referring to Douglas Scott of the Wilderness Society] to come into our State to create division among us, when no division has ever existed before. This man comes into our State for the first time and becomes an instant expert on our ecology, on our economy, and what's good for our people. North Dakota people can be trusted to take good care of our environment, as our people are doing today and have done in the past. This country hasn't always been easy to live in . . . but our people are a strong people and have practiced conservation of soil, water, and the natural resources, so that they will leave--they will leave for their children and their grandchildren a better land and environment than when they found it. (20)

In Medora the next day the situation was reversed. Of the eighteen statements made, only one was against wilderness designation. This is partly explained when one remembers that the NPS plan called for no wilderness areas at all in the South Unit.[21]

Some of the more sophisticated comments came from two North Dakota State University students. Dale Anderson invoked economic theory: he pointed out that, because wilderness values cannot be included in conventional pricing systems, such land had always been exploited as a "free good" to the point of scarcity. Now, just because of that scarcity, wilderness was attaining a tangible economic value. Extending these thoughts, Robert L. Burgess emphasized the monetary benefits of keeping wilderness areas as storehouses of genetic material and as buffers of "healthy land" between areas of depleted resources, land essential to maintaining biological energy flows.[22] And in another of the competing views on the purpose of national parks, the North Dakota Natural Science Society came out in favor of the Wilderness Society's proposal to create extensive statutory wilderness in the South Unit, asserting that "national parks were not designed nor created to satisfy economic desires and indeed if they do cater to the economic whims of the populace, then they will, in effect, destroy the very meaning, intent and purpose of their creation."[23]

Leading opinions

However, what proved to be the most influential

single comment was offered not at the hearings but in a letter a month later from Governor William Guy. He wrote to express his basic approval of the NPS proposal, with one exception: he favored a wilderness area in the South Unit west of the Little Missouri River. In contrast to Watford City opinion, Guy thought wilderness designation "would cause a dramatic enhancement of the park as a tourist attraction" and would "strengthen the position" of Theodore Roosevelt "among all national parks in the nation." For Guy, wilderness affirmed North Dakota's western heritage. It was also an antidote to the image of the state as nothing but one big wheat field.[24]

Guy's ideas struck Superintendent Thompson as "reasonably sound." Writing to the regional director toward the end of the public comment period, Thompson could find no good reason to exclude from consideration the South Unit west of the river because of old management roads or a tentative buckboard trail. He urged expanding the official plan to include the area Guy wanted. But Thompson did not go further and endorse the Wilderness Society's proposed wilderness areas east of the river, land hard by Interstate 94:

> We have a fear that much of our wilderness study program in this area is overly legalistic in approach. It would appear that the criteria for wilderness must be interpreted on the ground as well as on maps of the area. In the wide open Great Plains Grasslands and Breaks, we believe that the wilderness concepts and ingredients should be viewed differently than in the forest and mountain areas. Without the shielding influence of trees, sights, sounds and solitude become highly significant and it would seem

that the mere fact of lands being undeveloped
should not necessarily qualify them for wilderness
designation.

Thompson confessed to being "actually astounded at the
groundswell of public interest in wilderness in North
Dakota. . . ."[25]

At the time of his letter, he also was aware that
three-quarters of the written comments coming in to the
hearing officer favored enlarging the area proposed for
wilderness by the Park Service.[26] He advised the regional
director that NPS would do well to align themselves with
Governor Guy. "If the result of the Wilderness Hearings
is a 'no change' recommendation," Thompson wrote, "the
Service will be viewed in North Dakota as being unrespon-
sive to high public involvement, and as much oblivious to
reasoned arguments as to emotional rhetoric."[27]

In December 1971 the preliminary wilderness recommendation was published. Disdaining Watford City sentiment
(presumably the "emotional rhetoric" of which Thompson
wrote), the NPS plan for the North Unit went through
virtually unchanged, calling for 15,515 acres of wilderness. In the South Unit, however, an 8200-acre wilderness
west of the river now had the agency's official endorse-
ment.[28]

This preliminary recommendation was itself soon re-
drafted. In the North Unit, biologically important river-
ine habitat along the Little Missouri corridor was added
after it was determined that the stock driveway easement
was not a wilderness disqualification. The river proper

was still left out because it was considered state-owned and used as a frozen road in the winter.[29] Land set aside for a one-eighth-mile-wide buffer zone just inside the boundary fence of the park was also added, as were 520 acres below the rim of the upland prairie plateaus.[30] The addition of eleven hundred acres contiguous to the proposed South Unit wilderness brought the revised NPS recommendation to a total of 28,335 acres--a little less than half of all the roadless acreage in the park.[31]

Refining the wilderness

The publication of this revised recommendation in August 1972 prompted a three-way debate between the Wilderness Society, the Midwest Regional Office, and the staff at Theodore Roosevelt. That autumn the Wilderness Society sent a series of detailed letters to Omaha, objecting to various technical aspects of the recommendation. Basically, it could not understand why the land around the "ranch access" road near Sperati Point was left out. It questioned not only the road's placement on the map, but its very existence, calling it "a trail of less than 'unimproved dirt' standard." At stake were "significant rim-top lands, offering important contrast in physiography, ecology and scenic value to the basin wildlands to the south and east." It argued that "protection of this small but significant area against any future intrusion is important. . . ." The Society also accused the Service of unconscionable procrastination in responding to its "specific challenge."[32]

The delay was in reality caused by internal debate over how to answer the Wilderness Society. The public affairs division of the Midwest Regional Office had prepared an explanation not entirely satisfactory to John Lancaster, who had just taken over as Theodore Roosevelt's superintendent. The draft response letter that Lancaster received for review conceded the map's inaccuracy, but defended excluding the prairie plateaus from wilderness designation since the road had been created by man-made construction.[33] What Lancaster objected to was the draft letter's assertion that "the road could have been more precisely labeled 'ranch<u>ing</u> access road' than 'ranch access.' The access is to ranching activities and improvements, such as the fencing and watering installations at or near the boundary of the park." The letter left the impression that while the road did not lead directly to a ranch, it did give access to an important leased area of the Little Missouri National Grasslands. But Lancaster pointed out that according to the Forest Service such an implication would be "totally false," for the road was actually receiving no appreciable use. "There is no reason for this road," he concluded.[34] Eventually the Midwest Regional Office gave in and the land in question was included in the final North Unit wilderness.

Months were spent wrangling over this, all of three hundred acres, showing how the nature of the debate had changed since the end of 1970, going from consideration of the broad effects of wilderness to the particulars of its establishment. The Wilderness Society and the Service were arguing in technicalities. Left far behind were the comments and opinions so earnestly put forward by local residents. "What happened to all the papers and information presented at the hearings by the people of Western North Dakota is likely a good question," wondered the McKenzie County Farmer. "Efforts of North Dakota residents in the immediate area of the park were tossed aside and the recommendations of the 'Ecology Party' were taken."[35]

By 1973 the basic wilderness configuration was set. The only evident change reported in the final environmental impact statement, which appeared that summer, was the inclusion of the petrified forest in the South Unit wilderness proposal, the title to all the mineral rights there having been secured by the government.[36] Otherwise there was the usual presentation of alternatives, spiced only by new considerations of the propriety of dish tanks and rain making in a wilderness.[37]

The last stage of the designation process began after the publication of the environmental impact statement. Bills to create statutory wilderness areas were introduced in three successive congressional sessions beginning in 1975; all failed. The measure finally passed after it was included in the legislative portmanteau known as the National Parks and Recreation Act of 1978.[38] About forty-two percent of the park--29,920 acres--is now legally protected as wilderness. Only one thread was left dangling: in its report on the National Parks and Recreation Act, the House of Representatives requested NPS to evaluate one last time the Wilderness Society's position on the South Unit. During the hearings on the Act, both the Society and the Sierra Club contended that 28,000 more acres should be added east of the Little Missouri because the land there was already wild in character and grasslands were poorly represented in the Wilderness Preservation System. Moreover, the Society argued that the Endangered American Wilderness Act, by allowing designation of marginally wild areas near large cities, negated NPS's argument that extraneous noise from the interstate highway and the Burlington Northern Railroad disqualified the eastern South Unit.[39]

Its interpretation of the new law was not shared by the Park Service. In the re-evaluation of the South Unit, which appeared in 1980, NPS found no legal precedent for a look-see wilderness in the Endangered American Wilderness Act. On the contrary, the agency again relied almost exclusively upon aesthetic intrusions in making its case against the Wilderness Society's position. "In the bottom of the coulees it may be possible to escape the sight of motor vehicles," the NPS report stated, "but the sound is inescapable, destroying those 'outstanding opportunities for solitude or a primitive and unconfined type of recreation' identified in the Wilderness Act [of 1964] as one of the earmarks of wilderness. While the imprint of man's work may not be noticeable, the sound of his work is ever present." With the North Unit given over almost entirely to wilderness, the eastern South Unit remained "the only area left in the park where developments to accomodate the average day use park visitor can take place." The escalation of energy development in Billings County since the mid-1970s set the seal on NPS's conclusions. With all the new oil, gas, and coal extraction operations adjacent to the South Unit, there were now "far too many conditions present outside the park area which negatively impact and otherwise preclude wilderness designation."[40] With that the debate ended.

To place Theodore Roosevelt's designation process in perspective, to understand why the idea of a wilderness in the open spaces of North Dakota was slow to take hold, we might profitably turn to some observations on the topic by Roderick Nash, the conservation historian. In the preface to the second edition of his Wilderness and the American Mind, Nash discusses the sinister connotations of wilderness, the fear modern people have always had of untamed country. He traces these attitudes from their sources-- which predate even ancient Near East writings and legend-- to latter-day North America, where "the pioneers' obsession was to clear the land, to remove the vision-obscuring trees and vines, to bring light into darkness."

Wilderness, Nash says, has traditionally been associated with trees, and "the heart of the bias against wilderness" is "the ancient association between security and sight":

> In this connection it is interesting to note
> that many accounts of westward migration in
> North America contain expressions of relief
> on emerging from the Eastern forest wilderness
> to the opening of the Great Plains. All at
> once the pioneers could see, and their spirits
> immediately brightened. . . . The Midwestern
> plains, to be sure, were just as devoid of
> civilization as the Eastern forests, but from
> the pioneers' perspective they were a different
> kind of environment. This is evident from the
> fact that the term "wilderness" was seldom
> applied to the grasslands of the Middle West. (41)

The same perceptual barrier may have had its role in the Theodore Roosevelt wilderness designation process.

Notes to Chapter 7

1. _Wilderness Proposal: Theodore Roosevelt National Memorial Park_ (Washington, DC: NPS, 1970), 7. In 1956 an access road was bladed to Achenbach Spring to facilitate the installation of a dish tank. "North Unit District Ranger Monthly Narrative Report," memorandum, 3 December 1956 (THRO-S).

2. Osmer, 2.

3. _1963 Master Plan_, unpaginated.

4. Anthony Wayne Smith, introduction to _Preserving Wilderness in Our National Parks_ (Washington, DC: National Parks and Conservation Association, 1971), ix.

5. "Staff Meeting Minutes," 6 September 1966, and 7 November 1966, 3; "Superintendent's Monthly Narrative Report," 14 September 1966, 6; and 12 October 1966, 6.

6. George M. Johnson, "The Badlands and Teddy's Park," _Living Wilderness_ 31:96/97 (1967), 22-25.

7. Arthur L. Sullivan (Supt., THRO) to Reg. Dir. (MWRO), memorandums, 6 April and 2 May 1969 (THRO-S); and J. Stanley Fillmore (Acting Supt., THRO) to Reg. Dir. (MWRO), memorandum of 31 July 1969 (THRO-S). See also _Final Environmental Statement: Proposed Wilderness, Theodore Roosevelt National Memorial Park_ (Omaha: MWRO, 1973), 34.

8. Sullivan to Reg. Dir. (MWRO), memorandum, 2 September 1967 (THRO-S).

9. _Wilderness Proposal_, 8.

10. _McKenzie County Farmer_, 19 November 1970. See also "Staff Meeting Minutes," 23 October 1970.

11. _McKenzie County Farmer_, 28 November 1970.

12. Ibid., 28 November and 3 December 1970.

13. The Wilderness Society, "Joint Announcement of Hearings: Theodore Roosevelt National Memorial Park Wilderness," unpublished leaflet, 18 November 1970.

14. Ibid.

15. Joseph L. Sax, _Mountains Without Handrails: Reflections on the National Parks_ (Ann Arbor: University of Michigan Press, 1980), 63.

16. "Transcript of Proceedings of Public Hearings on Park

Wilderness Proposal, Theodore Roosevelt National Memorial Park, North Dakota," unpublished MS, December 1970 (THRO-A). Quote is from p. 60; Thompson's remarks from p. 19. See also pp. 39-46, 53, 56, 74-75, and 76-77.

17. "Transcript of Proceedings," 64, 50; and "Congressman Don Short," 65.

18. For the attitude of stockmen that public domain land is "theirs," see Phillip O. Foss, Politics and Grass: The Administration of Grazing on the Public Domain (New York: Greenwood Press, 1969), 18. Originally published by the University of Washington Press, 1960.

19. "Transcript of Proceedings," 26.

20. Ibid., 70. In the draft of his remarks, Stenehjem had "agitator" in place of "man from Washington." Scott was the Wilderness Society's liaison to the Theodore Roosevelt wilderness planning process. See Ibid., 27-30, 30-33, 36, 47-48, 50-53, and 61-64.

21. The only negative comment came from the Belfield Commercial Club, which introduced into the record a near-verbatim copy of the Watford City Association of Commerce position paper. Ibid., 115-118.

22. Ibid., 134-139 (Anderson) and 142-144 (Burgess).

23. Ibid., 122. See also 107-108, 110, 111, and 120-121.

24. Guy to Thompson, 8 January 1971, attached to Wilderness Recommendation: Theodore Roosevelt National Memorial Park, North Dakota (Washington, DC: NPS, 1972).

25. Thompson to Reg. Dir. (MWRO), memorandum, 30 January 1971 (THRO-S).

26. Of the 457 comments received during the allotted period:
   -- 340 favored enlarging the NPS proposal (74.4%);
   -- 55 favored the NPS proposal unchanged (12.0%);
   -- 23 expressed general support of wilderness (5.1%);
   -- 39 were against any designation of wilderness (8.5%).
A poll of the members of the Dickinson Chamber of Commerce produced this result:
   -- 47 favored the Wilderness Society's proposal (50.5%);

```
              -- 32 favored the NPS proposal (34.4%);
              -- 10 were against any wilderness designation
              (10.8%);
              --  4 had no opinion (4.3%).
```
See, respectively, Wilderness Recommendation (1972),
29; Don Wanner (Dickinson Chamber of Commerce) to
Hearing Officer (THRO), 6 January 1971 (THRO-A).

27. Thompson to Reg. Dir. (MWRO), 30 January 1971.

28. Wilderness Recommendation: Theodore Roosevelt Nation-
     al Memorial Park (Washington, DC: NPS, 1971).

29. Wilderness Recommendation (1972), 13-14, 27-28.

30. Ibid., 13-14. The buffer zone had been set aside to
     allow vehicles to enter the park for fence main-
     tenance, but in 1970 it was decided to henceforward
     perform such tasks on foot or by horse access. Final
     Environmental Statement: Proposed Wilderness, 15.

31. Wilderness Recommendation (1972), 23-24.

32. Douglas W. Scott (Coordinator of Special Projects,
     the Wilderness Society) to J. Leonard Volz (Reg.
     Dir., MWRO), 27 October 1972.

33. Dan Davis (Chief, Public Affairs, MWRO) to John O.
     Lancaster (Supt., THRO), memorandum with draft letter
     and attached comments, 6 December 1972 (THRO-S). See
     also "Revised Statement of Significant Issues, Theo-
     dore Roosevelt Wilderness Proposal," unpublished MS,
     27 February 1974 (THRO-S), 1.

34. Davis to Lancaster, 6 December 1972. MWRO wanted to
     present a united response and expressed "concern over
     revising [the] NPS position at this time." See also
     Robert D. Powell (Acting Supt., THRO) to Asst. Reg.
     Dir. (RMRO), memorandum, 28 February 1977 (THRO-A).

35. McKenzie County Farmer, 9 November 1972.

36. Lancaster to Joe Howe (no identification), memoran-
     dum, 27 February 1974 (THRO-S), 1. The rights were
     acquired on 12 September 1972, thus allowing seventy-
     six hundred acres to be added to the proposal.

37. For dish tanks see Final Environmental Statement:
     Proposed Wilderness, 4; Charles A. Evans (U. S. Soil
     Conservation Service) to Volz, memorandum, 20 Novem-
     ber 1972 (attached to the above, 40-41); Volz to
     James B. Thompson (Supt., THRO), memorandum, 25 May
     1972; and Wilderness Recommendation (1972), 14. For
     weather modification, see Warren Fairchild (Bureau of
     Reclamation) to Volz, 21 November 1972 (attached to

Final Environmental Statement: Proposed Wilderness, 38-39).

38. Legislative History of the National Parks and Recreation Act of 1978, 916.

39. U. S. Congress, Senate, Subcommittee on Parks and Recreation, 95th Cong., 2d sess., 26 July and 4 August 1978, Hearings on H. R. 12536, 118, 123, and 131.

40. Special Report: Re-evaluation of the South Unit for Wilderness, Theodore Roosevelt National Park (Denver: RMRO, 1980), 1-3.

41. Roderick Nash, Wilderness and the American Mind, revised ed. (New Haven, CT: Yale University Press, 1973), x-xi. First edition 1967. See also p. 2.

8) Terrestrial Research and Management

Water

All of Theodore Roosevelt National Park lies well into what used to be called, erroneously, The Great American Desert--that is, the area between the Rockies and the 100th meridian.[1] It is dry country, sometimes exceptionally so. As we have seen, drought was one of the factors which set about the land purchase program and can therefore be regarded as an indirect cause of the park's creation.

It is understandable that little water resources work has been done at Theodore Roosevelt. The only important surface water in the park is the Little Missouri River. It drains 4750 square miles of western North Dakota, but has no large tributaries; there are only a few other perennial creeks in the park.[2] The foremost concern about the river is pollution. Nevertheless, even given the recent oil boom there has been only one known incident, a 6000-barrel spill in 1971 forty miles upriver (south) from Medora. Fast response from the Shell Oil Company, and a fortuitous downpour, dispersed the oil enough to make its presence difficult to detect downriver in the park.[3] Other isolated surges in pollutant levels[4] are perhaps related to the wide fluctuation in the Little Missouri's flowage, but no one can be sure until a comprehensive water resources management program is developed for the park.[5]

A second concern is that the river might be dammed.

By law it is a state scenic river, wild and free-flowing, with a commission to coordinate its management. While it would take another act of the state legislature to allow it to be dammed, the most recent North Dakota water plan proposes doing so for the sake of irrigation. This plan is opposed by the Little Missouri Scenic River Commission, which claims that ever-present silt and bentonite make the water useless for crop growing, quite apart from a dam's effect on recreational interests and riparian ecology.[6]

Finally, there is the nettlesome issue of just who owns the Little Missouri as it flows through the park. The question turns on whether or not the watercourse is legally navigable. The state contends it is, and has in the past been backed by the Army Corps of Engineers.[7] Up until 1983 its position carried the day: North Dakota was adjudged owner of both the water and submerged land. But in May of that year the Supreme Court struck down the rulings that vested ownership in the state, sending the case back to lower courts for disposition on procedural grounds.[8] The case referred to began in 1978 when North Dakota sued the Department of the Interior over the Bureau of Land Management's issuing of oil and gas leases on river bottoms. The Park Service's main interest is not ownership per se but the extent to which winter recreational activities, such as snowmobiling and motorcycling, can be controlled on the frozen river.[9]

External threats to the quality of the park's ground

water have recently been acknowledged. Drilling for oil and natural gas takes place outside the park but within its aquifer, giving rise to the risk of depletion or contamination.[10] For example, the South Unit draws most of its drinking water from the Hell Creek aquifer, which at its deepest (nineteen hundred feet) is easily within the range of oil well drilling.[11] The staff hopes the issue will soon be addressed as part of a park-wide water policy plan.

Fire management

Given the region's low rainfall, it is surprising to learn that there have been no extensive wildfires in the immediate park area. From 1949 to 1981 only thirty-six were recorded, usually caused by lightning strikes.[12] There have not been many additional human-caused fires. Most burned just outside the boundaries of the park, such as those started by sparks from trains running along the Burlington Northern line in Billings County. Park personnel are often called to fight them, and NPS has a fire control agreement with the Forest Service for the Little Missouri National Grasslands.[13]

None of the fires within the park ever consumed more than three hundred acres.[14] This can be attributed partly to a long-standing policy of complete suppression. Since 1949 fire has been all but eliminated from Theodore Roosevelt's ecosystem. For years the management rationale was that "forest and range fires constitute one of the greatest menaces to National Parks and Monuments. Due to the great natural and historic values in this Memorial Park, fire control takes precedence over all other activities except the saving or safeguarding of human life."[15] At the core of this reasoning was a political reality: "natural fires must be extinguished within the Park where possible because of the danger to ranches outside the Park."[16]

The rigid approach applied to all fires, including those with little potential to damage private interests. By adopting it, the Service was once put in the awkward position of trying to get rid of the single most popular tourist attraction in the park.

In 1951 lightning ignited a coal vein southwest of Buck Hill. This phenomenon, unusual in recent years but historically an important force in shaping the geology of the badlands, soon became controversial. The Service wanted to put out the fire as it would any other, but, as a park report of the time put it, "local outside interests heard of the burning coal spectacle and publicized it as a tourist attraction. When these interests learned of the intentions of the Service to extinguish the fire, they exerted political influence and managed to temporarily stop suppression action. It has been decided that further study of the interpretive and aesthetic qualities of the lignite fire will be made before any further action is taken to suppress it." After reconsideration--and continued pressure from the Greater North Dakota Association—NPS agreed to let this "example of a geological process" run its course.[17]

A draft fire management plan was drawn up in 1974 that would have re-established wildfire to the park, but it never went beyond a preliminary stage.[18] Today the park continues its policy of fighting all fires as soon as possible. But the new Natural Resources Management Plan recognizes that "this tradition of suppression may be leading towards the creation of homogenous vegetation zones and may have some influence on normal plant succession within the park." It proposes returning to a natural fire regime. Aside from improving nutrient cycling, more natural burning is seen as a discouragement to the proliferation of exotic plant species.[19]

Two recent developments militate for a revised wildfire plan. A study done in 1982 by the Northern Prairie Wildlife Research Center showed that lightning-strike fires within Theodore Roosevelt consumed an average of about twenty acres when unfought, with rain or natural burn-out being most often responsible for extinguishment.[20] These small extents suggest that fears of a conflagration may be groundless. Second, the designation of wilderness in 1978 has changed the rule-making picture considerably. Park Service policy now treats lightning fires within wilderness areas as natural phenomena to be left to burn under most circumstances, and so for Theodore Roosevelt to continue to fight fires regardless of location or provenance is self-contradictory.[21]

Vegetation management

Until the advent of total ecosystem strategies for national park management, vegetation received scant attention at Theodore Roosevelt. Plant communities were left alone, mostly undifferentiated as to whether they were indigenous or exotic.[22] Occasional qualitative habitat typologies and single-species studies made up vegetation research.[23]

As might be surmised, the fertility of soil in arable parts of the North Dakota badlands was seriously degraded by homesteading in the early 20th century. In some instances overgrazing defoliated sites. Such areas now within the park have been allowed to revegetate, yet this hardly qualifies as active vegetation management.[24]

That has come only recently, as the park has moved away from case-by-case reactive management toward a strategy of managing "all resources together, considering the natural processes that are at work and the interactions of biotic and abiotic systems."[25] This total ecosystem strategy has particularly relevant applications in vegetation work, since plant life is at once important to both living and non-living processes: for instance, ground cover serves simultaneously as forage and as a barrier to erosion.

One goal of the new strategy is to explicitly promote the existence of plants indigenous to the northern mixed prairie. While attaining an absolutely unsullied flora is impossible, the park does now actively discourage certain exotic species. Twenty-three have been identified within the park. Some are innocuous, but others, in particular sweet clover (Melilotus spp.) and leafy spurge (Euphorbia esula), invade even undisturbed sites and compete with native plants for sunlight, nutrients, and moisture. As of 1985, four--Canada thistle (Cirsium arvense), Russian and spotted knapweed (genus Centaurea), and leafy spurge-- were being actively controlled.[26]

Spurge infestation presents a classic management dilemma. Left unchecked, it threatens communities of indigenous vegetation resulting in an as-yet unmeasured, but certainly adverse, effect on the mixed prairie. The only method of control proven effective is direct application of the herbicide Tordon. Also known as "agent white," this is a chemical so toxic that one formulation (Tordon 212; picloram +2, 4, D) was banned from all national park lands in 1970. Tordon 212 was apparently used on a limited basis prior to that date to fight selected patches of spurge at Theodore Roosevelt,[27] but all noxious weed control was suspended from 1970 to 1975 while NPS awaited approval of an alternative herbicide.[28]

Widespread spraying (and later, bead-treating) of spurge began in 1975 and has continued since; still, funding allows for only a small fraction of the infested area to be treated. Yet even if money for the program were increased, the unknown environmental effects of the herbicide would probably serve to constrain its use.[29] Currently the formulation Tordon 2K (picloram 4-amino-3,5,6-trichloropicolinic acid) is used. It is open to debate whether applying Tordon, even in small amounts, is worthwhile. Aside from possible environmental damage, the chemical's efficacy is limited by dry weather (1976 and 1981 were bad years for application); by the fact that leafy spurge enters the park via the drainages of the tributaries of the Little Missouri, drainages which have their headlands in heavily infested adjacent areas outside the park; and by evidence of a spillover killing of plants near sprayed areas.[30] These points seem to argue against the park's application of Tordon, but without clear-cut choices the Natural Resources Management Plan is left to endorse the status quo and hope that one of the many current university studies of the problem can come up with an environmentally sound control.

In the meantime Theodore Roosevelt is caught between the Service's philosophical, ecological, and financial constraints on the use of herbicides, and the desire to comply with North Dakota's noxious weed control law--to be in step with the surrounding agricultural community.

"The Service has many more, largely legitimate, constraints upon the use of herbicides and pesticides than is understood by the mainly agriculturally based population of the state," declares a recent park report. "We have spurge in the parks and it has come from outside the parks. We may have bans put on our chemical treatment of the weed in the parks and when this happens we will be at serious odds with state law regarding the control of it . . . . The natural process philosophy of the Service will at that point again be in direct conflict with official state policy. Part of the point is that even among our closest friends of the parks there often is still a failure to understand the philosophy of not tampering with the flora and fauna of the parks indiscriminately."[31]

Geological research

Overall, rather little has been accomplished in this field, though not for lack of potential topics.[32] One of the most immediately attractive is the petrified forest formations in the extreme northwestern South Unit. They have been promoted locally as a tourist attraction,[33] but remain not at all well-known outside of North Dakota, likely because of their relative inaccessibility. The formations have been the object of sporadic research.[34]

Notes to Chapter 8

1. Martyn J. Bowden conducts an illuminating discussion
   on how the Great Plains have been conceived and mis-
   conceived in "The Great American Desert in the American Mind: The Historiography of a Geographical
   Notion," in Geographies of the Mind: Essays in Historical Geosophy, David Lowenthal and Martyn J.
   Bowden, eds. (New York: Oxford University Press,
   1976), 119-147. See also Walter Prescott Webb, The
   Great Plains, reprint (Lincoln: University of Nebraska
   Press, 1981), 152-160. First published 1931 by Ginn
   and Company, Boston.

2. North Dakota Statewide 208 Water Quality Management
   Plan: Water Quality Report (Bismarck: Division of
   Water Supply and Pollution Control, NDSDH, 1979), 50.

3. "State Coordinator's Monthly Report," 29 October 1971.

4. See Dickinson Press, 23 September 1973; Williston
   Daily News, 5 August 1974; and 208 Water Quality
   Management Plan, 53. For flowage, see for example
   1974 Water Resources Data for North Dakota: Surface
   Water Records (Washington, DC: USGS, 1975), 106-110.

5. "NRM Plan," 29-30.

6. "Minutes, Little Missouri Scenic River Commission,"
   memorandum, 2 June 1983 (THRO-A).

7. "NRM Plan," 28.

8. "State Coordinator's Monthly Report," 7 June 1983.

9. Ibid., 26 February 1982, 30 March 1983. Interestingly, the river was first held navigable on the basis of
   a passage from the journal of Meriwether Lewis.

10. "NRM Plan," 28.

11. Lawrence O. Anna, Ground-Water Resources of Billings,
    Golden Valley, and Slope Counties, North Dakota (Bis-
    marck: USGS, 1981), 7, 15, and 45.

12. Kenneth F. Higgins, "Lightning Fires in Grasslands in
    North Dakota and in Pine-Savanna Lands in Nearby
    South Dakota and Montana (Review Draft)," unpublished
    MS, 1982 (THRO-A), 17.

13. "1982 Superintendent's Annual Report," 14; "1981
    Superintendent's Annual Report," 15.

14. 1973 Master Plan, 22; "Chief Ranger's Monthly Re-
    port," 22 August and 14 September 1978.

170

15. Einar L. Johnson, "Theodore Roosevelt National Memorial Park Forest Fire Control Plan," unpublished MS, 30 July 1965 (THRO-A), 1.

16. Lary D. Barney (Acting Supt., THRO) to Reg. Dir. (MWRO), memorandum, 31 January 1969 (THRO-S). This is an instance in which the park poses the external threat to adjacent land uses.

17. First quotation: "Annual Forestry Report: 1955," unpublished MS, 10 January 1956 (THRO-S), 1. Second quotation: Strand, 50-51.

18. "1974 Superintendent's Annual Report," 9.

19. "NRM Plan," 63 (quote), 64.

20. Higgins, 18.

21. John O. Lancaster (Supt., THRO) to Associate Reg. Dir. (RMRO), memorandum, 8 July 1977 (THRO-A); and "NRM Plan," 63, 26.

22. Grazing of domestic livestock within the park--an open invitation to exotic species--was allowed well into the 1950s (see 1963 Master Plan, unpaginated) and into the 1980s in the case of the Elkhorn, supposedly in order to maintain the historical character of the site (but see text at nn65-69, Chapter 1): "Chief Ranger's Monthly Report," 18 September 1974; "1980 Superintendent's Annual Report," 11. There is a brief reference to restoring native vegetation to heavily disturbed areas in "Mission 66 for Theodore Roosevelt National Memorial Park," unpublished MS, ca. 1956 (THRO-S), 2-3.

23. Osmer included a covert description, rough map, and photographs in his 1937 wildlife report (p. 9 ff.). The map seems to have been lost, or at least it is not extant with the park's original copy of the report.

Single-species research includes Donald Hazlett, "An Ecological Study of Artemisia Dominated Vegetation in Western North Dakota With Special Reference to the Concept of Allelopathy," master's thesis, University of South Dakota, Vermillion, 1972; Robert Dean Ralston, "The Structure and Ecology of the North Slope Juniper Stands of the Little Missouri Badlands," master's thesis, University of Utah, Salt Lake City, 1960; Benjamin L. Everett, "Use of Populus Sargentii in Tracing the Recent History of a River Channel," senior thesis, Princeton University, Princeton, NJ, 1965.

24. "NRM Plan," 25. In the 1950s old homesteads within the park were overseeded. "Annual Forestry Report: 1958," memorandum, 16 January 1959 (THRO-S).

25. "NRM Plan," 6.

26. Ibid., 18; Hellickson to author, 14 May and 8 October 1985.

27. Final Environmental Statement: Wilderness Proposal, 16.

28. "1974 Superintendent's Annual Report," 9.

29. "NRM Plan," 18; "1975 Superintendent's Annual Report," 8.

30. "NRM Plan," 18, 20.

31. "North Dakota and the National Park Service," 3.

32. Geologic research includes: Michael B. Clark, "The Stratigraphy of the Sperati Point Quadrangle, McKenzie County, North Dakota," master's thesis, University of North Dakota, Grand Forks, 1966; Mark A. Steiner, "Petrology of Sandstones from the Bullion Creek and Sentinel Butte Formations (Paleocene), Little Missouri Badlands, North Dakota," master's thesis, University of North Dakota, Grand Forks, 1978; Bernard M. Hanson, "Geology of the Elkhorn Ranch Area, Billings and Golden Valley Counties, North Dakota," North Dakota Geological Survey Report of Investigations #18 (Grand Forks: NDGS, 1955), reprinted 1959; and John R. Tinker, Jr., "Rates of Hillslope Lowering in the Badlands of North Dakota," doctoral dissertation, University of North Dakota, Grand Forks, 1970. Also useful is the booklet by John P. Bleumle and Arthur F. Jacob, Geology Along the South Loop Road (Medora: Theodore Roosevelt Nature and History Assn., 1973).

33. See Yoder, 50.

34. For example, Donald J. Berg and John A. Brophy, "An Investigation of Fossil Wood From the South Unit, Theodore Roosevelt National Memorial Park," unpublished MS, 1963 (THRO-L), 9. The authors ventured "a highly tentative guess" that identified the wood as Sciadopitys, but the research done in 1983 by Harold Coffin of Loma Linda University might contradict this.

9) Wildlife Management

One of the pleasures of visiting Theodore Roosevelt today is to see the uncommon community of animals who make the park their home. Majesty and understatement live next to one another, as is readily apparent when one happens upon a bison wallow in a prairie dog town. In the North Unit, creatures both wild and secretive, such as the coyote, inhabit the same area as semi-domesticated long-horn cattle.

These unexpected contrasts are the stuff of insight. One cannot fully know the badlands--and what being in the badlands can do for a man--without knowing how it is that seemingly incompatible animals can live together. Roosevelt had a keen sense of the unexpected and the meaning it holds. Some of the most revealing turns in his western narrative were occasioned by a chance crossing of the ways with wild creatures:

> In the hot noontide hours of midsummer, the broad ranch veranda, always in the shade, is almost the only spot where a man can be comfortable; but here he can sit for hours at a time, leaning back in his rocking-chair, as he reads or smokes, or with half-closed, dreamy eyes gazes across the shallow, nearly dry river-bed to the wooded bottoms opposite, and to the plateaus lying back of them. Against the sheer white faces of the cliffs, that come down without a break, the dark green tree-tops stand out in bold relief. In the hot, lifeless air all objects that are not near by seem to sway and waver. There are few sounds to break the stillness. From the upper branches of the cottonwood trees overhead, whose shimmering, tremulous leaves are hardly ever quiet, but if the wind stirs at all, rustle and quiver and sigh all day long, comes every now and then the soft, melancholy cooing of the mourning-dove, whose voice always seems far away and expresses more than

any other sound in nature the sadness of gentle, hopeless, never-ending grief. (1)

This passage, one of the most beautiful Roosevelt ever wrote, distils his Dakota experience: the repose he sought at the Elkhorn seeming at one moment so clear, only to shimmer away at the calling of a bird. The recent loss of his mother and wife was never far from him.

It is a pity, then, that the biotic community he knew in the 1880s is incomplete today. Even as his own well-known hunts of buffalo and bear played a bit role in its demise, his actions never struck him as sordid or a contradiction of his basic conservationist bent.[2] In any estimation, Roosevelt's days in the badlands came toward the end of the decimation of its native fauna, not the beginning--although the time separating the two was disgracefully short.

Of the large game animals existing in the 19th-century badlands only white-tailed deer, mule deer, and pronghorns (also misleadingly known as "pronghorn antelope") were in the immediate vicinity of the park at the time of its creation in the 1940s. The others now there have been reintroduced. Three--the grizzly bear, gray wolf, and Audubon mountain sheep--are still missing, the last being completely extinct.

Large-scale hunting depredations were only part of the reason for the end of the indigenous living community. Open range ranching, and later fenced ranching and homesteading, put more and more habitat in grazing or under the plow, forcing what big game was left into marginal areas such as the rugged river breaks. It was not long before some species populations became inviable. By the 1920s there was no doubt that a number of species were no longer present locally. This was hinted at in the article on North Dakota in the Ecological Society of America's 1926 report on "all preserved and preservable areas in North America in which natural conditions persist," in which it was declared that "the proposed national park in the heart of the Badlands near Medora should have the generous encouragement of every one who is interested in the preservation of the native life of the state." Writing in 1935, Nate Halliday, the state game warden for the Medora District, was more explicit:

> In those days which were the latter part of the last century a great many species of wild game roamed this section of our state among them being the Bear, Elk, Mountain Sheep, Mountain Lions, Buffalo and many others as well as all species of game birds. Today is a great contrast to those old days. Practically all we see in this area today is the deer and antelope and the upland game consisting of Partridge, Grouse and Pheasant. During the last 40 years that I have lived along the Little Missouri River, which was always known as an ideal game sanctuary, truthfully I am at a loss to understand the disappearance of the game unless it was thru the carelessness of the hunters during the past ten or twelve years. During the season just past my territory had very little game in it. . . .

Once upon a time Indians had traveled great distances solely to partake of the rich game in the badlands.[3]

The dearth of big game was confirmed two years later by Thomas Osmer's informal but extensive survey of the wildlife of the north part of the Roosevelt Recreational

Demonstration Area. Osmer made exactly five sightings of game animals, all white-tailed deer. "Successive surveys made of game, fur bearers, and their known predators, revealed low census figures, both in numbers of species and individuals," he reported.

> This condition should, perhaps, be expected due to the natural limitations caused by the climatic and other environmental factors of the country. However, in addition, the past years of drought, over-grazing, and the common mistake of trying to farm a cattle country, plus excessive hunting and trapping, legal and other-wise, have greatly interfered with the above classes of animals and their natural habitats, and has reduced their numbers well below average figures. Many years must pass before the environment for animal wildlife will approach a return to natural conditions. Even then some species of valuable forage plants will not return because they are as extinct as the Audubon mountain sheep. (4)

A systematic professional wildlife survey of the park (Osmer was a student) was not undertaken until 1949, when FWS and NPS personnel trooped the area with big game reintroduction in mind.[5] Yet for a long time wildlife management remained haphazard, hindered by the administrative emphasis on cultural resources and by a lack of basic field data (for example, no records of wildlife sightings in the North Unit during the 1950s are extant). Only in the last few years have some much-needed baseline studies and censuses been finished, the capstone being the final Natural Resources Management Plan of 1984.[6]

Reintroduced species

In 1951 the Service began a program of big game

replenishment--twelve years in advance of the Leopold Report, which is now accepted as a seminal statement of what NPS wildlife management policy should be, and which also was the first really influential expression of the idea that biotic communities might and ought to be re-created in the national parks.[7] Is this a suggestion that Theodore Roosevelt was somehow ahead of the vanguard in wildlife management? In a very limited way, yes; for it appears that the park's reintroduction program was begun under the influence (if not at the instigation) of Olaus Murie, the wildlife biologist. Murie toured the park in late 1949 with, among others, Superintendent Allyn Hanks, and in a brief memoir of the visit he wrote that they had discussed concepts such as biological units; the effects of reintroducing elk and bighorn sheep and bison on each other, on vegetation, and on other species; and carrying capacities. His aim, however, if we are to judge from the context of the complete memoir (Appendix F), was to re-create, not the biotic community of Roosevelt's time, but those elements of the biotic community that Roosevelt would have been most interested in--the big game animals, the game birds, the "look" of the badlands before overgrazing.[8] The Leopold Committee's conception of bio-tic re-creation went deeper than Murie's valuable, but ultimately anthropocentric, prescription for the park.

Though the rationale behind the reintroductions has never been fully debated, NPS has gone ahead and tried to re-create the biotic community that existed before Roose-velt arrived in the badlands--up to a point. There is not now nor has there ever been serious thought given to bringing back grizzlies or wolves, for instance.

It can be little surprise that the park authorities chose a relatively innocuous species, the pronghorn (An-tilocapra americana), for the first reintroduction. Ex-tensively hunted in the early years of this century, pronghorns were never totally exterminated from southwes-tern North Dakota; however, by the 1950s there were still too few in the region to hope for a natural recolonization of the park. So in January 1951 seventy-five pronghorns were captured in Yellowstone National Park by using air-planes to herd them into corrals. After transport to Theodore Roosevelt they were released about a mile north-west of park headquarters at Peaceful Valley. The seed herd comprised seventeen mature bucks, thirty-nine mature does, ten buck kids, and nine doe kids. They immediately went up onto the Big and Petrified Forest plateaus.[9] The size of the herd varies as the animals move into and out of the park; indeed, Theodore Roosevelt has no popula-tion as such, with park merely serving as one portion of the herd's range (which itself is centered in that area of the Lindbo Flats located outside the park).[10] These nimble animals, seldom seen by the casual summertime visi-tor, demand little time from the park's resource man-agement staff.[11]

The same does not hold for two of the other species

reintroduced to Theodore Roosevelt.

Bison are the creatures most closely identified with the Great Plains and remain the single most popular subject of wildlife watching in the park. The gregarious nature of buffalo--surely a contributing factor to their near-extinction (whether by indiscriminate slaughter or, as has been suggested lately, by contagion)--is today a source of delight to visitors of both the North and South Units. The sight of a hundred buffalo running across the Little Missouri River, the agogic rise and fall of their backs making a low, dark, off-the-beat wave in the thick, still air, trailing calves and puffs of dust of nearly equal size and color--this is a memory many visitors to Theodore Roosevelt carry down the years.

But the other side of the coin is the cost of maintaining bison. They are the most intensely managed species at Theodore Roosevelt.[12] Large sums have been spent in trying to keep them in the park, getting them back after they get out, and rounding them up so a few can be taken someplace else. It is patently true that "the question of how the park should manage large ungulate populations to simulate natural conditions remains unanswered. . . ."[13]

Reintroduction of bison was delayed until the South Unit could be fenced to inhibit free movement of a herd onto adjacent ranch and crop land. The first release was in December 1956 when twelve yearling heifers, twelve mature cows, and five young bulls were brought from the Fort Niobrara National Wildlife Refuge near Valentine, Nebraska. Although buffalo had probably not lived in the North Dakota badlands for nearly seventy-five years (it took Roosevelt two weeks to find and shoot a poor specimen in 1883), many relict wallows were reported at the time of the initial release.[14] The park's herd is likely a cross between American bison (<u>Bison</u> <u>bison</u> <u>bison</u>) and Wood bison (<u>B</u>. <u>b</u>. <u>athabascae</u>).[15] Entrance road construction and the high number of inholdings delayed release in the North Unit until November 1962, when twenty from the South Unit herd were transferred.[16] The present estimated management capacity is 300-500 for the entire park.[17]

The problem with buffalo has been that the size of the herd has repeatedly risen above that capacity. Not only does this necessitate periodic reductions, but as their numbers increase so do escapes from the park. The boundary was originally fenced with four-strand barbed wire, which is little more than an admonishment to a charging buffalo.[18] On many occasions the entire North Unit herd escaped, sometimes roaming as far away as Grassy Butte, fifteen miles to the south.[19] After one such fiasco, in which the entire ranger staff spent a week recapturing the herd, Superintendent Arthur Sullivan had a proposition for the regional director. "We understand the Crow Indians in Montana are attempting to acquire buffalo, and we would be only too happy to make a donation of the entire herd," he wrote in exasperation. "With the removal of the buffalo, we could then concentrate our efforts in the North Unit on the management and interpretation of the Longhorn cattle."[20]

Ranchers too have learned to their dismay what damage a group of half-ton animals can do. Claims against the park in the thousands of dollars have been upheld in court. Between 1974 and 1977, for example, four out of six claims were allowed, costing the Service $8687.00. Even leaving out the cost of lawsuits, recent figures show that it costs the government $65.00 per escape.[21]

Setting aside Sullivan's remarks, a partial reduction of the herd was the obvious management response. How to go about it was less readily apparent. The earliest plans called for scheduled distribution of bison among Indian tribes "to avoid the need for slaughtering animals and handling carcasses in the park."[22] Still, for a few years buffalo were on occasion rounded up and slaughtered "to order," usually to provide meat for tribal ceremonies. Eventually the practice became too "difficult, expensive, and dangerous to both participant riders in the round-up and to the herd as well" and was discontinued after 1970.[23] Free distribution of excess animals is still the preferred method of herd reduction, but now it takes place exclusively through live shipping after a general round-up (see Table 9.1).[24]

A veteran park wildlife manager gives us this description of a buffalo round-up at Theodore Roosevelt.

The roundup and shipment of buffalo is in theory a relatively simple straight-forward wildlife management project. Buffalo are gregarious herd animals and it would seem from their bovine-like appearance and general tranquil nature that it would be a simple matter to herd them into confinement and then load and ship. Not so. Buffalo are wild animals: swift, powerful, quick to frighten or anger and totally unpredictable. A buffalo or herd of buffalo will go where they want to go. . . .

The roundup effort generally consists of an airborne spotter plane to locate the herds, from 15-20 mounted riders to move the buffalo to the corral, and the accompanying support forces of vehicle operators, communicators, and remounts.

The plan developed for each drive is generally finalized after a herd is located. Best results in moving animals have been obtained when the herd can be pushed to the boundary fence and then herded along it to the corral. In the north unit of the park, this is impractical as the corral is not located at a junction with the boundary fence. In instances such as this, an attempt is made to drive the animals along drainages or other topographical features in the direction of the corral. Drives of this nature leave the buffalo escape routes either to the right or left of the line of drive. With the boundary fence along one flank, the buffalo can generally only escape in one direction. One other escape exists in either case and that is to escape straight ahead along the line of the drive by simply outrunning the riders. This happens most frequently in the more broken terrain. Attempts to gather and again move animals that have broken and escaped, generally prove fruitless until they settle down and gather together again. If all goes well and the herd does not escape the riders, they are driven into the corral holding pasture.

At this point, the actual corral work of culling, ear tagging and loading takes place. Much innovation and many improvements have been made in the corrals since they were first constructed in the early 1960s. Although still somewhat hazardous and at times exasperating, animals can generally be moved from the holding pastures, into the corrals, through the chutes and onto the waiting trucks. The corral operation requires a crew of at least 8-9 men plus the veterinarian and truck driver. If all goes well

and the crew has some experience, 100 animals
can be loaded out in a day's time.

This description of a roundup is quite simplistic. In actuality, it can become quite complicated. Should, as has happened, a herd be
driven several miles to the corral location and
then at the final moment break and escape, many
of the horses will be beat. Replacement mounts
must then be available or else the roundup
efforts must cease until the horses can be adequately rested. In the corral operation, if a
piece of equipment such as a gate or a chute be
broken, all culling and loading operations must
wait until repairs or a replacement can be made. (2!

Despite all the problems inherent in capture and
live-shipping, it appears that the park will continue to
rely upon this method,[26] for round-ups have controlled
the bison population. However, an important secondary
goal has not been met. It had been hoped that buffalo
donated to Indians would form the basis of self-sustaining
herds for their tribes. This was the intent of an agreement signed in 1965 with the Bureau of Indian Affairs.
Hopes were especially high because Theodore Roosevelt's
herd was (and is) one of the only ones in the country free
from brucellosis, an infectious bacterial disease. Unfortunately, some of the tribes accepted shipments of buffalo
without having prepared for their care, and, in one case,
without even knowing what to feed them.[27]

Replacing the boundary fence has facilitated bison
management. Flimsy four-strand barbed wire, five feet in
height, is now giving way to seven-foot-high woven wire.
The latter was first used in the park in the late 1960s
along the right-of-way of Interstate 94; complete re-
fencing was begun in 1977. Nearly all of the park is now

bounded by woven wire. It is tall enough and strong enough to foil charging and jumping buffalo, yet requires less maintenance than barbed wire--an important consideration when all repair work in the wilderness areas must be done by horse or foot access. The woven wire fence has special panels designed to allow pronghorns, deer, and other migratory species to move into and out of the park.[28]

Bighorn sheep, the most recent species reintroduced, has in a different way proven to be as vexing a management problem as the bison. Whereas buffalo have been engagingly prolific, bighorns have never been able to sustain a regenerative population within Theodore Roosevelt.

With the bighorn, the park has had to deviate slightly from its policy of reintroducing only indigenous fauna. By the time Roosevelt arrived in the badlands in 1883, Audubon mountain sheep (Ovis canadensis auduboni) were well on their way to being routed from Dakota by the impinging cattle industry. None, anywhere, survived the end of Roosevelt's presidency.[29] Even if bighorn sheep did not figure prominently in his writings, their importance to a simulation of a 19th-century ecosystem, their desirability as a game animal, and, one imagines, their nobility and beauty of movement made it incumbent upon the park to try to re-establish a herd. Since Audubons had gone completely extinct, California bighorn sheep (Ovis canadensis californiana) were chosen instead.

Bighorn reintroduction started out as a joint venture of the Service and the North Dakota State Game and Fish Department, which had already built two breeding enclosures, one south of Medora and another on Magpie Creek west of Grassy Butte.[30] The park followed suit, constructing pens in both the North and South units during 1959 and early 1960 in anticipation of the project.[31] In fact, the Game and Fish Department donated five rams to NPS which were released in 1959 before the park's enclosures had been stocked with ewes. The next year the two agencies made a formal agreement: for each bighorn provided by North Dakota, the federal government would pay back two from the animals born in its breeding pens, with any surplus to be retained by the park.[32]

Most of the park's initial stock was trapped near Williams Lake, British Columbia, and transported to the South Unit by the Game and Fish Department (there were never any significantly large releases of sheep within the North Unit). Close tabs were kept on them, including forage and browse studies within the pens, but the plan soon went awry. Hopes for controlled breeding were ruined when it was discovered that mature rams could leap into the enclosure over the seven-foot-high fence at will. The fence also proved to be no deterrent to coyotes, and all lambs were lost for the first three seasons.[33]

From this bad start came only more disappointment. By 1965 the total population was still less than twenty, and the cooperative agreement was dissolved. A year later the enclosures were written off as useless, and dismantled.[34] This admission was all the more galling because of the state's success with its own bighorn breeding program in the badlands outside the park, so much so that a special twelve-ram hunting season was put on in 1975.[35]

The disparity is puzzling, for it would seem that the textbook sheep range conditions to be found within the park would more than offset the relatively higher incidence of natural predation that one might expect there. But Theodore Roosevelt's bighorn population never recovered from its early setbacks, reaching a peak of perhaps thirty-six in 1975 and 1976. It has since dropped precipitously. As of 1982, two rams and four ewes were all that were left.[36]

Researchers from the park staff, the Game and Fish Department, and North Dakota State University have tried everything from radio collars to medication in an attempt to pinpoint the reasons for the general mortality, but "no concrete explanations" have been uncovered.[37] The actual cause of death is known--pneumonia in association with lungworm infestation of the bronchial system[38]--but why state herds are surviving similar infestations is not. The Theodore Roosevelt staff is now planning for another bighorn restoration.[39]

The original reintroduction of bighorns left one last viable candidate for such projects among the larger mammals: elk (<u>Cervus</u> <u>elaphus</u> <u>canadensis</u>), also known to Roosevelt by its original Indian name, "wapiti." For reintroduction purposes, elk had the inestimable advantage over bear and wolves of preferring plants to flesh. Yet even though elk are no direct threat to livestock, the Park Service was aware that, if they were reintroduced, only to escape the park's boundaries, they could conceivably compete with cattle for range cover or damage crops in the field. Nevertheless, elk were experimentally reintroduced to Theodore Roosevelt in early 1985 when forty-seven head (eight bulls, thirty-nine cows) were transferred from Wind Cave National Park in South Dakota. Thirteen were born in the first season. A contract has already been let to study the new herd.[40]

The missing animals

These reintroductions encompass only a few of the species which have the northern badlands as part of their historical range. As was said before, while the general principle governing reintroductions has been to restore the faunal community of the last century, the program has been necessarily selective.

For example, two important carnivores once present in the region stand almost no chance of making a reappearance. One, the grizzly bear (<u>Ursus</u> <u>horribilus</u>), is somewhat abundant elsewhere, although its status, like all large wild carnivores, is precarious. The second, however, is a bona fide endangered species in this country.

187

The gray wolf (<u>Canis</u> <u>lupus</u>) is now limited to Alaska and very small parts of four other states, none providing a badlands habitat.[41] In terms of the choices the Park Service must make it is a bad turn of fortune that the two are pitted against the local ranching economy. Bears, wolves, and livestock are not a happy mix.

Where badlands and relict prairie come together a possible refuge for a few other rare species is formed. Two are of outstanding interest. Whether the extremely rare blackfooted ferret (<u>Mustela</u> <u>nigripes</u>) lives in the park is not confirmed, but they favor prairie dog towns, of which Theodore Roosevelt has an abundance. The discovery in October 1981 of a colony of blackfooted ferrets near Meeteetse, Wyoming, has rekindled hope that they may also be somewhere in the North Dakota badlands.[42]

The presence of peregrine falcons (<u>Falco</u> <u>peregrinus</u>) is also uncertain. Both in 1981 and 1982 a single peregrine was spotted during the Audubon Society's annual Christmas bird count but there has been no confirmation of a nesting pair in western North Dakota for thirty years. Rough terrain offers fine nesting to falcons, so perhaps peregrines will soon be found in Theodore Roosevelt. Increased censusing of such endangered and rare species is an important wildlife management objective for the park.[43]

Other wildlife

Unlike Wind Cave National Park (representing a some-

188

what similar ecosystem in South Dakota), Theodore Roosevelt has had no problems with a population explosion of blacktailed prairie dogs (Cynomys ludovicianus). Still, the park does have one of the largest concentrations of them anywhere, for prairie dogs are routinely exterminated outside of protected areas since they are hardly more than yipping pests to ranchers, who like neither the amount of grass they consume nor the injuries their burrows can cause to roaming stock. Somewhere between four hundred and five hundred acres of park land is taken up with active prairie dog towns, an extent which has remained steady over the last decade.[44] Measuring the size of these towns and repairing damage to undercut asphalt roadbeds is all the attention they now require.

The only other small mammals which have been managed are porcupine and beaver. Concentrated along the Little Missouri River's wooded bottomland, they feed there upon the cambium of trees (a thin organic layer between the bark and the interior vascular system). Cambium gives rise to new cells; if destroyed, further secondary growth is halted. So it is that visitors to Squaw Creek or Cottonwood campgrounds encounter places where the crowns of the trees look like they have been stripped of their leaves. In response, the park has tried all sorts of controls ranging from trapping and relocation to outright shooting; each has proven undesirable. Future control of porcupine and beaver will likely depend upon the use of repellents.[45]

Little direct avian management has been done at Theodore Roosevelt. Golden eagles (_Aquila chrysaetos_) are a case in point. In the late 1950s and early 1960s the park engaged in the construction of observation blinds and specimen banding,[46] but recently the accent has been placed on aerial surveys along with a conscious decision to depublicize locations of eagle nests within the park.[47]

Sharp-tailed grouse (_Pedioecetes phasinaellus_) and ring-necked pheasant (_Phasianus colchicus_) are given separate treatment in the Natural Resources Management Plan, the former by virtue of their ritual dancing grounds and the latter because they are the most prominent of the three exotic bird species in the park.[48] In general, the park's bird population is healthy and self-regulating.

It is likewise with Theodore Roosevelt's amphibian, insect, reptile, and fish life. While acknowledging that their role in badlands ecology "may not be fully understood,"[49] the Natural Resources Management Plan concludes that these communities are sustaining themselves without human help--the best management of all.

Notes to Chapter 9

1. Theodore Roosevelt, Ranch Life and the Hunting-Trail, reprint (Lincoln: University of Nebraska Press, 1983), 39-40. Originally published 1888.

2. There is no greater "problem" with Roosevelt's character than trying to reconcile the hunter and the conservationist. To my mind this has never been adequately worked out, but is sensibly treated in Paul Schullery's introduction to American Bears: Selections From the Writings of Theodore Roosevelt (Boulder: University of Colorado Press, 1983).

3. J. T. Sarvis and J. E. Switzer, "North Dakota," in Naturalist's Guide to the Americas, Victor E. Shelford, ed. (Baltimore: The Williams & Wilkins Co., 1926), 546; Nate Halliday, "Report of Activity," in Sixth Annual Report of the State Game and Fish Commissioner of the State of North Dakota (N.p., 1935), 37. Phelps Wyman, a consultant to the early park promotional groups, in 1930 recommended to them "the restoration of much of the wild life. . . ."; see Strand, 26. See also Byrne, "Final Project Report, Roosevelt Regional Park," unpaginated.

4. Osmer, 4.

5. Petty, "Draft History," 66. The group included the noted wildlife biologist Olaus Murie (see text at nn 8-9 below).

6. Edwin C. Alberts, "Regional Naturalist's Summary Notes," unpublished MS, June 1962 (THRO-S), 24.

   Examples of wildlife research include: Paul L. Hansen, Ricky B. Hopkins, and George R. Hoffman, An Ecological Study of the Habitat Types and Their Animal Components at Theodore Roosevelt National Park, North Dakota (Vermillion: Department of Biology, University of South Dakota, 1980); Paul L. Hansen, "An Ecological Study of the Vegetation of Theodore Roosevelt National Park, North Dakota," master's thesis, University of South Dakota, Vermillion, 1980; Patrick W. Theisen, "Age-Specific Reproduction in the Black-Tailed Prairie Dog," master's thesis, University of North Dakota, Grand Forks, 1981; Robert W. Seabloom, Richard D. Crawford, and Michael W. McKenna, Vertebrates of Southwestern North Dakota: Amphibians, Reptiles, Birds, Mammals, Research Report #24, Institute for Ecological Studies, University of North Dakota, Grand Forks, 1978. Finally, Jack Norland, Clayton Marlow, and Lynn Irby of Montana State University have recently finished an important study of the bison population at Theodore Roosevelt: their ranges and seasonal feeding habits, and general forage conditions.

7. A. Starker Leopold, Stanley A. Cain, Clarence M.
    Cottam, Ira N. Gabrielson, and Thomas L. Kimball,
    "Wildlife Management in the National Parks," Transac-
    tions of the North American Wildlife and Natural
    Resources Conference 28: 28-45. This report is cited
    in virtually every professional paper on the subject.
    Its publication has been called the manifestation of
    "the most important shift in national park philo-
    sophy"--the shift away from the precepts of MISSION 66
    and toward those of total ecosystem management, or
    biocentrism. See Brian C. Kenner, "The Philosophical
    Basis for National Park Management," The George Wright
    Forum 4:3, 27.

8. In his memoir, Murie freely admitted that ever since
    his boyhood the badlands had seemed to him "legend-
    ary," a quality imputed to them by Roosevelt's pre-
    sence there. Although it is only speculation, it
    appears that Murie may have been implicitly advocating
    that NPS manage the wildlife of the park so as to re-
    create those parts of the Rooseveltian landscape of the
    1880s that had appealed to him as a youth, and which
    now were flooding his memory as a man (see Appendix
    F). If so, the park's reintroduction program was
    predicated upon a spurious principle--one which does
    not stand alone, if D. B. Houston is to be believed.
    Writing of Yellowstone's northern elk herd, he con-
    tended that by the 1960s the Park Service had fallen
    into managing the animals for a kind of ecological
    "scene" that it found (or thought park visitors would
    find) aesthetically appealing, but which was without
    sound scientific basis: lush vegetation, fat elk, and
    unburned forests. Houston, The Northern Yellowstone
    Elk, quoted by David M. Graber, "Managing for Uncer-
    tainty: National Parks as Ecological Reserves," The
    George Wright Forum 4:3, 4-5.

9. Russell Reid, "The Mammal and Bird Life of the North
    Dakota Badlands," unpublished MS, 1948 (WL Papers), 2-
    3; McKenzie County Farmer, 25 January, 8 February, and
    24 May 1951; Strand, 47-48.

10. Micki Hellickson (Chief Naturalist, THRO) to author, 8
    October 1985.

11. "NRM Plan," 48-50.

12. "1975 Superintendent's Annual Report," 6.

13. "NRM Plan," 38.

14. Howard W. Baker, "Items of Interest from the Regional
    Director," memorandum, 25 January 1963 (THRO-S).

15. "NRM Plan," 38.

16. "North Unit District Ranger Monthly Narrative Re-
     port," memorandums, 1 October 1959, 1 August 1960,
     and 1 September 1960 (THRO-S); McKenzie County Far-
     mer, 28 September 1975.

17. Hellickson to author, 8 October 1985.

18. "1974 Superintendent's Annual Report," 7; Robert D.
     Powell, "Reduction and Disposal of Surplus Wildlife,"
     paper prepared for the NPS Chief Ranger's Conference,
     Jackson, WY, 21-24 March 1977, 2.

19. "Staff Meeting Minutes," 27 April 1966; "Chief Ran-
     ger's Monthly Report," 8 August 1974, 7 November
     1977, 14 November 1978, and 30 August 1979; "Superin-
     tendent's Monthly Narrative Report," 11 May 1967, 3.

20. Arthur L. Sullivan (Supt., THRO) to Reg. Dir. (MWRO),
     memorandum, 15 April 1969 (THRO-S). In 1975 a map
     was prepared showing the location and frequency of
     buffalo escapes in the North Unit. "Chief Ranger's
     Monthly Report," 8 October 1975.

21. For 1974-1977, see Powell, "Reduction and Disposal,"
     5. The latter figures are from 1976-1979, when 143
     escapes cost the park $9300. See "1979 Superinten-
     dent's Annual Report," 9-10. The most recent tabula-
     tion of total claim payments is nearly $18,000: "NRM
     Plan," 60.

22. Walter H. Kittams (Regional Research Biologist, NPS)
     to Asst. Reg. Dir., memorandum, 7 July 1961 (THRO-S),
     2.

23. James B. Thompson (Supt., THRO) to Area Director,
     Bureau of Indian Affairs (Aberdeen, SD), 29 June 1970
     (THRO-S). It should be noted, though, that in 1974 a
     park buffalo was slaughtered specifically for a
     museum exhibit at the Jefferson National Expansion
     Memorial in St. Louis. "State Coordinator's Monthly
     Report," memorandum, 27 November 1974 (THRO-A).

24. In 1977, Chief Ranger Robert Powell estimated the
     value of buffalo given away since 1963 at over
     $258,000. Powell, "Reduction and Disposal," 2.

25. Ibid., 3-4. See also Catherine Rutherford, "Theodore
     Roosevelt roundup corrals buffalo," Courier: The
     National Park Service Newsletter 4:1 (January 1981),
     13.

26. If so, Powell suggested a study of bison reaction to

forced herding. See "Reduction and Disposal," 7. A lone bison bull behavioral study was completed in the park in 1966. "Superintendent's Monthly Report," 13 January 1967, 2.

27. Powell, "Reduction and Disposal," 2, 8. For brucellosis status, see "NRM Plan," 38, and Belfield News, 3 October 1968.

28. "NRM Plan," 60, 38. See also "Superintendent's Monthly Report," 13 January 1967, 3.

29. "NRM Plan," 45.

30. "North Unit District Ranger Monthly Narrative Report," 31 July 1959; Lary D. Barney, "Final Report on Status of Bighorn Sheep in Theodore Roosevelt National Memorial Park," unpublished MS, ca. 1967 (THRO-A), 2.

31. Barney, "Final Report on Status of Bighorn Sheep," 3; "North Unit District Ranger Monthly Narrative Report," 4 April 1960. The South Unit enclosure was between 160 and 200 acres in size and was located on Big Plateau. See Sullivan to Charles G. Hansen (Research Biologist, Death Valley NM) 11 April 1969 (THRO-S); Barney, 3; and Petty, "Draft History," 82. I have been unable to ascertain the location of the North Unit enclosure.

32. Barney, "Final Report on Status of Bighorn Sheep," 9, 1.

33. For trapping and initial release: Sullivan to Hansen, 11 April 1969; and "NRM Plan," 45. For range studies, Walter H. Kittams (Regional Research Biologist) to Asst. Reg. Dir. (MWRO), memorandum, 2 April 1963 (THRO-S); Barney, "Final Report on Status of Bighorn Sheep," 8; "Superintendent's Monthly Narrative Report," 10 August 1964. For breeding problems: Sullivan to Hansen, 11 April 1969; and Barney, 3. For lamb predation: Barney, 3; Sullivan to Reg. Dir. (MWRO), memorandum, 7 May 1968 (THRO-S); Sullivan to Hansen, 11 April 1969. For North Unit release: 1963 Master Plan, unpaginated. In his "Draft History," (p. 85) Petty states that the first bighorns were inoculated against brucellosis, hemorrhagic septicemia, and black leg while in the enclosure. No other source corroborates this.

34. Sullivan to Hansen, 11 April 1969. See also Barney, "Final Report on Status of Bighorn Sheep," 3, 9; and "Superintendent's Monthly Report," 8 October 1965.

35. "Chief Ranger's Monthly Report," 10 December 1975.

36. Steven D. Fairaizl, "Investigations of Bighorn Sheep
     Lamb Mortality Factors," unpublished MS, ca. 1978
     (THRO-A), unpaginated; "NRM Plan," 45.

37. Fairaizl, unpaginated; "1978 Superintendent's Annual
     Report," 12; "1979 Superintendent's Annual Report,"
     7.

38. Stephen H. Richards, "Preliminary Report on Bighorn
     Sheep Deaths in Theodore Roosevelt Memorial Park",
     unpublished MS, 25 September 1980 (THRO-A).

39. Hellickson to author, 8 October 1985.

40. See also "NRM Plan," 58; Hellickson to author, 14 May
     and 8 October 1985; Harvey D. Wickware (Supt., THRO)
     to Dick Hanegar (Commissioner, ND Game & Fish Dept.),
     12 July 1983 (THRO-A). The McKenzie County Farmer
     reported in its 24 May 1951 issue that elk were to be
     reintroduced along with bison as soon as the park was
     fenced. See 1973 Master Plan, 3; The New York Times,
     3 May 1954, 27, and 8 August 1954, 2:25.

41. "NRM Plan," 55.

42. Joan Nice, "Endangered Species: A Wyoming Town Be-
     comes Ferret Capital," Audubon 84:4 (July 1982), 106-
     109. Even in Roosevelt's day the blackfooted ferret
     was a "rather rare animal": Ranch Life and the
     Hunting-Trail, 41. The 24 May 1951 issue of the
     Farmer also reported that blackfooted ferrets were to
     be brought in to control the growth of two prairie
     dog towns in the park.

43. "NRM Plan," 55.

44. "Chief Ranger's Monthly Report," 17 September 1973,
     gives 435 as a figure, as does the "NRM Plan" (1983).
     The census for 1977 gives 500 acres: "Chief Ranger's
     Monthly Report," 7 November 1977. See also Final
     Environmental Statement: Wilderness Proposal, 10.
     One general study of the park's prairie dogs is Carl
     B. Koford, Prairie Dogs, Whitefaces, and Blue Grama
     (The Wildlife Society: Wildlife Monographs #3, 1959).
     His research was also conducted at Wind Cave NP and
     Devils Tower NM.

45. "NRM Plan," 53-54.

46. "North Unit District Ranger's Monthly Narrative
     Report," 3 May and 12 July 1960; and May 1958.

47. "Chief Ranger's Monthly Report," 14 March 1983; "NRM
     Plan," 74-75.

48. "NRM Plan," 65-66, 70-71. The other two are chukar
     (Alectoris chukar) and wild turkey (Meleagris
     gallopavo), the latter entering the park after being
     released elsewhere in the badlands by sportsmen's
     clubs. 1963 Master Plan, unpaginated.

49. "NRM Plan," 76-77. Reference may also be made to
     George C. Wheeler, The Amphibians and Reptiles of the
     North Dakota Badlands (Medora: Theodore Roosevelt
     Nature and History Assn., 1954), and to Seabloom et al.
     at n6 above.

10) Cultural Resources Management

In a park where the history of human activity necessarily depends so much on natural resources, one might ask whether it is possible to consider cultural resources management apart and alone. For instance, a most valuable cultural resource is the historic scene Roosevelt knew, part of which was the badlands landscape of the late 19th century. Should its care be called cultural resources management or natural resources management? Likewise, does one comment on the park's museum collection, replete as it is with artifacts, under cultural resources management or under its main function, interpretation? What to do with the subjects of feral horses and longhorn cattle?

It will be seen that, in the last analysis, cultural resources management at Theodore Roosevelt is inseparable from--and sometimes synonymous with--management of natural resources and provision of visitor services. The park staff is now preparing a Cultural Resources Management Plan which proposes "interim or final treatment and use of all human cultural resources within the park area," but will also be open to minor changes as agreed upon by the superintendent and regional director.[1]

Before European contact

Until recently, our understanding of the badlands before the appearance of Jean Baptiste LePage in 1804 was limited by a scarcity of material evidence. Few thorough archeological surveys were completed before the 1970s.[2]

This state of affairs might still prevail were it not for the development of mineral leases on federal lands (primarily USFS-controlled) in western North Dakota. The National Historic Preservation Act and Executive Order 11593 require a cultural resources survey of federal land prior to its disturbance. When Dakota oil boomed in the 1970s, so did the business of finding out what sort of human use has been made of the badlands.

Of course the boom did not extend to the surface lands of Theodore Roosevelt, since no surface exploration for oil can take place in the park. So, much more is now known of the early culture of the badlands lying outside the park than inside. The irony of this outpouring of information is that it comes from sites being disturbed or destroyed, rather than those which can be protected in situ--making the few early culture sites known to exist within the park all the more significant.[3]

In 1968 and 1969 James Sperry of North Dakota's State Historical Society conducted a first-time survey of pre-modern sites inside Theodore Roosevelt. He found forty, and thought twelve might be worth nominating to the National Register of Historic Places. Oddly, though, he did not complete his survey report until 1981; in the interim, at just the time when badlands archeology was being advanced, the staff had no means of comparing these new finds with Sperry's park sites.[4] It is therefore a matter of some urgency, as the park's draft Cultural Resources Management Plan puts it, that "a systematic, 100 percent archeological survey to record and evaluate for the National Register all sites within the park" is done. Such a study would not only bring the Park Service into full compliance with Executive Order 11593, but would also, in effect, establish interpretation of the aboriginal use of the park area where none exists today.[5]

However, the value of even the most complete survey would be compromised if it were undertaken as though the recent regional finds had not happened. The Cultural Resources Management Plan points out that before any ground survey is begun, NPS would do well to have at hand a summary of the hundreds of survey reports filed since 1975 on western North Dakota sites.[6] Context is essential to archeology. This is brought home by the fact that Sperry estimated the oldest site in his preliminary survey at about 5000 years BP (Before the Present), whereas one badlands site outside the park is thought to date from 6000 BP and one in the Knife River quarries area from 10,000 BP.[7] Although one may not expect to find sites inside Theodore Roosevelt quite as old as this last (apparently the badlands were occupied only during parts of each year), clearly the extent and duration of early human use of the park area awaits discovery.

Some general patterns have emerged. People moving overland through the badlands seem to have used ridge lines more than wash bottoms. A site typical of ridge lines was the Hidatsa-Mandan eagle trapping pit. Eagle feathers and claws were highly valued for adornment and the making of calumet ceremonial pipes; characteristically, the Hidatsa-Mandan people also made use of the meat and hides of the bird. Pits were usually dug in groups of four to ten, each deep enough for a man to crouch under a protective cover of brush upon which a bait was placed. They often were made just below the crest of west-facing ridges so eagles could glide in on the prevailing wind and land easily on the trap. When the birds alighted, the trapper would reach through the brush and catch them by the legs.[8]

Wood frame hunting lodges were often associated with trapping pits. Anywhere in the badlands where a good water source exists (or once existed) close by a ridge top with a western exposure, one might come upon the site of a lodge. Stands of juniper or cottonwood alongside tributaries of the Little Missouri were preferred most of all. Just as elsewhere in the northern Plains, badlands lodges were made either of grass or of sticks arranged in a cone shape; hence, the latter are sometimes referred to as "wooden tipis" and the circle of stones which braced them as "tipi rings."[9]

Eagle trapping probably ended with white settlement of Dakota in the 1880s.[10] Even so, evidence of this activity has survived into our own time. Osmer photographed an intact wood hunting lodge near Achenbach Spring in 1937, and remains of lodges and trapping pits have been positively identified in recent park surveys.[11] As one researcher has said, obviously more sites remain to be found in the badlands, and those already known deserve more study.[12]

Little is known about the role of the badlands in an extensive east-west trade network which is conjectured to have existed before European contact, and still less about how European-American use of the area correlates with that of earlier people.[13] We have the broadest outlines of pre-modern badlands life, and that is all. Here is undoubtedly the part of the park's history in which the greatest advances in knowledge remain to be made, and it may be here that the greatest challenges of NPS cultural resources management will fall.

Historic sites and structures

The people of European descent who filled western Dakota in the 1880s brought with them their own ways of doing things, ways incompatible with the old life. Roosevelt spent part of his "manhood's prime vigor" watching the transformation. To date, cultural resources management in the park created to commemorate him has been largely preoccupied with documenting the few years he spent in Dakota Territory, a time he called "the pleasantest, healthiest, and most exciting phase of American existence."[14]

Yet even this task has not been without complications. Most sources, for example, readily admit the im-

possibility of drawing anything but the slightest historical connection between Roosevelt and the area that is now
the North Unit.[15] He is known to have been there once,
and then only briefly during the storied chase of the boat
thieves in 1886.[16] Beyond this there is nothing.

Nevertheless, despite the minuscule amount of archeological work that has been completed in the park, we
probably know more about the North Unit in pre-contact
times than we do about it in the period between 1880 and
1930. In 1925 the State Historical Society reviewed the
history of the northwestern counties and made mention of
the North Unit area only twice, both times vaguely. Later
researchers have found no better luck. In 1974 Merrill
Mattes, an NPS historian, surveyed the North Unit just
before Squaw Creek campground was refurbished and found
"distressingly meager" evidence for the Long X cattle
trail, long thought to be a major historic feature of the
park.[17] Mattes concluded--in frustration, no doubt--that
"the North Unit, while scenically superb, is virtually a
historical desert."[18]

Of course this is not so with the other two units.
The Elkhorn has been exhaustively studied, so we are now
well-supplied with accounts of Roosevelt's favorite retreat. Between 1948 and 1956 background research was
completed by Olaf Hagen, Ray H. Mattison, and Chester
Brooks, Park Service historians who worked out of Medora
and the Region II Office in Omaha.[19] Mattison's identification of the boundaries of the ranch site was based in

part upon oral histories of early ranchers.

Building on their work, in September 1957 Regional Archeologist Paul Beaubien made a study of the grounds. He established a baseline and located several foundations.[20] This in turn led to a complete archeological reconnaissance by Dee C. Taylor of Montana State University, who hoped his work would "recreate a picture of the Elkhorn Site as it had been when it was Roosevelt's 'home ranch'."[21]

Working from Beaubien's baseline, Taylor was able to locate the main buildings (which are now marked with cement pilings) by spot-checking old photographs, digging exploratory trenches, and sweeping with metal detectors. He could not explain some anomalies in the fence-post holing, nor did he locate a utility shed or outhouse.[22]

Taylor had an eye for detail and found many artifacts which enrich our knowledge of Roosevelt's life on the Little Missouri: cans of Maine oysters (the home state of his foremen, William Sewall and Wilmot Dow); a lard bucket from the N. K. Fairbank Company of New York; bottles of sarsparilla, wine, and "Dr. Pierce's Favorite Prescription"; suspenders and rubber boots; a coyote skull.[23]

The work of these historians and archeologists is authoritative. When the park's Historic Structure Report was published in 1980, the author, Louis Torres, found nothing which added to or contradicted earlier material history research except a changed vegetative cover at the ranch site from the loss of some large cottonwood trees.[24]

The history of Roosevelt's first home in Dakota, the Maltese Cross (or Chimney Butte) Ranch, is less fully documented because its site is still privately owned. Since July 1959 his cabin which stood there has been part of the park. Between September 1960 and June 1961 it was restored to nearly its original appearance,[25] having been altered by years of rough use and neglect. Again, the restoration was based on studies by Brooks and Mattison.[26] In 1978 the cabin was "rehabilitated" using more up-to-date historic preservation techniques.[27]

The Maltese Cross cabin is fitted out in accordance with a Park Service furnishing plan written in 1959.[28] Most of the items inside are either reproductions or period pieces, but a few, such as the writing desk, were almost certainly Roosevelt's. Should the Elkhorn Ranch house ever be reconstructed, the Service can also consult Lenard E. Brown's Furnishing Plan for a Badlands Ranch House. The book goes well beyond its title. It is a treatise on the culture of western Dakota and eastern Montana in the last decades of the 19th century. Drawing on primary and anecdotal sources, Brown describes not only furnishings but the games people played, what they read and ate, and how they spent their free time.[29]

The Elkhorn Ranch site and the Maltese Cross cabin are the two most significant historic resources in the park. It should be remembered, however, that for the duration of the national memorial park--that is, for as long as Theodore Roosevelt was managed as a historical area--everything in the park was officially considered to be of historic importance, at least with regard to the National Register of Historic Places. This was because all historical units of the National Park System were automatically listed in their entirety on the Register unless and until portions were excluded through documentation.

Since 1966, when the National Historic Preservation Act was passed, federal agencies have been required to evaluate the effects of any of their undertakings involving National Register properties. Because this requirement, spelled out in Section 106 of the law, prevails in "every planning context from the preparation of a general management plan to the smallest construction project,"[30] strictly speaking every act of the park's management was liable to conform with NHPA (and with its adjunct, Executive Order 11593, issued in 1971). Quite obviously certain projects (such as those affecting parts of the park which, while listed on the National Register because of Theodore Roosevelt's overall administrative status, did not possess true historic significance) could have been subject to undue constraint.[31]

The redesignation in 1978 did not immediately resolve the problem: the park had to be officially expunged from the Register before Section 106 compliance could be obviated. This was not done until October 1982, and even then, in a last ironic twist, everything in the park had to be delisted, including such eminently worthy candidates as the Elkhorn site and Maltese Cross cabin. The staff then had to oversee preparation of renomination forms for them so they could again enjoy the full measure of legal protection.[32]

Possibly, buildings other than the Maltese Cross will also be renominated. If so, they will be chosen from the park's List of Classified Structures. The LCS is an inventory of all historic and prehistoric structures under Park Service care which merit preservation for their archeological, historic, architectural, or engineering values. Anything on the LCS can be considered eligible for nomination to the National Register, though acceptance does not necessarily follow. Theodore Roosevelt's LCS (Table 10.1) is based on surveys begun in the mid-1970s, including a comprehensive Historic Structure Report (published in 1980). A Historic Structure Report is simply a compilation of the known history of a building: who used it, what it was used for, when it was built, what it is made of, and how it has been altered.[33]

All this documentation is meant to further preservation efforts whose thrust, according to the Cultural Resources Management Plan, "will be routine and cyclic maintenance of those structures which have reached their intended ultimate level of treatment."[34] There are three final treatments: continued use, wherein the resource keeps on serving the purpose for which it was originally designed; adaptive use, wherein it is given a new purpose consonant with, but different from, that which was originally intended; and removal or benign neglect, in cases where a resource deemed beyond preserving is documented (according to the method specified by the Historic American Buildings Survey) and removed, or allowed to molder. Within these levels of treatment fall the possibilities of preservation or restoration.[35]

Living history: longhorns and feral horses

Currently, the presence of these two domestic species is tolerated within the park because of their historical significance. They are officially regarded as "living history demonstrations," and, as long as the park was considered a historical area, they presented no inconsistencies of managerial philosophy. However, since Theodore Roosevelt's redesignation as a national park it has been questioned whether these species, exotic to the badlands, conflict with NPS policies on ecosystem management in natural areas.[36]

Of the two, longhorns have been the easier to manage. It seems the Service first contemplated introducing some kind of cattle to Theodore Roosevelt about the time of the initial push to reconstruct the Elkhorn. The original suggestion appears in the 1963 Master Plan. Why longhorns were preferred to other breeds is not clear, for, as the master plan admitted, "interpretation of the longhorns [would have to] emphasize that though this type of cattle was brought here in the open range era, Roosevelt, himself, preferred to stock and breed-up with shorthorns."[37]

There is some evidence that placing longhorns in the park was the brainchild of Hal Davies, an influential editor of the Minot Daily News. Davies wanted them as part of the Elkhorn's development, or, failing that, in the South Unit. In this he had the support of Senator Milton Young. Perhaps deferring to their wishes, in 1964 the park staff proposed a longhorn herd for the Elkhorn Unit, but the Midwest Regional Office turned down the idea precisely because Roosevelt never ran longhorns at that ranch.[38] The political overtones of the situation occupied a good part of the September 1966 staff meeting, and a telling remark is recorded in the minutes. "Perhaps the North Unit could handle them," someone present mused. "If we do not accept the longhorn cattle, appropriations might be cut."[39] Six months later the North Unit received a shipment of six steers from the Fort Niobrara National Wildlife Refuge in Nebraska.[40] While it cannot be said that the influence of Davies and Young caused the introduction of longhorns to Theodore Roosevelt,[41] certainly political considerations played a part in the decision.

Twenty-one more steers have been placed in the North Unit since 1967. While they have the run of the park, the herd prefers a 750-acre sagebrush flat of the Little Missouri near the buffalo corral. They are readily visible from the scenic drive and have become a favorite of visitors, providing some of the atmosphere of the open-range cattle industry of the last century.[42]

Since it is a non-breeding herd (steers are gelded males) the longhorns require only to be fed (hay), given salt licks, and have river water kept open to them in winter. Mortality has been low, with replacements obtained from Fort Niobrara. The only management concerns are their authenticity and whether to bring in breeding stock. As for the latter, the park staff has decided that problems on the order of those caused by buffalo would result, and prefer to continue present minimal management of the cattle. As for authenticity, despite Roosevelt's preference for shorthorns and the shaky documentation of the Long X Trail, the staff believes "retention of the herd in its present state is desirable as a historical display."[43] Undoubtedly the longhorns have a place at Theodore Roosevelt so long as the reasons for their presence are made explicit to visitors.

No one is sure of the ancestry of the fifty or so horses now living in the South Unit. Although often loosely referred to as "wild," they are certainly feral. A common explanation of their origin holds that they descend from two escaped ranch mares bred by a white stud of unknown provenance.[44] But this is only an informed guess.

The animals can be considered feral on the authority of Roosevelt himself, who wrote that "in a great many--

indeed, in most--localities" of western Dakota in the 1880s

> there are wild horses to be found, which, al-
> though invariably of domestic descent, being
> either themselves runaways from some ranch or
> Indian outfit, or else claiming such for their
> sires and dams, yet are quite as wild as the
> antelope on whose domain they have intruded.
> Ranchmen run in these wild horses whenever pos-
> sible, and they are but little more difficult to
> break than the so-called "tame" animals. But
> the wild stallions are, whenever possible, shot;
> both because of their propensity for driving off
> the ranch mares, and because their incurable
> viciousness makes them always unsafe companions
> for other horses still more than for men. A
> wild stallion fears no beast except the grizzly,
> and will not always flinch from an encounter
> with it. . . .

"Invariably of domestic descent": it is evident that the "wild" horses he saw a hundred years ago were like those in the park today. Their habits and behavior were wild, yet they retained enough cultivated traits to be recognized as descendants of domestic stock.[45]

This passage from Ranch Life and the Hunting-Trail is used to justify the horses's presence in the South Unit.[46] They are regarded as a "historic livestock display" and as such are not subject to provisions of the Wild Free-Roaming Horse and Burro Act of 1971.[47]

The herd has been actively managed since the 1950s. Early on the Service wanted to rid the South Unit of all feral horses. During those years several round-ups were sponsored by local grazing associations. Most of the captured bore brands from neighboring ranches. Unbranded horses were either auctioned off for charity or claimed under North Dakota's estray laws.[48] Newspapers gave these early round-ups widespread publicity (The New York Times covered one in 1954), in the process creating confusion about and criticism of the methods used by the Park Service. Nevertheless, the 1963 Master Plan called the feral horses "a recent, exotic intrusion and a management problem" and recommended their removal.[49]

One of the problems referred to was that of ownership. For a time the staff seemed to be under the impression that the government held title to all stock left unclaimed at the completion of the fencing of the park. This notion prompted an ultimatum to be issued in 1962: local ranches were given two years to remove any stock they could prove to be theirs. After the deadline, all title was to be vested in the government; then NPS would hold one last round-up to dispose of the horses by allowing any ranch to put in a claim for part of the herd.[50]

The deadline passed with many horses left behind, so in the late spring of 1965 the park held its "final" round-up. It can only be described as a public relations disaster. The methods of capture--running the horses to exhaustion with shifts of riders and then corraling them into the buffalo holding pen--were unpopular in themselves, and even more so because so many local people still thought of the herd as wild. Many area newspapers, especially the Dickinson Press, were critical of the round-up. They urged the park to make plans for keeping and maintaining the horses which had escaped capture.[51]

Local sentiment in favor of the herd was so strong that in May 1966, a year after the final round-up, Super-intendent Arthur Sullivan proposed to the Midwest Regional Office a reversal of policy, asking permission to keep a small herd of horses on the strength of Roosevelt's refer-ence to them. The Regional Office agreed that the remain-ing horses should be maintained at least until the next review of the master plan, but warned the staff not to solicit opinion one way or the other about the herd. "In fact," wrote Fred Fagergren, the regional director, "the less publicity given to these horses is probably all for the best."[52]

So things stood until 1972, when almost all private claims to the herd were waived after the state asked for and received legal release of its ownership. North Dakota then donated the horses to the federal government on the condition that they be managed by NPS. The Service for-mally claimed them in June 1974.[53] In anticipation of gaining clear title, the park held another round-up in the autumn of 1973 in which twelve were captured.[54]

The 1973 round-up was not as controversial as the one in 1965, but the staff realized that if they were now to maintain the herd a coherent plan of management was called for. Just such a plan was drawn up in 1976 and revised in 1977. It identified two concerns: the tendency of the herd to a small range, and suspected inbreeding. The horses have always spent most of their time in the extreme southeastern part of the South Unit, watering at Boicourt,

Southeast Corner, and Sheep Butte springs (all dish tanks) and Olson Well (undeveloped). The plan voiced worries about fence damage, trail erosion, and overgrazing.[55] Since the herd rarely dispersed, it was also thought that inbreeding might be excessive: "jugheads," colts with crooked legs, horses with "poor overall conformation," and little color variation within the herd had all been observed.[56]

Admitting that the number was arbitrary, the herd management plan nevertheless affirmed the decision made after the 1965 round-up to keep about forty horses in the park.[57] Removal was eliminated as an option because of past adverse public reaction. Moving part of the herd west of the Little Missouri, while not ruled out, was presented as an unlikely choice because of the "potential negative impacts on the Bighorn Sheep population." Direct reduction of the herd by round-up every few years was the recommended course of action.[58]

In between the original appearance of the plan and its revision, NPS commissioned a report on the horses by Milton Frei, a range specialist working for the Bureau of Land Management. He spent three days in the field, and his findings disputed those of the park. Frei discounted overuse of the range. He could find no support for the existence of genetic deficiencies and recommended against introducing new blood lines. Although his was an evaluation, and did not offer any overall management prescriptions, he did suggest five other possible methods of herd reductions besides round-ups.[59]

Perhaps because of the brevity of his fieldwork, Frei's conclusions have not been followed by the park staff in subsequent management. It was instead decided to keep the herd down to forty by means of periodic round-ups and to introduce new animals to increase genetic variability.[60]

Round-ups have since been held in 1978 to 1981.[61] Both made use of helicopters, ostensibly to guide the riders driving the herd. But some private citizens on the scene accused NPS of using the helicopters to directly chase the herd. One complainant called the 1981 round-up "obscene" and "an inhumane circus."[62] Obviously the truth lies somewhere between this extreme and the Park Service's assertion that "every consideration is given to the humane treatment of the animals."[63] Round-ups are an imperfect way to control an animal population, but the alternatives appear even less attractive. The next one, scheduled for autumn 1986, will reduce the current herd of eighty by half. It too will no doubt take place in an atmosphere filled with the strong emotions many people reserve for "wild horses."[64]

The ranching way of life

One last cultural resource the park may be charged to protect in the future is exactly the one that has historically been taken most for granted in western North Dakota:

214

the ranching way of life. To be sure, ranching in Roosevelt's time is well-represented, and the park supports the Gold Seal Company's restoration of Medora to a semblance of its 1880s appearance. But over the years the remains of many more-recent homesteads inside Theodore Roosevelt were "cleaned up" and cleared entirely.[65] At the time it seemed a good idea to restore the park land to its most natural appearance, whatever that may have been. Now, with energy production threatening to supplant ranching as the economic mainstay of the region, it is not inconceivable that Theodore Roosevelt National Park will one day be called upon to interpret the way people ranched in the middle-to-late 20th century. In this sense, it may be said that it is not always enough for cultural resource managers to look to the past; they must also be watchful of the present while thinking of the needs of the future.

Notes to Chapter 10

1. "Cultural Resources Management Plan, Theodore Roosevelt National Park (draft)," unpublished MS, 1983 (THRO-A), 1 (hereafter cited as "CRM Plan").

2. Not so with ethnographic work. In his "Eagle Trapping Along the Little Missouri River" (North Dakota History: Journal of the Northern Plains 50:1, Winter 1983, 4-22), Walter E. Allen gives a number of citations.

3. "CRM Plan," 3-4.

4. Apart from the information gleaned from circumscribed pre-construction surveys. Ibid., 3; James E. Sperry, "A Preliminary Archeological Survey of Theodore Roosevelt National Memorial Park," unpublished MS, 1981 (THRO-S). See also Sperry to John J. Reynolds (Chief, Division of Planning, DSC), 29 July 1974, attached to Final Environmental Assessment for Squaw Creek Campground, Theodore Roosevelt National Memorial Park (Denver: DSC, 1976), 104; and "Draft Environmental Statement, Proposed Master Plan, Theodore Roosevelt National Memorial Park, North Dakota," unpublished MS, ca. 1975 (THRO-A), 17. For a partial list of pre-construction surveys, see "CRM Plan," 23-25.

5. No archeological sites in the park are now listed on the National Register of Historic Places. "CRM Plan," 45, 51-52.

6. Ibid., 53-55.

7. Ibid., 3.

8. Allen, 4-5, 7-8.

9. Ibid., 4-8.

10. Ibid., 12.

11. See Osmer, appendix; and "CRM Plan," 4. In the mid-1960s George M. Johnson reported the remains of wooden lodges in the Achenbach Hills. See his "The Badlands and Teddy's Park," Living Wilderness 31:96-97 (1967), 24.

12. Allen, 12 ff.

13. "CRM Plan," 4.

14. Ranch Life and the Hunting-Trail, 24.

15. See for example the "Interpretive Prospectus, Theo-

dore Roosevelt National Memorial Park, North Dakota,"
unpublished MS, ca. 1973 (THRO-L), 8.

16. For an account, read Ranch Life and the Hunting-
Trail, 111-129, or Hermann Hagedorn, Roosevelt in
the Bad Lands (Boston: Houghton Mifflin Co., 1921),
365-386.

17. Merrill J. Mattes, "Historic Resource Survey, North
Unit, Theodore Roosevelt National Memorial Park," 19
June 1974, attached to Final Environmental Assessment
for Squaw Creek Campground, 96-97. Mattes thought
its supposed route up the Squaw Creek drainage to be
"rooted in a vague oral tradition."

18. Ibid.

19. For a bibliography of these studies, see "CRM Plan,"
72-74. See also Dee C. Taylor, "Archeological Investigations of the Elkhorn Ranch Site," unpublished MS,
1959 (THRO-L), 10, 13-14; and Russell Reid (Supt.,
SHSND) to WL, 6 April 1948 (WL Papers).

20. Petty, "Draft History," 79; Taylor, 14, 18, 70.

21. Taylor, 3.

22. He did find a path that likely led to the privy, but
couldn't find its exact location even after diligent
searching, "much to the delight of local cowboys who
thought the whole thing was ridiculous." Ibid., 69.

23. Ibid., 70.

24. Louis Torres, Historic Structure Report, Theodore
Roosevelt National Park, North Dakota (Denver; NPS,
1980), 56, 60.

25. Petty, "Draft History," 81.

26. See n19 above.

27. John O. Lancaster (Supt., THRO) to Rodd Wheaton (His-
toric Preservation Officer, RMRO), memorandum, 24
June 1978 (THRO-A); "1978 Superintendent's Annual
Report," 14.

28. Sally Johnson, "Furnishing Plan for the Maltese Cross
Cabin," unpublished MS, 1959 (THRO-A).

29. Lenard E. Brown, Furnishing Plan for a Badlands Ranch
House (Washington, DC: NPS, 1969).

30. Cultural Resources Management Guidelines: NPS-28
(Washington, DC: NPS, 1981), 6-1, 6-4 (quotation from

p. 6-4).

31. See "CRM Plan," 9.

32. James B. Thompson (Acting Reg. Dir., RMRO) to James Sperry (Supt., SHSND, and State Historic Preservation Officer), 1 July 1982 (THRO-A); Bruce MacDougal (Chief of Registration, National Register Programs, NPS) to Federal Preservation Officer (NPS), memorandum, 29 October 1982 (THRO-A); "CRM Plan," 2-3, 10; "1976 Superintendent's Annual Report," 8.

33. "CRM Plan," 16-18; Richard A. Strait (Associate Reg. Dir., RMRO) to Superintendents of the Rocky Mountain Region, open memorandum, 12 May 1983 (THRO-A); Torres, passim.

34. "CRM Plan," 17. "Routine" maintenance is done seasonally during any one year; "cyclic" maintenance takes place only occasionally.

35. Ibid., 39, 47, 21.

36. "NRM Plan," 51. The desirablity of having feral horses in the park was also questioned before Theodore Roosevelt was officially categorized as a historical area in 1964: see text at n49 below.

37. 1963 Master Plan, unpaginated.

38. Jackson E. Price (Asst. Director, NPS) to Reg. Dir. (MWRO), memorandum, 14 October 1964 (THRO-S); A. Clark Stratton (Asst. Director, Design and Construction, MWRO) to Reg. Dir. (MWRO), memorandum, 7 October 1968 (THRO-S); "Staff Meeting Minutes," 19 September 1966.

39. "Staff Meeting Minutes," 19 September 1966, 2.

40. "Staff Meeting Minutes," 8 March 1967; "Basic Operations Declaration," unpaginated.

41. At the time (1967) the route of the Long X Trail, over which longhorns were driven, was considered to be a certainty. The work of Mattes and other historical archeologists (referred to above) had not yet occurred, so it was thought a fact that the Long X followed the Squaw Creek drainage through the North Unit. This, not politics, might have been the justification for placing longhorns in the North Unit.

42. "NRM Plan," 51; "Basic Operations Declaration," unpaginated.

43. "NRM Plan," 52. The herd is regarded as having an

insignificantly small impact on the park's natural environment.

44. Robert D. Powell, "Draft Resource Management Plan for Wildlife--Feral Horses," unpublished MS, 16 August 1977 (THRO-A), 1 (revision of 1976 original). The explanation is repeated in "NRM Plan," 42.

45. Ranch Life and the Hunting-Trail, 33.

46. The "historic significance of horses to [the] cattle industry" has also been cited as a reason: "Basic Operations Declaration," unpaginated.

47. The horses are not "free-roaming" under the terms of the law and so are not available under the "Adopt-a-Horse" program. Harvey D. Wickware (Supt., THRO) to Leonard S. Boser (Pierz, MN), 27 October 1981 (THRO-A); Powell, "Draft Resource Management Plan for Wildlife--Feral Horses," 13.

48. McKenzie County Farmer, 6 May 1954; "Superintendent's Monthly Narrative Report," 9 July 1965.

49. The New York Times, 3 May 1954, 27; Petty, "Draft History," 71-72; 1963 Master Plan, unpaginated.

50. Sullivan to Fred C. Fagergren (Reg. Dir., MWRO), memorandum, 31 May 1966 (THRO-S).

51. "Staff Meeting Minutes," 15 June 1965; Dickinson Press, 29 May, 11 June, and 9 July 1965; Powell, "Draft Resource Management Plan for Wildlife--Feral Horses," 2; "Basic Operations Declaration," unpaginated.

52. Sullivan to Fagergren, 31 May 1966; Fagergren to Sullivan, memorandum, 5 July 1966 (THRO-S).

53. "State Coordinator's Monthly Report," 27 December 1972, 4 October 1973; "Basic Operations Declaration," unpaginated; "Chief Ranger's Monthly Narrative Report," 10 May and 9 July 1974 (the last Tescher claim was forfeited in June 1974); John O. Lancaster (Supt., THRO) to Governor Arthur Link (ND), 2 July 1974 (THRO-A).

54. "Chief Ranger's Monthly Narrative Report," 5 October 1973.

55. Powell, "Draft Resource Management Plan for Wildlife--Feral Horses," 1-2; "Environmental Assessment: Proposed Feral Horse Reduction, Theodore Roosevelt National Memorial Park," unpublished MS, 19 April 1978 (THRO-A), 1.

56. Powell, "Draft Resource Management Plan for Wildlife--Feral Horses," 1.

57. "It has also been determined"--how is not told--"that with a herd of not less than 35-40 head, representative sexes and age classes can be displayed." Ibid., 3.

58. Ibid., 2-3.

59. Milton N. Frei, "Wild Horse Herd Evaluation for Theodore Roosevelt National Memorial Park," unpublished MS, April 1977 (THRO-A), passim.

60. For a short time the staff thought about using "direct reduction"--shooting, in other words--as that seemed "the most economical [method] and the least disruptive to other park resources." Wrote Superintendent Lancaster: "We are well aware of public sentiment regarding this method of reduction but consider Theodore Roosevelt National Memorial Park to be a special case since the animals are captive and under closer management than other wild horses in the western United States." Lancaster to Assoc. Reg. Dir. (RMRO), memorandum, 11 August 1976 (THRO-A). He might also have championed shooting in the name of historical authenticity, since that was the preferred method of "reduction" in Roosevelt's day. See text at n45 above.

61. The 1978 round-up was preceded by an environmental assessment and a month-long public comment period, during which the plan drew no disapproval. "Environmental Assessment: Proposed Feral Horse Reduction," passim; "Chief Ranger's Monthly Narrative Report," 8 September 1977; Lancaster to Reg. Dir. (RMRO), memorandum, 5 July 1978 (THRO-A).

62. Jay V. Brevold (Medora, ND) to Powell, 6 October 1981 (THRO-A).

63. "Basic Operations Declaration," unpaginated.

64. Hellickson to author, 8 October 1985. Sources do not agree on the exact number of horses captured in the two NPS-sponsored round-ups of 1978 and 1981. Cf. "Chief Ranger's Monthly Narrative Report," 14 November 1978; Powell to Lancaster, memorandum, 13 September 1978; and "Basic Operations Declaration," for the 1978 round-up. Cf. "Chief Ranger's Monthly Narrative Report," 9 November 1981; "1981 Superintendent's Annual Report," 14; and "Basic Operations Declaration" for the 1981 round-up.

65. Restoration of Medora: Warren D. Hotchkiss, "Information and Interpretive Services Report for 1965,"
memorandum, 26 January 1966 (THRO-S).   Clearing of
homesteads: "Chief Ranger's Monthly Narrative
Report," 10 December 1975; "1981 Superintendent's
Annual Report," 13 (Paddock Cabin); Petty, "Draft
History," 72, 89.

A Forest Service management plan for the Little
Missouri National Grasslands, published in 1975,
mentions the desirability of preserving the "tradi-
tional way of life" of the region--a clear reference
to balancing the needs of energy development with
those of ranching.   Final Environmental Statement:
Management Plan, Rolling Prairie Planning Unit,
Little Missouri National Grasslands (Billings, MT:
Custer National Forest, USFS, 1975), 34.

Part 4:

People in the Park

I pictured in my mind the future visitor to the
badlands, we'll say the visitor who is attuned
to the message [of] wild open country. I pictured him climbing up to a grassy plateau, and
sitting there on a knoll to contemplate the
scene. There would be the scent of the sod at
his feet. He would look with interest at the
curled heads of the grama grass, the grama grass
of Roosevelt's day, the grama grass of the tumultuous days when this country was formed. . . .

Not a serrated mountain range here, not a mossy
forest, nor a lake studded paradise. Rather an
open country; its trees are twisted and storm
worn, and grow sparingly along the river banks.
A raw country, a country in the making perhaps.
This very fact, this character, the attributes
of chiseled buttes and domes, the clay and the
prairie grass, the eagle, the prairie dogs,
deer, coyote; the flocks of grouse at the heads
of the wooded draws--all these spell one phase
of our west--not to be compared with different
ones--to be taken and enjoyed for its own singular beauty and character. Ordinary country, but
with an aura of the west. . . .

                          -- Olaus Murie, December 1949

11) Recreation

Most people come to Theodore Roosevelt to have fun. They come to relax, take a scenic drive, perhaps to car-camp for the night. Only one in ten stays longer. Nearly a third never even contact a ranger during their stay. Most are just passing through on their way to somewhere else--the general fate of all of North Dakota, it must be said.[1] This suggests that quite a few visitors to Theodore Roosevelt engage in a self-directed, self-reliant park experience, which is in itself no bad thing.

Backcountry use

And of course, there are always a few who, in the course of being on their way to somewhere else, find themselves compelled to abandon their cars, venture away from the asphalt, and explore a river bank or scramble up a butte or wander through a draw. Itineraries are discarded, if only for a few hours. Like Roosevelt, these people--far removed from Edward Abbey's infamous description of the typical national park tourist[2]--have succumbed to a desire to get out into the backcountry.

The challenge of the park's backcountry lies in mastering extremes, and not merely those of climate. Badlands topography offers little of the familiar. Narrow coulees quickly become confining; buttes and defiles seem to alternate endlessly with a disorienting repetition. The open prairies of the plateaus can be more forbidding yet, for in a sea of grass there is no shelter and nowhere to hide--quite unsettling to a species with a marked preference for being on the edge of the open.[3] It seems one must choose between claustrophobia and the tyranny of the open sky. There is little middle ground in the Theodore Roosevelt backcountry.

Few are ready to meet the challenge entirely alone, and so horseback trips have always been the favorite method of getting into the backcountry. A 1970 survey found that they constituted seventy-five percent of overall backcountry use, which itself had increased sixfold since 1960. At the time of the survey there were designated sites for camping and a couple of marked trails but no formal trail system, resulting in a proliferation of tracks in grassland areas of the park.[4] Group rides were particularly popular; some saddle clubs even bought or leased private land just outside the park for base camps, while others used group campgrounds within.[5] Plans to institute buckboard rides into the backcountry, although much debated by high-echelon NPS officials in the late 1960s and early 1970s, did not catch on.[6]

Hiking has never competed with horse use in popularity. Foot travel is hindered by the rugged terrain, lack of drinking water, and capricious Plains weather. A comprehensive trail system for both hikers and riders has just lately been put together. There were no maintained long-distance trails at all for the first fifteen years of the park, and only three nature trails: Long X, Ridgeline, and Wind Canyon.[7] Backpacking may yet become more popu-

lar, especially in the North Unit given the recent congressional approval of the Lewis and Clark National Historic Trail, which is planned to run nearby.[8]

River recreation is seasonal. Late spring runoff
raises the water in the Little Missouri channel to truly
navigable levels for a few weeks each year, but by mid-
summer flowage drops and the river takes on the consis-
tency of old coffee, discouraging canoeist, swimmer, and
wader alike.

The other "high season" on the river is winter. The
Little Missouri is usually frozen from the first of December to early March. As the sole natural thoroughfare in
the badlands it has been used for decades as an ice highway by local residents in pickup trucks, on horseback, or,
most recently, on snowmobiles.

Snowmobiling is prohibited in national parks unless
the superintendent permits it in carefully circumscribed
areas. Recreational snowmobiling was first allowed in
Theodore Roosevelt on a trial basis in 1969, confined to
the frozen river in the North Unit and to a twenty-nine-
mile trail of river and loop road in the South Unit. When
the time came to form a definite policy on snowmobile use,
the park staff did an environmental impact assessment. It
recommended a compromise solution: restrict snowmobiles to
the Little Missouri. The cost of damage to ephemeral
river features (e.g., sandbars) and of noise pollution in
the river corridor was thought far less than that of tread

erosion and wildlife disturbance over a much wider land area. To have banned snowmobiles altogether, on the other hand, would have meant alienating a small but vocal part of the local community.[9] There was no challenge to the assessment's conclusions, so in 1975 the river was permanently opened to snowmobiles, though their use has not been unduly encouraged.[10]

No changes in river recreation have come about because of the designation in 1975 of the Little Missouri as North Dakota's first state scenic river, but until ownership of the river bed is finally established the possibility remains open.[11] Nor has wilderness designation made a significant difference: the backcountry was already being managed de facto as a wilderness, and, because of the ownership problem, the river was not included in the designated area anyway.[12]

MISSION 66: the connecting parkway

Backcountry use is slight compared with conventional automobile touring. The park has therefore devoted a proportionate amount of money and expertise to the latter, and never so much as during the MISSION 66 program. Begun in the mid-1950s in anticipation of the Service's fiftieth anniversary in 1966, a major part of MISSION 66 was an agency-wide push to build new visitor facilities. A 1954 "wish list" for the park drawn up by the Greater North Dakota Association, a group devoted to promoting tourism in the state (and successor to the Roosevelt Memorial

National Park Association), prefigured the kind of projects that were soon actually undertaken at Theodore Roosevelt as part of MISSION 66: new entrance roads, campground utilities, visitor centers, boundary fencing, and headquarters buildings.[13]

At Theodore Roosevelt the task was not only to expand facilities to accommodate increasing visitation (Table 11.1), but to re-do what was built before the park's admittance to the National Park System. "When Theodore Roosevelt National Memorial Park was created," a MISSION 66 circular explained, "an area which had already undergone some development as a Recreational Demonstration Area became subject to some new concepts. Under the recreational area program, campgrounds and picnic areas were provided as were horse trails and roads, all without emphasis upon historical significance. When the area became a part of the National Park System, largely on the basis of its historical associations, the concepts of appropriate development had to be adjusted accordingly."[14] In terms of its own goals MISSION 66 was a success: the park headquarters was moved from an antiquated situation at Peaceful Valley to a new visitor center in Medora, a new South Unit entrance road was built, and interpretive signs were erected along the loop drive. The North Unit also got a set of road-signs, improvements to Squaw Creek campground, and other facilities.[15]

Easily the most ambitious proposal to come out of MISSION 66 was for a parkway connecting the three units.

The idea had been bandied about since the 1920s, but nothing came of it until it was revived by the Greater North Dakota Association in 1957. It proposed a scenic highway starting from U. S. Route 12 at Marmarth and ending at U. S. Route 2 near the present-day Fort Union Trading Post National Historic Site, west of Williston.[16] The idea was picked up by the Service and became part of the elaborate plans to make the Elkhorn Unit the focal point of the park (see Chapter 2).

The parkway was never built because there was no agreement on its purpose or worth. For the park staff it was a means to an end: a connecting highway would assure some development of the Elkhorn, which in turn would mean that the park was fulfilling its prescribed mission as a historical area. The Washington leadership of the Service saw an opportunity for regional recreational development: as part of a longer Prairie Tourway, the proposal suited the increased emphasis NPS was giving to recreation at the time of the Outdoor Recreation Resources Review Commission. The parkway was also consonant with the personal philosophies of Director Conrad L. Wirth and Secretary of the Interior Stewart L. Udall, and received their explicit support.[17] Politicians smelled a porkbarrel (indeed, the parkway became a central issue in the 1964 congressional race between Don Short and Rolland Redlin), and North Dakota representatives repeatedly tried to get Congress to fund the project.[18] Booster groups dreamed of it as part of "a non-mountainous, non-metropolitan, Great Plains gateway to southern winter resorts and northern recreation areas."[19]

The Forest Service, on the other hand, was never enthusiastic about the parkway and by the early 1970s had decided that "it would cause irreversible damage to the virtually virgin Little Missouri River flood plain" if it were ever built. It is also quite possible that USFS anticipated the escalation of energy exploration (although they, like most others, probably thought the boom would come in coal, not in petroleum) and did not want an inconvenient parkway tying up their options in the Little Missouri National Grasslands. They flatly declared that it would never be constructed--at least not using USFS lands.[20]

The position of the ranchers, by virtue of their diversity, was the least easy to gauge. Some were unalterably opposed because the planned route crossed too many "base lands" used to produce crops and pasture for livestock in winter; others, because they had already seen the government take plenty of agricultural land out of production as part of the Garrison Dam diversion on the Missouri River. Still others thought a parkway useless as a farm-to-market route, promising nothing but stock kills and scenic easements. And some thought it an invasion of their tenaciously-held privacy.[21] But a sizable number were in favor, especially those families living in Billings County away from the proposed route.[22]

An inordinate amount of time was spent trying to amass the political wherewithal needed to gain approval. Meetings and briefings and more meetings were held. The issue was debated over the coffee table and at the polls. Theodore Roosevelt's superintendent kept the Midwest Regional Office apprised with special monthly reports for three years running. But as the end of MISSION 66 drew near, sentiment for large-scale development projects faded.[23] Congress as a whole showed no great interest in the parkway bills, and the disparate opinions of the project prevented a coalition of effective political support from forming. Like the Elkhorn Ranch restoration, the parkway was quietly dropped from the park's agenda. A different set of priorities was coming into view.

This is not to say that no physical plant expansion has taken place in recent years. Two major changes in North Unit recreational facilities have been made: the remodeling of Squaw Creek campground and the paving of the scenic road all the way to Oxbow Overlook. The campground is beautifully situated in a grove of cottonwoods near the confluence of Squaw Creek and the Little Missouri--making it susceptible, unfortunately, to erosion and violent springtime flooding. River bank stabilization was but one of the improvements carried out: abandoned campground roads were obliterated, the loop re-routed, campsites modernized, and a small campfire circle built.[24] Even more important was the long-awaited paving of the entire scenic road, previously hard-surfaced only as far as Squaw Creek. The rough drive on to Oxbow had discouraged visitation to the North Unit.[25] Both projects met with the approval of local residents who probably considered them partial compensation for NPS's support of the North Unit wilderness areas (see Chapter 7) and who, in any event, thought "improved facilities in the park will correspond to better facilities elsewhere and that without improved facilities in the park, outside development will be deterred."[26] Recent construction of note in the South Unit includes the Painted Canyon visitor contact station, a separate park administration building, and the remodeling of the Medora visitor center.

It should be mentioned in passing that concessioners have played just a small role in the park's history. The tone was set by Julius Krug, the secretary of the interior, at the dedication ceremony in 1949. He told the audience that no concessions would be necessary within the park as long as local businesses provided services that kept pace with demand.[27] This view went unchallenged by MISSION 66. Concessions were not made part of its program "since most of the visitors can obtain a satisfying experience from daytime use of the area and food and lodging are available in places not too distant from the north and south units. . . ."[28] Since 1967 Peaceful Valley Ranch has been operated as a trail ride outfit, but this is the only important concession Theodore Roosevelt has ever had.[29]

Notes to Chapter 11

1. Michele Hellickson, "General Statement for Interpretation and Visitor Services: F[iscal] Y[ear 19]82,"
unpublished MS, 28 April 1983 (THRO-A), part I.3;
National Park Statistical Abstract, 1982 (Washington,
DC: NPS, 1983), 21.

2. See Edward Abbey, Desert Solitaire: A Season in the
Wilderness (New York: Ballentine, 1968), 51-52.

3. "Even today we find few peoples adapted to entirely
open or entirely forested areas. For most humans the
contrasts seem important. . . . The phenomenon of
edge, or interspersion, well known to wildlife biolo-
gists, may have entered into man's original choice of
habitat." Raymond F. Dasmann, A Different Kind of
Country (London: Collier, 1968), 55-56. See also
Thomas Justin Gallagher, "Preference for Alternative
Natural Landscapes," doctoral dissertation, University
of Michigan School of Natural Resources, Ann Arbor,
1977, 16-17, 116-117. Cf. n41, Chapter 7.

4. "Backcountry Use and Management Survey," unpublished
MS, 11 February 1970 (THRO-S), unpaginated; James B.
Thompson (Supt., THRO) to Senator Milton R. Young
(ND), 11 December 1970 (THRO-S). No statistics on
backcountry use were kept before 1967. See 1967 Mas-
ter Plan, 31.

5. 1973 Master Plan, 24; "Summary of Meeting Between
U. S. Forest Service and National Park Service Conducted at Theodore Roosevelt National Memorial Park,
Medora, North Dakota, Tuesday, April 22, 1969," memorandum, 25 April 1969 (THRO-S); "Staff Meeting
Minutes," 6 September 1966, 3. The most popular group
campground was the Roughrider, situated on an old
ranch access road leading off from U. S. Route 10,
west of the Little Missouri River in the South Unit.
It was not sited advantageously: a landslide closed it
in 1969 and a flood inundated it in 1978 before it was
abandoned in 1980. There is still pressure from horse
clubs to either re-open or replace it. See Final
Environmental Statement: Wilderness Proposal, 36;
"1978 Superintendent's Annual Report," 9; "1980 Superintendent's Annual Report," 21; "State Coordinator's
Monthly Report," 3 June 1980; "Chief Ranger's Monthly
Narrative Report," 2 December 1982; "North Dakota and
the National Park Service," 5-6.

6. See Fred C. Fagergren (Reg. Dir., MWRO) to Director
(NPS), memorandum, 6 March 1967 (THRO-S); "Staff Meeting Minutes," 20 August 1970.

7. Thompson to J. J. Dipboye (Richmond, VA), 21 September

1970 (THRO-S); <u>1963 Master Plan</u>, unpaginated; "North
Unit District Ranger's Monthly Report," 2 November
1958.

8. Governor Allen I. Olson (ND) to Harvey D. Wickware
    (Supt., THRO), 21 January 1983 (THRO-A).

9. "Environmental Assessment for Snowmobile Trails,"
    unpublished MS, ca. 1975 (THRO-A), unpaginated.

10. "1975 Superintendent's Annual Report," 8; <u>Dickinson
    Press</u>, 6 January 1978.

11. "1975 SFM" (fourth revision, 1980), 5; "Environmental
    Assessment: Elkhorn Unit Development," 9. See also
    text at n9, Chapter 8. The Little Missouri State
    Scenic River Act of 1975 stipulated that the waters
    of the main stem and its tributaries could not be
    made available for industrial purposes (but see text
    at n6, Chapter 8). The Act was a response to a
    number of proposals, beginning in late 1973, which
    would have dammed the main stem for use by a coal
    gasification plant. Gary Leppart, "A State Scenic
    River for North Dakota," <u>North Dakota Outdoors</u> 37:10
    (April 1975), 18.

12. <u>Final Environmental Statement: Wilderness Proposal</u>,
    13-14.

13. Strand, 51. See also Robert N. Henry (Director of ND
    Economic Development Commission) to Warren D.
    Hotchkiss (Supt., THRO), 17 February 1964 (THRO-S).
    For a description of MISSION 66, see Wirth, 237-284;
    Shankland, 323-340; and Ise, 546-550.

14. "Mission 66 for Theodore Roosevelt National Memorial
    Park," unpublished MS, ca. 1956 (THRO-S), 3.

15. Ibid., 4; Petty, "Draft History," 75-76, 78, 80-82.

16. For early highway study plans, see Phelps Wyman, "A
    Preliminary Park Study of the Badlands of Western
    North Dakota," <u>Landscape Architecture</u> vol. 20 (April
    1930), 184-185, quoted in Strand, 26. For GNDA's
    proposal, see Strand, 55-56. When he was working to
    get the park established, William Lemke strongly
    implied to his correspondents that adding the North
    Unit to the new national memorial park would compel
    the government to build a parkway connecting the
    three units. WL to Carl Indergaard, 2 June 1947 (WL
    Papers).

17. Wirth's support, expressed in 1959, is credited with
    getting the project off to a start. S[am] Serrano,
    "Study of Proposed Scenic Road Along the Little

Missouri River Gorge Connecting Units of Theodore Roosevelt National Memorial Park," unpublished MS, June 1962 (THRO-A), 1; see also p. 7. Udall indicated his support during a 1965 visit to the North Unit. Warren D. Hotchkiss, "Park highlight briefing statements for 1965," memorandum, 4 January 1966 (THRO-S). See also Udall to Representative Rolland Redlin (ND), 6 October 1966 (THRO-S).

18. Udall to Redlin, 6 October 1966; Hotchkiss to Reg. Dir. (MWRO), "Special Report on Public Affairs and Related Responsibilities," memorandums, 1963-1966 (THRO-S): 2 November 1964, 2 August 1965, 3 January 1966. "Annual Narrative Report, Theodore Roosevelt National Memorial Park, 1965," unpublished MS, 1966 (THRO-S). See also George Magnus Johnson (Bismarck, ND) to Richard Montgomery (Acting Asst. Director, NPS), 22 September 1965 (THRO-A).

19. F. W. Barnes and Constance Barnes, "Report of Activities: 385 International Park Highway Association," memorandum, 6 March 1963 (THRO-S). See also McKenzie County Farmer, 9 June 1955 and 29 July 1950; "Special Report on Public Affairs," 2 August 1963.

20. Stanley D. Doremus (Deputy Asst. Secretary of the Interior) to D. C. MacIntyre (Supervisor, Custer National Forest, USFS), 12 August 1974, 1, in Addendum to Management Prescription for the Badlands Planning Unit, Little Missouri National Grasslands (Billings, MT: USFS, ca. 1974). See also Management Prescription for the Badlands Planning Unit, Little Missouri National Grasslands (Billings, MT: Custer National Forest, USFS, 1974), 49.

21. Weldon W. Gratton, "Report of NPS Study (June 1964) of proposed Theodore Roosevelt Memorial Parkway," unpublished MS, 1964 (THRO-A), 4-10.

22. George F. Baggley (Acting Reg. Dir., MWRO) to Director (NPS), memorandum, 14 August 1964 (THRO-A); Lemuel A. Garrison (Reg. Dir., MWRO), to Director (NPS), memorandum, 22 June 1964 (THRO-A).

23. For the scope of the somewhat similar Park Restoration and Improvement Program, see "1982 Superintendent's Annual Report," 12.

24. Final Environmental Statement for Squaw Creek Campground, 1-10. See also "North Unit District Ranger's Monthly Report," 2 July and 3 August 1957, and 2 June 1960; "1975 SFM," 5; John W. Jay, Jr. (Supt., THRO) to H. L. Hills (District Engineer, U. S. Army Corps of Engineers), 1 June 1954 (THRO-S); Jay to Reg. Dir. (Region II), memorandum, 4 November 1960 (THRO-S).

25. "Draft Environmental Assessment: Proposed Reconstruc-
tion of Park Road, North Unit, Theodore Roosevelt
National Memorial Park, North Dakota," unpublished
MS, ca. 1974 (THRO-A), passim.

26. Final Environmental Statement for Squaw Creek Campground, 26. See also p. 36.

27. McKenzie County Farmer, 9 June 1949.

28. "Mission 66 for Theodore Roosevelt National Memorial
Park," 5.

29. "Summary of Meeting Conducted Between U. S. Forest
Service and National Park Service," unpaginated; and
1973 Master Plan, 25. In 1968 a prospectus was
circulated investigating the possibility of turning
Cottonwood Campground over to a concessioner, but the
idea fell through. Arthur L. Sullivan (Supt., THRO)
to Reg. Dir. (MWRO), memorandum, 13 December 1968
(THRO-S). For years (until 1981) the park provided
firewood free of charge to campers, sometimes under
private contract, but strictly considered this is not
a concession since nothing was sold. See the
following memorandums: "Annual Forestry Report:
1953," 18 January 1954, 3; "Annual Forestry Report:
1954," 4 January 1955, 3; "Annual Forestry Report:
1958," 6 January 1959, unpaginated; "Annual Forestry
Report: 1960," 13 January 1961, unpaginated (all
THRO-S). The Theodore Roosevelt Nature and History
Association currently has a concession permit to sell
soft drinks in the North Unit: Hellickson to author,
14 May 1985.

12) Interpretation

The purpose of a national park is not served if its resources are not understood by the public. Interpretation is therefore a crucial part of resource management.

Theodore Roosevelt National Park is challenged to uphold the high standard of its namesake, who was one of the more talented amateur descriptive naturalists of his time. Roosevelt had in abundance the single most important quality of a good interpreter: a keen, curious eye.[1] Few pages of his western writing pass but some vivid image of the natural scene is conveyed to the reader. Today, a goal of the park's interpretive program is to imbue visitors with Roosevelt's enthusiasm for nature while explaining the human background of that enthusiasm.

Facilities and the Interpretive Prospectus

In the early to mid-1950s, before the installation of any interpretive facilities, park historians Chester Brooks and Ray Mattison conducted extensive research into Roosevelt's time in the badlands.[2] Thanks to their diligence, by 1956 the park's MISSION 66 planners could declare that "historical research has now progressed to the point where the story can be told in simple, accurate terms. Only the facilities to tell this story in an interesting manner are needed."[3] Theodore Roosevelt used money made available under MISSION 66 to build its interpretive program from the ground up. The Service saw the park as "perhaps the best place in the entire National

236

Park System in which to bring to life the important American history of the pioneer cattleman. . . ."[4] While attempts to rejuvenate the Elkhorn failed, in general MISSION 66 was able to provide the park with many needed visitor facilities: a new visitor center in Medora (1959); an entrance station for the North Unit (1961); the relocation of Roosevelt's Maltese Cross cabin from Bismarck to Medora and its restoration. (1959, 1961); and the building of the Long X (later Caprock Coulee) nature trail (1957, 1962). These new facilities (but especially the completion of Interstate 94) made it possible for the old East Entrance station in the South Unit to be closed in 1965.[5] Without them interpretation would have remained limited.

One major park planning document, the Interpretive Prospectus, directly addresses these sorts of needs. It is a statement of ideal facilities, of what the park staff would like to see in place. Theodore Roosevelt's prospectus was completed in 1973. It echoed the emphatic insistence of the master plans on developing the Elkhorn Unit so as to fulfill the historical mandate of the park. The entire interpretive program was to be built around the Elkhorn (for details, refer to Chapter 2), but the prospectus admitted that as long as the ranch site remained "virtually inaccessible" plans for its restoration might as well be written in the sky.[6]

One of the more insightful moments in the document came when it made a real distinction between the North and

South units, one which seems to have always been there in the minds of Service personnel but never before articulated. Because Roosevelt had only the slenderest connection with the North Unit region, the prospectus called for fewer facilities there in keeping with its unspoiled ambience. Away from the tourist center of Medora and the interstate highway, the North Unit was relaxed, its "speech" laconic, as it were. The North Unit scenic drive offered a "low-keyed, pleasant experience, an experience that should not be changed significantly, but enhanced."[7] Unburdened by the contrived need to spotlight Roosevelt, North Unit interpretation could be devoted to natural history. For example, the prospectus hoped that the scenic drive would be divided into six sections corresponding to different plant communities, culminating in a "modest interpretive facility" at Oxbow Overlook.[8]

This certainly was a useful contrast to the South Unit, where everything somehow had to tie in with Roosevelt, from having him be the "leading actor" in each museum exhibit to constructing a nature trail at Painted Canyon around the theme "A Walk With T. R." All the stops along the loop road were to have a tie-in except for Peaceful Valley Ranch, which, to avoid confusion with the Elkhorn, was not to be associated with Roosevelt. At the time it was thought the existing waysides could benefit from "a stronger thread of Rooseveltian outlooks."[9]

As laid out in the prospectus, the interpretive program was to "help visitors understand the need for conservation as Roosevelt saw it and compare this with the need for environmental conservation today."[10] While no doubt still a goal of today's interpretation, a short visit to the park is long enough to see how little of the prospectus has come to pass. There is no development at the Elkhorn or at Oxbow, no thread of Rooseveltian outlooks woven through the stops along the South Unit loop road. The reasons why were foreseen even before the prospectus was written. "The real problem in preparing the Prospectus is in determining how to merge the natural history of the Badlands and the actions of Mr. Roosevelt as President in later years," wrote an NPS interpretive specialist in 1967. He concluded that "this is something that will take a good historian to work out,"[11] partly because "verification of Roosevelt's history with the natural surroundings is lacking."[12]

Exactly so. There is no convincing evidence that the conservation ethic Roosevelt displayed as president was shaped entirely, or even primarily, by his time in Dakota Territory. There is much evidence to suggest that his experience in the badlands was precipitated and shaped by a predisposition toward conservation, and that his ranch life there formed a vital part of a cumulative tendency in his adulthood toward a conservation ethic, but to attribute his actions as president directly to his Dakota years--as again and again Theodore Roosevelt National Memorial Park seemed to be asked to do--is simplistic.

Roosevelt was nothing if not a complex man, one who had already had what many would consider a lifetime's worth of experience before he even stepped off the train at Medora in 1883. But the national memorial park honoring him had an institutional mandate to emphasize human history, Roosevelt's history, and to above all else make connections between his intangible presence and the tangible natural resources of the park. In short, the prospectus was charged with finding connections that were not always there, for it is impossible to "merge" the natural history of the northern badlands with what Roosevelt accomplished in the White House. In this respect, the Interpretive Prospectus reflected the miscasting of the park as a historical area.

Museum collection and exhibits

Using both artifacts and specimens in interpretation is one way the park now attempts to balance human and natural history. The museum collection is frequently consulted by the staff for exhibits, research, campfire programs, and demonstrations. Its purpose is interpretation and interpretation alone; anything not furthering this end is not accessioned. For example, there is no attempt to have one specimen of each species in the park-- just those useful for visitor programs.[13] Artifacts must relate directly to Roosevelt or to the open range cattle industry of the period from 1880 to 1898.[14] Not surprisingly, the collection was originally mostly devoted to human history; the natural history holdings were "very meager and of little benefit to staff or visiting scholars."[15]

In 1962 an evaluator from the Regional Office in Omaha described how the collection was displayed at the new Medora visitor center. He found the museum room "jam-packed with exhibits," leaving no room for short-term displays. Human and natural history themes were kept strictly separate, the latter having "little tie-in to Roosevelt's residence here." None of this surprised him, for he knew the museum room had been built expressly to showcase human history. Most natural history interpretation was supposed to take place in situ.[16]

Another study was made of the museum in 1975, and while it does not mention overcrowding specifically, the checklist of displays it gave included a diorama, stuffed animals, artifact exhibits, audio-visual exhibits, flat-wall panels, and human history display cases.[17]

No such criticism can be made of the museum today. After the visitor center was remodeled in 1979 and 1980, the Harpers Ferry Center designed new exhibits in accordance with the latest tenets of museology. No longer is most of the floor taken up by display cases and most of the wall with text. Gone are the obtrusive audio-visual devices. A disembodied effect is sought, the visitor stepping out of time, drawn naturally around the room by a logical mixture of human and natural history. There is plenty of open space on the floor and white space on the walls. Plexiglas panels, aluminum rods, and wooden cut-outs make the exhibits seem to float in the air. In the center of the room is a life-sized horse sculptured from thin wood slats, stained lightly. It is an accomplished and beautiful work which succeeds as art without detracting from its utilitarian purpose, which is to support a Roosevelt mannequin dressed in articles of clothing that actually belonged to him. Some of his rifles and other personal effects are also on view, as are natural history specimens in a series of informative "spoiler" panels.[18] The authenticity of all these items is enhanced by the reticence of the museum-makers in designing the exhibits.

Sureness in handling a theme is the hallmark of the new park museum. The ambience is so natural that one leaves with the feeling that it could not have been done in any other way. But it could have been, of course, and in fact almost was. In the late 1950s the Service was approached with a proposal that, had it been carried through, would have made for very different interpretation than that existing today.

In 1959 a Twin Cities frontier history buff came forward and made what was to be the first in a series of fanciful offers to develop an elaborate living history site in the park. He began by proposing to donate $500,000 toward the restoration of Peaceful Valley Ranch. The man was a rather well-known manufacturer and the Service was fully cognizant that he had the means to make good on his offer. Understandably, the Midwest Regional Office was excited about the possibility and wasted no time in dispatching Ray Mattison, who by then had been promoted from his post at Theodore Roosevelt to the position of Site Survey Historian, to the man's home for a follow-up interview. Their first meeting uncovered a major problem, however. It came out that he wanted to build a museum in the park for the sole purpose of housing his western memorabilia, which might not have been an insurmountable demand except that Mattison found his collection to be mostly exotica picked up during the course of his travels. Little of it was authentic and none suitable for display at Theodore Roosevelt.[19] The Regional Office spent the next three years trying to coax him into a realistic restoration plan, but he responded by proposing even more grandiose projects.[20] He eventually found an appropriate outlet for his largesse in the Cowboy Hall of Fame in Oklahoma City.

Personal services

As any Chief of Interpretation will admit, a park's program stands or falls with its interpreters. Thought-provoking person-to-person contact has always been the goal of NPS interpretation, setting it apart from the purveyors of "industrial tourism." The same qualities that make personal services successful make them difficult to write about. The best interpreters gently prod visitors to discover the park for themselves, and there are no written accounts of the prodding. All one can do is indicate the variety of formal programs tried at Theodore Roosevelt over the years. It is not possible to measure in any meaningful sense how well this all-important phase of interpretation has succeeded.

Although records for the period are scant, personal services were apparently rather limited until the beginning of the facilities expansion in 1956. Self-guided automobile tours, probably the most popular visitor activity from 1951 to 1961, can be taken as typifying the early years.[21]

Personal services really began to take off with the opening of the Maltese Cross cabin, the development of nature trails, and the other improvements remarked upon at the beginning of this chapter. Not until 1961 were any seasonal interpreters hired for the North Unit, and not until the next year were there regularly-scheduled campfire programs.[22] But even then guided walks and hikes were not offered because it was observed that "no Park travellers have exhibited any interest in remaining long enough to take, say, a half-day tour"; overall, Theodore Roosevelt had "scarcely any long-stay visitors."[23]

From these modest beginnings has come a most diverse program. Over the last twenty years visitors have been offered horse-mounted ranger talks along the rim of Painted Canyon, sun viewing, midnight caravans to the burning coal vein, Bicentennial caravans to the Elkhorn, and free surrey rides.[24] Interestingly, unlike the park's overall management, personal interpretive services seem to have always tended toward the kind of balance between natural and human history suggested by this short list. In fact, the 1963 Master Plan exhorted the staff to make them "the dual interpretive themes for the park with nearly equal emphasis placed on each. A deeper appreciation of this historical period, of western and national development, a national pride stirred by the accomplishments of Theodore Roosevelt, and a cultivated perception of the wilderness character of the badlands should be conveyed to each visitor."[25] Despite lapses of coordination between the park historian and the chief naturalist during the years both were on staff,[26] because of this balance the interpretive program was probably affected least of all by the park's redesignation in 1978.

If interpretation has not shown the swings in emphasis we have seen elsewhere, it has changed in other ways. Nearly all interpretation now includes precepts of environmental awareness. At Theodore Roosevelt environmental education per se began in 1968 as part of a Servicewide project composed of three parts: the National Environmental Education Development program, which aimed to "introduce the total environment concept without preaching" in a network of outdoor study camps; Environmental Study Areas (ESAs), sites in national parks to be made available to local school groups for day use; and environmental awareness messages to be delivered as part of regular park interpretive programs. "Basic needs of living things" and ecosystem relationships were the themes to be gotten across.[27]

The Service saw parks joining the array of "educational resources" available to the classroom. NPS personnel would provide schools with preparatory material and teacher training but would not plan or lead actual field trips to the park.[28] For the most part, parks were to carry out the project locally, even if geography limited them to working with a single school.[29]

Isolation turned out to be the main obstacle to the success of the project at Theodore Roosevelt. The three cities nearest the park--Dickinson, Beach, and Watford City--were full of enthusiasm, but feared travel time (they are thirty-three, twenty-six, and fifteen miles away, respectively) would be a fatal problem.[30] The park went ahead anyway and designated part of Halliday Wells in the South Unit as an Environmental Study Area in 1969, but declined to set up outdoor study camps, declaring that "the expense and logistics are beyond the means of local schools."[31]

This observation was soon borne out for the Environmental Study Area as well. Not nearly enough field trips were able to be made to justify setting aside 160 acres as an ESA.[32] "After several years of no response from nearby schools,"[33] in 1975 it was decided that "elimination of the ESA would not result in a serious impact to the local school system."[34]

Still, the environmental awareness component of the NPS project did work out.[35] In fact, the environmental education progam can be considered an overall success because of the alacrity the interpretive staff has shown in incorporating the tenets of ecology into their presentations. If any one message runs through all the formal and informal person-to-person interpretation, it is the total environment concept, the idea that there exist relationships, seen and unseen, which tie together everything in the park, both the living and the inanimate. This message, delivered over and over in every sort of ranger-visitor situation, is probably more powerful in its totality than even a successful Environmental Study Area would have been.

Support services

Helping to carry the message to the public is the function of the Theodore Roosevelt Nature and History Association. The park's cooperative association sees itself as supporting "a public educator in ecological principles as well as environmental problems." As its name implies, the TRNHA tries to keep a balanced thematic perspective, even though it was founded in 1951 by a historian, Chester Brooks.[36] Despite its small size, the TRNHA has long been regarded as a particularly active and innovative park cooperative association; it was, for example, one of the first to incorporate and gain tax-exempt status.[37] Although it reaches visitors directly through its own publications, the TRNHA also gives NPS personnel the latitude to make their interpretation more professional. This means purchasing books for the park library, or buying support equipment which otherwise would never find its way into the annual budget, such as mopeds for roving interpretation. The TRNHA also funds resource management projects, such as the recent study of lichens as indicators of changing air quality, and helps defray the costs of other special research, such as the compilation and publication of this administrative history.

Notes to Chapter 12

1. See John Burroughs's assessment in the epigraph to the Afterword of this history.

2. A bibliography of their work can be found in "CRM Plan," 72-74.

3. "Mission 66 for Theodore Roosevelt National Memorial Park," 4. The park had also received some development money in the early 1950s in anticipation of the celebration of the centennial of Roosevelt's birth. See The New York Times, 11 September 1955, 83.

4. Howard W. Baker (Reg. Dir., Region II) to Harry V. Johnston (Minneapolis, MN), 15 December 1959 (THRO-S).

5. See, respectively, Strand, 48; Richard H. Maeder, "Annual Report of Information and Interpretive Services: 1961," memorandum, 10 January 1962 (THRO-S); Strand, 50; Newell F. Joyner (Regional Museum Curator) to Asst. Reg. Dir., memorandum, 25 May 1961 (THRO-S); "North Unit District Ranger Monthly Report," 2 July and 1 September 1957; Wallace O. McCaw, "Annual Report of Information Services: 1962," memorandum, 22 January 1963 (THRO-S).

6. "Interpretive Prospectus," 7-8.

7. Ibid., 15.

8. Ibid., 15-16.

9. Ibid., 10-14.

10. Ibid., 1.

11. Charles H. McCurdy (NPS) to Asst. Reg. Dir. (MWRO), memorandum, 29 August 1967 (THRO-S).

12. McCurdy to Assoc. Reg. Dir. (MWRO), memorandum, 2 June 1966 (THRO-S).

13. John O. Lancaster (Supt., THRO) to Reg. Dir. (MWRO), "Scope of Collection Statement," memorandum, 12 November 1973 (THRO-A). This document is scheduled to be revised at the end of 1985.

14. Ibid. Parts of the park collections were photographed in 1974 as part of preservation measures begun a year earlier. "Chief Ranger's Monthly Narrative Report," 5 October 1973 and 4 April 1974.

15. Edwin C. Alberts, "Regional Naturalist's Summary Notes," unpublished MS, June 1962 (THRO-S), 25-26.

The thematic imbalance in the museum collection can
be traced to its origins in the late 1940s when it
was conceived as a vital part of the commemoration of
Roosevelt. In fact, William Lemke wanted a museum
specifically as a replacement for the statue of
Roosevelt called for in P. L. 80-38. See WL to M. J.
Connolly (Asst. Secretary, Greater North Dakota
Assn.), 9 March 1948, and to Hermann Hagedorn (Secretary, Roosevelt Memorial Assn.), 10 March 1948; and
John W. Jay, Jr. (Supt., THRO) to Mrs. William Lemke,
14 September 1953 (all WL Papers).

16. Alberts, 1-3, 10. The most popular exhibit featured
a 90-second recording of Roosevelt's voice. See
Ibid., 4-5; "Superintendent's Monthly Narrative
Report," 8 October and 9 November 1965.

17. Alan David Capelle, "An Observation and Analysis of
the Visitor Center Complex at Theodore Roosevelt
National Memorial Park," master's thesis, University
of Wisconsin--Stevens Point, 1975, 9.

18. These new exhibits were installed in June 1982.
"1982 Superintendent's Annual Report," 7.

19. John W. Jay, Jr. (Supt., THRO) to Reg. Dir. (Region
II), memorandum, 12 November 1959 (THRO-A); Ray H.
Mattison (Historian, Region II) to Regional Chief of
Interpretation (Region II), 27 November 1959 (THRO-A).

20. At one point he proposed to buy, restore, and stock
with longhorns the Bellows (now McLeod) Ranch about
ten miles south of the Elkhorn Unit, which he would
then donate to the government to be made a part of
the park. His proposal was rejected because, among
other things, it required an act of Congress to
authorize new park boundaries: Harrison V. Johnston
to Ann Brown, n.d. (THRO-A). See also Howard W.
Baker (Reg. Dir., Region II) to Supt. (THRO), memorandum, 5 July 1962 (THRO-A); and Conrad L. Wirth
(Director, NPS) to Asst. Secretary of the Interior,
memorandum, 20 July 1962 (THRO-A).

21. Maeder, "Annual Report of Information and Interpretive Services: 1961," unpaginated.

22. Ibid.; Alberts, 6-7.

23. Alberts, 17. Guided nature walks were finally begun
in 1966. Arthur L. Sullivan, "Annual Information and
Interpretive Service Report for 1967," memorandum, 26
January 1968 (THRO-S); "Superintendent's Monthly
Narrative Report," 12 August 1966, 3.

24. Horse mounted rangers: Billings County *Pioneer*, 25

July 1968. Coal vein: McCurdy to Asst. Reg. Dir., 29
August 1967. Elkhorn Unit: Bismarck Tribune, 12 July
1976. Sun viewing: "Chief Naturalist's Annual Report
for 1981," memorandum, 23 February 1982 (THRO-A), 3.
Surrey rides: McCurdy to Asst. Reg. Dir., 29 August
1967. There have been few living history programs
given; see McKenzie County Farmer, 21 August 1975,
but for an exception see "1976 Superintendent's
Annual Report," 4-5.

The most popular interpretive activity in the park's
history was the caravan to the burning coal vein near
Buck Hill in the South Unit (now burnt out). The
auto tour left Cottonwood Campground nightly after
the regular campfire program. Even though the hour
was late, and it was a twenty-mile round trip to the
burning seam, few passed up the opportunity. A
ranger described the turnout this way: "Although the
duration of the tour averages about 2 hours, visitor
response is unbelievable, averaging 30 to 60 people
each night but sometimes the tours numbered in excess
of 100 people. . . . The trip is more a curiosity
about the view [of the red-hot coal] at night." Lary
D. Barney, "Annual Information and Interpretive Service Report for 1968," memorandum, 31 January 1969
(THRO-S).

25. 1963 Master Plan, unpaginated.

26. Ibid., and Alberts, 16.

27. First quote: Barney, "Interpretive Service Report for
1968." Second quote: "Recapitulation of Environmental Education Program to Schools in Vicinity," memorandum, 1972 (THRO-S). See also Paul F. McCrary
(Environmental Education Coordinator, MWRO), open
memorandum, 1 November 1968 (THRO-S).

28. Sullivan to Reg. Dir. (MWRO), memorandum, 26 February
1969 (THRO-S); "Recapitulation of Environmental Education Program," unpaginated. See also McCrary to
Glen Sherwood (Northern Prairie Wildlife Research
Center), 5 March 1969 (THRO-S).

29. McCrary, "Environmental Study Areas," memorandum, 12
December 1968 (THRO-S).

30. Sullivan to Reg. Dir. (MWRO), memorandum, 3 September
1968 (THRO-S).

31. Glenn D. Gallison (Acting Asst. Reg. Dir., MWRO),
open memorandum, 24 June 1969 (THRO-S); James B.
Thompson (Supt., THRO) to William F. Hodny (Bismarck,
ND), 16 October 1970 (THRO-S). Quote from Thompson,

"Annual Information and Interpretive Service Report for 1969," memorandum, 9 February 1970 (THRO-S).

32. See "Recapitulation of Environmental Education Program," unpaginated; "1975 Superintendent's Annual Report," 5.

33. "1972 Superintendent's Annual Report," 3.

34. "Draft Environmental Impact Statement: Proposed Master Plan, Theodore Roosevelt National Memorial Park, North Dakota," unpublished MS, ca. 1975 (THRO-A), 50. See also p. 47.

35. A later program which has been an unqualified success and can be traced to the environmental education project is the Youth Conservation Corps. Theodore Roosevelt has hosted YCC enrollees since 1974. The young men and women in the YCC have performed valuable maintenance tasks while learning about the natural history of the park. See Annual Management Review, Theodore Roosevelt National Park, North Dakota (Medora: NPS, 1980).

36. Quotation from TRNHA, "Publications Program: Theodore Roosevelt National Memorial Park," unpublished MS, May 1971 (THRO-A), 6. See also Petty, "Draft History," 68. Edward C. Blackorby, the biographer of William Lemke, was on the first board of directors.

37. Alberts, 19-20; Michael O. Wintch, "Narrative Annual Report of Cooperating Association: Theodore Roosevelt Nature and History Association," unpublished MS, 1 March 1966 (THRO-S), 2.

Afterword

At some point in the Dakotas we picked up the former foreman of his ranch, and another cowboy friend of the old days, and they rode with the President in his private car for several hours. He was as happy with them as a schoolboy ever was in meeting old chums. He beamed with delight all over. The life which those men represented, and of which he had himself once formed a part, meant so much to him; it had entered into the very marrow of his being, and I could see the joy of it all shining in his face as he sat and lived parts of it over and over again with those men that day. He bubbled with laughter continually. The men, I thought, seemed a little embarrassed by his open-handed cordiality and good-fellowship. He himself evidently wanted to forget the present, and to live only in the memory of those wonderful ranch days,--that free, hardy, adventurous life upon the plains. It all came back to him with a rush when he found himself alone with these heroes of the rope and stirrup. How much more keen his appreciation was, and how much quicker his memory, than theirs! He was constantly recalling to their minds incidents which they had forgotten, and the names of horses and dogs which had escaped them. His subsequent life, instead of making dim the memory of his ranch days, seemed to have made it more vivid by contrast.

When they had gone, I said to him, "I think your affection for those men very beautiful."

"How could I help it?" he said.

> -- John Burroughs, traveling
> by train with Roosevelt to
> Yellowstone, 1903

13) Living Up to One's Name

This history began with a reference to the "national park idea" without explaining exactly what the idea was, or is today. Many perceptive writers have addressed the meaning of the national parks: John Muir, Frederick Law Olmsted, Robert Underwood Johnson, and John C. Merriam from long ago; Freeman Tilden, Bernard DeVoto, Joseph L. Sax, and Alfred Runte more recently. They are but a short list. One person cannot presume to sum up what they have to say about the national parks in a few words. It is enough to note that each detected the existence of a meaning, an underlying philosophy, a way of looking at the world, that is associated with the national parks. Their writings try to evoke various aspects of the national park idea, the idea that certain places have an intrinsic worth and should perforce be managed with vision and stewardship.

As we have seen, the national park idea can be easily misinterpreted. People bring diverse perspectives to the parks. Some support them as money-makers for tourism or as an acceptable way to use lands with no other obvious economic value. Some see them as playgrounds on a grand scale. And some see them as dead weight to be carried by society.

Whether such people are in the majority or the minority is of little importance. What is important is how well the amorphous, undisciplined national park idea will hold its own over the next quarter-century, a time of

254

critical decisions concerning land-use values, depletion of resources, and, ultimately, this country's standard of living.

The experience of Theodore Roosevelt National Park over its first thirty-five years, and particularly over its last ten, is in many ways merely a harbinger of this upcoming critical period. The park is on the cutting edge of problems the entire System will have to face. If the national park idea is not to be subsumed by "progress" as we have traditionally defined it, clear thinking and resourceful, even courageous, leadership will be required of the Park Service in the years to come.

As for Theodore Roosevelt itself, the park can be instructed by the example of the man. Roosevelt's greatest characteristic was his ability to cut through to the heart of the matter and take decisive action once he got there. It is to be hoped that the park's staff will be able to do the same when they are confronted by those who present the national park idea and economic development as mutually exclusive choices. They need not be.

So, in a sense, the powerful presence of Roosevelt's personal example--what might be called his "extended incumbency"--is the ally of the park's staff today. Yet his conservation record, perhaps still the most admirable of any president, also sets a level of expectation for the park's management, even if only unconsciously. Theodore Roosevelt is the only national park that has to live up to its name.   The challenge, of course, is to do it.

APPENDIXES

Appendix A:

Chronology of Legislation and Executive Actions

date	legislation	description
1934	cooperative agreement	Federal Emergency Relief Administration, NPS, CCC, & state of North Dakota create Roosevelt Regional Park
3-25-35	(Harry L. Hopkins)	Federal Emergency Relief Administration director turns Roosevelt Regional Park into a Recreational Demonstration Area (RDA)
4-30-35	EO 7027 EO 7028	Resettlement Administration created & receives jurisdiction over RDAs from FERA
11-14-36	EO 7496	Transfers RDAs to Department of the Interior; placed under NPS control but not official part of NP System
6-6-42	PL 77-594 (56 Stat 326)	Secretary of the interior authorized to convey RDAs to states with proviso that land be used for recreation or conservation only
8-11-42	(Franklin D. Roosevelt)	President approves list of "special status" RDAs; Roosevelt RDA included
6-1-45	(Harry S Truman)	President releases Roosevelt RDA from "special status," clears way for transfer to Fish & Wildlife Service (FWS)
2-26-46	(Oscar L. Chapman)	Acting secretary of the interior transfers Roosevelt RDA to FWS; becomes Theodore Roosevelt National Wildlife Refuge
4-25-47	PL 80-38 (61 Stat 52)	Theodore Roosevelt National Memorial Park enabling act

6-10-48	PL 80-620 (62 Stat 352)	adjusts boundaries of South Unit; eliminated provision in PL 80-38 for statue of Roosevelt in Medora
6-12-48	PL 80-631 (62 Stat 384)	adds North Unit to park; reserved stock driveway easement to ranchers
6-29-48	PL 80-827 (62 Stat 1102)	boundary description corrected
3-24-56	PL 84-438 (70 Stat 55)	boundary adjustments along U. S. Rtes. 10 & 85: 880 acres deleted from North Unit, 60 added to South Unit
8-31-61	PL 87-193 (75 Stat 423)	authorizes secretary of the interior to modernize water & sewerage facilities in Medora on reimbursable basis
11-6-63	(Stewart Udall)	Secretary of the interior deletes 398 acres of South Unit cut off by realignment of U. S. 10 & I-94; 459 acres added to South Unit from USFS, state, & private land
7-8-64	PLO 3420	91 acres deleted to USFS
11-10-78	PL 95-625 (92 Stat 3467)	National Parks and Recreation Act of 1978 approves North & South Unit wilderness areas; redesignates park as Theodore Roosevelt National Park; adjusts North Unit boundary

Abbreviations

EO. . . . . . Executive Order
PL. . . . . . Public Law (old law citation in parentheses)
PLO . . . . . Public Land Order

Appendix B:

Superintendents of Theodore Roosevelt National (Memorial) Park

Allyn F. Hanks	September 1947 to January 1953
John W. Jay, Jr.	February 1953 to December 1960
Wallace O. McCaw	January 1961 to April 1963
Warren D. Hotchkiss	May 1963 to February 1966
Arthur L. Sullivan	March 1966 to July 1969
James B. Thompson	July 1969 to October 1972
John O. Lancaster	October 1972 to May 1979
Harvey D. Wickware	June 1979 to present

Appendix C:

Land Ownership

LAND ACQUISITION METHODS, 1951-1980

method	number of tracts	number of acre
donation	7	216.76
purchase[a]	6	379.80
declaration of taking	6	75.95
exchange[b]	14	10,002.26
condemnation[c]	1	160.00
transfer	3	231.72
withdrawal from other public domain[d]	2	59,145.67
subtotal	**39**	**70,212.16**
less land disposed of (see Appendix A)		(-)536.28
inholdings[e]		(+)740.51
TOTAL		**70,416.39**

SOURCE: National Park Service Division of Land Acquisition, "Master Deed Listing," memorandum, 31 July
1980 (Medora: THRO-A).

Notes

a) Purchases were reserved for special cases, such as the
    necessary acquisition of the souvenir shop on the rim
    at Cedar Canyon along U. S. 10. The property there
    was bought in 1959 to make way for Interstate 94, but
    the owner was allowed to operate until 1964. 1963
    Master Plan.

b) When the National Memorial Park was created, the Ser-
    vice retained some old Recreational Demonstration Area
    lands just outside the official boundaries to use in
    exchange for private land within. Most of the RDA
    surplus had been exchanged for inholdings by 1965.
    1963 Master Plan; Warren D. Hotchkiss, "Park highlight
    briefing statements for 1965," memorandum, 4 January
    1966 (Medora: THRO-S).

c) The only condemnation proceeding the government ever had to make was against the owner of a 160-acre parcel in the middle of the South Unit along the south side of Jones Creek. The owner had purchased the property in 1955 and used it to operate a small ranch; it was fenced and included a 12 x 32 house. Although his principal residence was not on the property, he ran a herd of about fifty head of cattle there from 1955 to 1966 (including driving them to and from his property over park land using the stock easement), at which time, according to him, repeated damage to his fence and harassment of his cattle by the park's bison herd made it impossible for him to raise domesticated livestock any longer. The park had been trying to buy him out since at least the early 1960s, but his asking price was too high. In 1974 the Service finally had his property condemned. He was paid $150 per acre and $5624 in severance damages for a total purchase price of $29,624. By the autumn of 1975 he had vacated the premises; the house, fencing, and other improvements were soon removed. See 1963 Master Plan; Robert W. Jackson to Asst. Regional Director, Operations (MWRO), memorandum, 16 July 1968 (Medora: THRO-S); Dickinson Press, 28 November 1974 and 19 September 1975; David L. Olson, "Report of Real Property Transaction," memorandum, 2 June 1976 (Medora: THRO-A).

d) This acreage was reserved in November 1936 for the park from part of the land recently acquired for the public domain under the submarginal land purchase program.

e) The Park Service is currently trying to clarify the confusing inholding situation within Theodore Roosevelt, and late in 1985 published the results of a two-and-a-half-year investigation into non-federal mineral ownership interests in the park ("Summary of Mineral Title Project, Theodore Roosevelt National Park," unpublished MS, 10 October 1985, THRO-A); even after this exhaustive study, uncertainty remains, due not in small part to errors in plat maps, unresolved judicial claims, and so on. The most recent information on surface rights is as follows: South Unit, two tracts (176.3 acres total); Elkhorn Unit, none; North Unit, six tracts (approximately 512 acres total). "Land protection Plan and Boundary Issues--Concerns and Recommendations, Theodore Roosevelt National Park," unpublished MS, 7 September 1984 (THRO-A), 1-4.

Appendix D:

Park Statistics

DATE ESTABLISHED: South Unit -- 25 April 1947
                  Elkhorn Unit -- 25 April 1947
                  North Unit -- 12 June 1948

LOCATION: southwestern North Dakota, Billings and McKenzie
            Counties
                 South Unit -- N 46 degrees 57 minutes
                               W 103 degrees 27 minutes
               Elkhorn Unit -- N 47 degrees 18 minutes
                               W 103 degrees 38 minutes
                 North Unit -- N 47 degrees 43 minutes
                               W 103 degrees 25 minutes

AREA: South Unit -- 46,128.07 acres (18,675.33 ha)
               Elkhorn Unit -- 218 acres (88.26 ha)
                 North Unit -- 24,070.32 acres (9745.07 ha)
                      TOTAL -- 70,416.39 acres (28,508.66 ha)

BOUNDARIES: 65 miles in circumference (104.84 km);
             38 miles adjoin public land (61.29 km; 58.5% of
             total); 27 adjoin private land (43.55 km;
             41.5% of total)

DIMENSIONS: South Unit -- 15.4 miles (24.84 km) by
                                8.8 miles (14.19 km)
               Elkhorn Unit -- 1.0 miles (1.61 km) by
                                0.5 miles (0.81 km)
                 North Unit -- 10.56 miles (17.03 km) by
                                7.8 miles (12.58 km)

ALTITUDE: South Unit -- 2250 feet above mean
                               sea level (686 m) to
                               2855 feet msl (870 m)
               Elkhorn Unit -- 2110 feet msl (643 m) to
                               2420 feet msl (738 m)
                 North Unit -- 1952 feet msl (595 m) to
                               2572 feet msl (784 m)

WILDERNESS: South Unit -- 10,510 acres (4255.06 ha)
               Elkhorn Unit -- 0 acres (ha)
                 North Unit -- 19,410 acres (7858.30 ha)
                      TOTAL -- 29,920 acres (12,113.36 ha)

```
ZONING:  Historic Zone: 245 acres (99.19 ha)
         Natural Zone:  70,204 acres (28,422.67 ha)
             Wilderness sub-zone: 29,920 acres (12,113.36 ha)
             Natural environment sub-zone: 40,284 acres
                                           (16,309.31 ha)
(some        Outstanding natural feature sub-zone:
areas                                80 acres (32.40 ha)
approximate) Development sub-zone: 600 acres (242.91 ha)
             Special use sub-zone (private land):
                                   740.51 acres (299.80 ha)

IUCN LAND CLASSIFICATION:  Nearctic realm, temperate grasslands

ROAD MILEAGE WITHIN PARK:  56.5 (91.13 km) of which 47.6
                           (76.77 km) are paved

TRAIL MILEAGE WITHIN PARK: 67.7 (109.19 km)
                           61.1 recreational (98.55 km),
                            6.6 interpretive (10.64 km)

RIVER MILEAGE WITHIN PARK: 25.5 (41.13 km)

WELLS:  13 developed springs, 18 dish tanks (wildlife wells)
```

SOURCES:

International Biological Programme, "Check Sheet (Mark VII) for Survey of IBP Areas," unpublished MS, 24 March 1969 (Medora: THRO-S).

John O. Lancaster (Supt., THRO) to E. Jennifer Christy (Man and theBiosphere Program Asst.,NPS),letter,27 September1978 (Medora: THRO-A).

"Natural Resources Plan and Environmental Assessment, Theodore Roosevelt National Park, North Dakota (draft)," unpublished MS, 1983 (Medora: THRO-A).

"Basic Operations Declaration, Theodore Roosevelt National Park," unpublished MS, ca. 1982 (Medora: THRO-A).

Miklos D. F. Udvardy, A Classification of the Biogeographical Provinces of the World. IUCN Occasional Paper #18. Morges, Switzerland: International Union for the Conservation of Nature and Natural Resources, 1975.

APPENDIX E:

Ambient Air Quality Standards

pollutant	federal primary standard	North Dakota standard
total suspended particulates (TSP)	75 ug/m^3 annual geometric mean	60 ug/m^3 annual geometric mean
	260 ug/m^3 24-hr. average	250 ug/m^3 maximum 24-hr. average
settled particulates (dustfall)	none	15 tons/sq. mile, maximum 3-month arithmetic mean in residential areas
		30 tons/sq. mile, maximum 3-month arithmetic mean in heavy industrial areas
sulfur dioxide	0.03 ppm (80 ug/m^3) annual arithmetic average	60 ug/m^3 (0.02 ppm) maximum annual arithmetic mean
	0.14 ppm (365 ug/m^3) 24-hr. average	260 ug/m^3 (0.10 ppm) maximum 24-hr. concentration
		715 ug/m^3 (0.24 ppm) maximum 1-hr. concentration
reactive sulfur	none	0.24 mg/100 cm^2/day, maximum annual arithmetic mean
		0.50 mg/100 cm^2/day, maximum for 1-month period

pollutant	federal primary standard	North Dakota standard
suspended sulfate	none	4 ug/m^3
		12 ug/m^3 maximum annual arithmetic mean; maximum 24-hr. concentration not to be exceeded over 1% of the time
		30 ug/m^3 maximum 1-hr concentration not to be exceeded over 1% of the time
foliar fluoride	none	none
sulfuric acid mist, sulfur trioxide, or combination	none	4 ug/m^3 maximum annual arithmetic mean
		12 ug/m^3 maximum 24-hr. concentration not to be exceeded over 1% of the time
		30 ug/m^3 maximum 1-hr. concentration not to be exceeded over 1% of the time
hydrogen sulfide	none	45 ug/m^3 (0.032 ppm) maximum half-hour concentration not to be exceeded more than twice in any five consecutive days
		75 ug/m^3 (0.054 ppm) maximum half-hour concentration not to be exceeded more than twice a year

266

pollutant	federal primary standard	North Dakota standard
carbon monoxide	9 ppm (10 mg/m^3) 8-hr. average*	10 mg/m^3 (9 ppm) maximum 3-hr. concentration*
	35 ppm (40 mg/m^3) 1-hr. average*	40 mg/m^3 (35 ppm) maximum 1-hr. concentration*
nitrogen dioxide	0.05 ppm (100 ug/m^3) annual arithmetic average	100 ug/m^3 (0.05 ppm) maximum annual arithmetic mean
		200 ug/m^3 (0.10 ppm) maximum 1-hr. concentration not to be exceeded over 1% of the time in any 3 months
photochemical oxidants (ozone)	0.12 ppm (235 ug/m^3) 1-hr. average*	235 ug/m^3 (0.12 ppm) maximum 1-hr. concentration*
hydrocarbons (less methane)	24 ppm (160 ug/m^3) 3-hr. concentration (6-9 AM)*	160 ug/m^3 (0.24) ppm maximum 3-hr. concentration (6-9 AM)*
lead	1.5 ug/m^3 calendar quarter average	1.5 ug/m^3 quarterly arithmetic mean
visibility	none	0.4 coefficient of haze per 100 linear feet maximum annual geometic mean (coefficient of haze)

abbreviations:

* not to be exceeded more than once per year
ug = micrograms
m^3 = cubic meter
mg = milligrams
ppm = parts per million
cm^2 = square centimeter(s)

SOURCES:

National Ambient Air Quality Standards 1978
North Dakota Air Pollution Regulations 1978

Appendix F:

Olaus Murie at Theodore Roosevelt National Memorial Park

Murie, a noted wildlife biologist, wrote this short memoir after a late-autumn visit to the park in 1949. The manuscript, heretofore unpublished, is dated December 16, 1949.

The Little Missouri had been to me a legendary stream. I think I could hardly have described my vicarious impression of the river, so vague can a purely imaginary picture be. Now, here before me, was the reality.

It was the 4th of November [1949], when winter should have settled [in] with snow flurries, somber skies, and [the] threat of more to come. But we were enjoying a remarkably pleasant week of clear blue skies.

Allyn [Hanks][1] had driven us through the Badlands of North Dakota, over crude roads leading north from National Park Headquarters. Eventually we had pulled off the road. Vic, Jim,[2] and I followed him as he pushed his way through weeds and rose bushes, among the gray cottonwoods, until we assembled on the river bank. Over there, across the river, somewhere back in those cottonwoods, was the site

---

1. The park superintendent.

2. Victor Cahalane, NPS Chief Biologist, and James E. Cole, NPS Regional Biologist.

of Roosevelt's Elkhorn Ranch.

It was hard for me to comprehend all that our guide was telling us, for my thoughts went back to boyhood days, when I had sought adventure in "Hunting Trips of a Ranchman." I recalled the virile writings of our hunter-naturalist President, how they had pictured in the boyhood mind the antelope and bison, the calling of geese, the sage grouse--the appeal of far places--the boyhood yearning for adventure in wilderness. With a sort of wonder at the chain of events, I mentally reviewed more recent sequences. North Dakota now had a national park. Congress had created the Theodore Roosevelt National Memorial Park. I understood it was to commemorate the wilderness life of an outstanding President. And here we were, a group of us, with an assignment to study the wildlife of this new park, its historic and wilderness aspects, and to make recommendations on what might be done to restore the animal life that was part of the scene in Roosevelt's day.

We looked about us on the river bank. Several cottonwoods had been cut up by beavers years ago, and we looked at the gnawed lengths. There were the tracks of a white-tailed deer in the mud near the water. The muddy river, flowing silently by, was at low stage this time of year, but we could see the high scars in the cottonwoods where the ice in spring flood had cut and bruised them. And over across there was the historic site. What a memorial--the muddy banks and muddy water of a small river, and a line of twisted, leafless cottonwoods! Behind them rose a low bluff, rising to the upland beyond.

But its very simplicity was eloquent. There at one time had stood a significant log cabin. By recognizing this humble spot on the bank of the Little Missouri we do more than establish a reminder of a prominent national political figure. It pleased me that this was not a mountain spire, a figure carved in a cliff, or some other obtruding feature. By selecting a spot where had once stood a cabin, representative of the bigger scene, a spot no different from the rest of it up and down the river (rather less striking, in fact, than the rest of it) we effectively recognize an adventurous era, a significant experience of mankind, a stretch of country that is capable of instilling in us something that can hardly be named in ordinary prose, but may only be guessed by the poet.

A bald eagle appeared and settled for a moment in a big cottonwood. Then he rose in the air and we ourselves seemed to feel a lift as we watched him soar upward on the air-currents near the bluff. He swerved downward again and we watched his shadow moving across the cliff--then up again, and he slanted off behind the hill.

Theodore Roosevelt National Memorial Park. That is the imposing title bestowed by Congress. I don't know who drew the boundaries, or why they were drawn as they are. The park is made up of three different pieces. The South

Area, containing park headquarters, abuts on highway 10 at Medora. It comprises a picturesque section of the badlands, with the Little Missouri running through it, and consists of [   ] acres. Northward, down the river, is the site of the Elk Horn [sic] Ranch, a small acreage dedicated to preserve that historic location. Still farther down river is the North Area, another rugged section of the badlands, containing [   ] acres.

As we looked over the area during these autumn days and contemplated the grasslands, the supply of browse, the thin line of trees, the forage resources contained within the park boundaries, we could have wished the area was a little bigger, that the two [main] areas were somehow connected. We discussed concepts such as biological units. We scrutinized the species of bushes present and judged their palatability for various "big game" species. We gratefully estimated the carrying capacity of some remnants of original grama grass prairie which had been included within the boundary. Bison? Mountain sheep? Elk? What would they do to the limited supply of red ozier dogwood, plum, cherry? They would have to be fenced in, and stray cattle fenced out, for farms adjoin the park on all sides and we can t have bison and elk running loose over the countryside.

We were thrilled to find flocks of sharp-tailed grouse, apparently thriving. What would reintroduced grazing and browsing animals [do] to the security for grouse? I was acutely conscious of the small population of such grouse [in] the National Elk Refuge in Wyoming some years ago, and how they dwindled year by year, until they disappeared. Had the intensive winter feeding of elk on this refuge, over a long period of years, affected the food supply of those grouse by destroying the willow growth?

Such are the considerations. Such is the problem in trying to keep some sort of biological balance in a national park of limited area. The natural vegetation is also a part of the biological assets. These bits of short grass prairie, for instance, in a land that is steadily going under the plow. When prairie has given way to plowed fields elsewhere, and has become but a memory in the minds of men, how precious then must be these fragments.

I pictured in my mind the future visitor to the badlands, we'll say the visitor who is attuned to the message [of] wild open country. I pictured him climbing up to a grassy plateau, and sitting there on a knoll to contemplate the scene. There would be the scent of the sod at his feet. He would look with interest at the curled heads of the grama grass, the grama grass of Roosevelt's day, the grama grass of the tumultuous days when this country was formed.

Here is history! Our visitor looks across the badlands--the broken, tumbled badlands, domes and bluffs and color banded rims. Traces of ligite coal are there, speaking of ages still farther back in time. And the colored [scoria?], the product of native clay baked by burning coal seams. Traces of petrified forest. A landscape of clay and sandstone, persistently, patiently carved by muddy water, through infinite ages, until these rugged land forms took shape, worthy of being declared a National Park by a modern Congress. Our visitor will visualize the broad undulating North Dakota plains, here in the west broken open and dissected to reveal for him the long Nature´s history of the State, which is elsewhere deeply hidden beneath plowed fields, and [the] dwelling[s] of the Dakota homeland.

The first morning we had gone up Munsen Creek, and came to a prairie dog town. At the far edge we saw two coyotes trotting about, and examination of some droppings we found revealed that they had previously fed on prairie dogs and wild plums. A few days later we saw a badger and coyote in another "dog town," and they had apparently nearly depopulated this prairie dog village. The badger glared at us before he disappeared down the enlarged burrow he had taken from a prairie dog. In the stream bottom nearby we found the tracks of a bobcat.

A guard in the North Area told us of seeing a badger, a coyote, and a bobcat in a prairie dog town. The bobcat had a prairie dog in its mouth. The acquisitive coyote made a run at him, but the bobcat ran up a tree a little way and calmly devoured his game. When he came down, the coyote again made a run at him and they disappeared in the woods. The badger had been nosing about at the far end of the "town."

These are the experiences this new park holds for the appreciative visitor who will quietly seek them out. These were the thoughts we had in mind as we went over the country day after day, sizing up range land, seeking proper habitat for mountain sheep in case they should be brought back, trying to anticipate the impact of one animal population on another, the impact of both on the plant life, and the impact of hordes of people on all of it. We tried to visualize as much of the historic animal life, restored as nearly as practicable, on a sustained basis, all within the boundary of land allowed by the act of Congress.

We were continually intrigued by the prairie dogs. We visualized mountain sheep restored to the area, at home once more on the pinnacles and bluffs overlooking [the] grassy bottom domain of the prairie dogs; bison lazily moving about on the adjacent bits of prairie. In short, our study was a mixture of routine biological study and intense personal enjoyment of what we found. After all, in a national park the end product is the enjoyment of the natural scene by people. Our studies and recommendations should necessarily contribute to those ends.

To me one of the most enjoyable experiences occurred on the last day of our stay. The superintendent had invited a group of people from the state, representatives of various organizations--[the] State Historical Society,

Soil Conservation Service, Fish and Wildlife Service, and particularly the North Dakota Game and Fish Commission. They were most enthusiastic about the prospects for the National Park. Heartening, indeed, was the assurance from the head of the Game and Fish Commission: "We are all for it. When you need help, just call on us."

I remembered what I had been told about the dedication on [June 4, 1949]. The people of North Dakota had turned out 30,000 strong, and the parking problem was something to be concerned about. Evidently North Dakota appreciates its National Park. When a people understands and cherishes a natural treasure, I believe they are in the frame of mind to get the most out of it in historical significance, enjoyment, and inspiration.

I like to remember one evening on the rim of the deeply chiseled valley in the North Area. We had been looking down on the winding course of the Little Missouri far below us, with its typical line of cottonwoods, and bordered by the typical badlands formations. I had thought of those high school days in Minnesota, when I had borrowed Roosevelt's books from the library. I remembered Frederic Remington's drawings, remembered the burning desire to find this western scene. Will the people of today, the people of tomorrow, continue to feel the pull of land that beckons to a sample of our country as it was, a country of space and beauty and a sense of freedom?

The sun went low and dusk was creeping over the valley below us. We watched that poetic quality of light envelop the cliffs and rims about us, and settle over the river bottom where we glimpsed the gleam of water in the bends.

Not a serrated mountain range here, not a mossy forest, not a lake studded paradise. Rather an open country; its trees are twisted and storm worn, and grow sparingly along the river banks. A raw country, a country in the making perhaps. This very fact, this character, the attributes of chiseled buttes and domes, the clay and the prairie grass, the eagle, the prairie dogs, deer, coyote; the flocks of grouse at the heads of the wooded draws--all these spell one phase of our west--not to be compared with different ones--to be taken and enjoyed for its own singular beauty and character. Ordinary country, but with an aura of the west--something that drew Roosevelt, the adventurous ones.

Figure 2.1.   Land management and constraints, South Unit

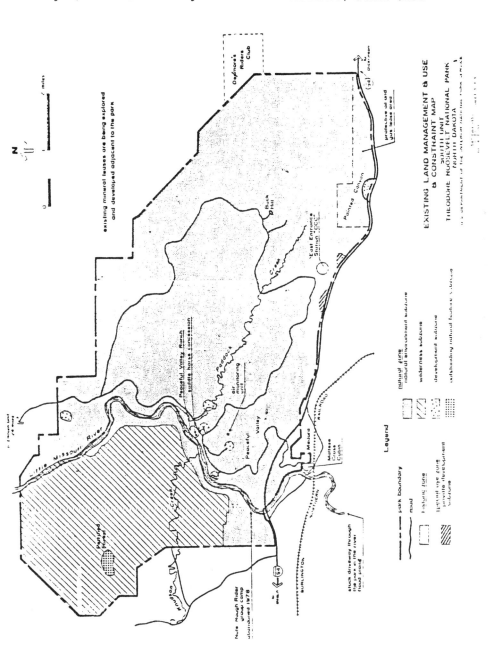

Figure 2.2. Land management and constraints, Elkhorn Unit

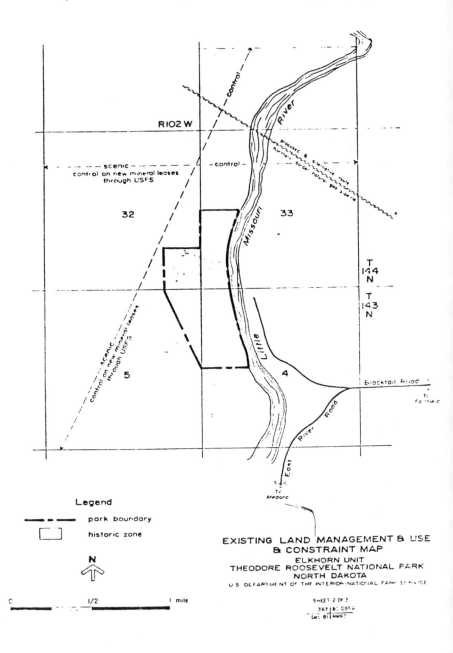

R102 W

scenic
control on new mineral leases
through USFS

control

process & distribute route
Northern border natural gas pipeline

32

33

Missouri River

scenic
control on new mineral leases
through USFS

T
144
N

T
143
N

Little

5

4

Blacktail Road

To
Fairfield

River Road

East

To
Medora

Legend

— · — · — park boundary

☐ historic zone

N
△

EXISTING LAND MANAGEMENT & USE
& CONSTRAINT MAP
ELKHORN UNIT
THEODORE ROOSEVELT NATIONAL PARK
NORTH DAKOTA
U S DEPARTMENT OF THE INTERIOR NATIONAL PARK SERVICE

0   1/2   1 mile

SHEET 2 OF 2
367 80 035A
Det 81 HMEC

igure 2.3. Land management and constraints, North Unit

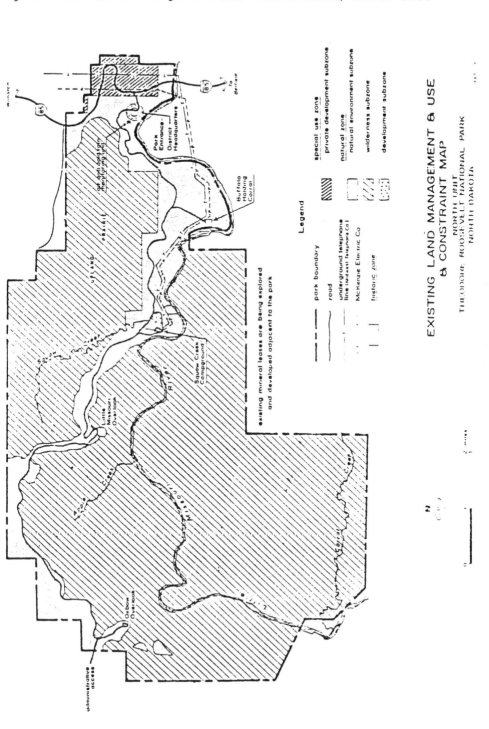

Legend

park boundary

road

underground telephone
line (Midwest Telephone Co)

McKenzie Electric Co

historic zone

special use zone
private development subzone

natural zone
natural environment subzone

wilderness subzone

development subzone

EXISTING LAND MANAGEMENT & USE
& CONSTRAINT MAP
NORTH UNIT
THEODORE ROOSEVELT NATIONAL PARK
NORTH DAKOTA

Figure 3.1. Location, Williston Basin

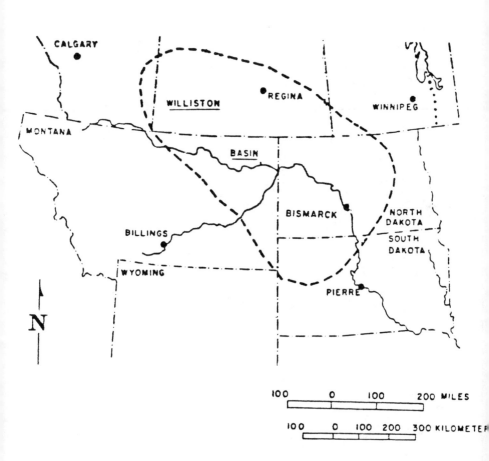

Figure 3.2. Major geologic features, Williston Basin

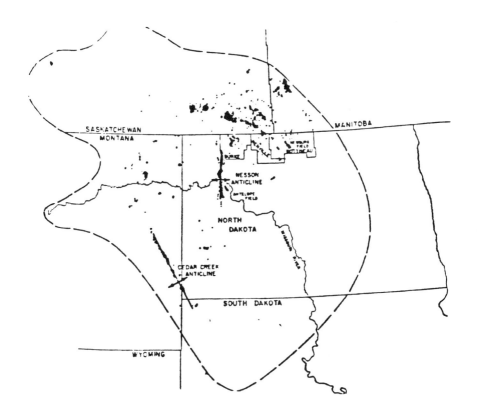

Figure 3.3. Oil traps

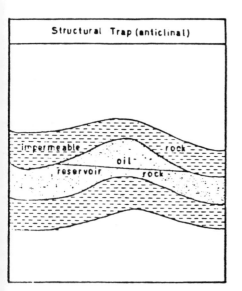

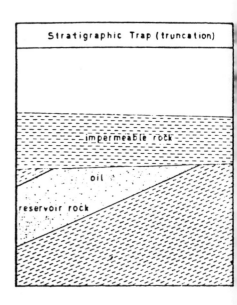

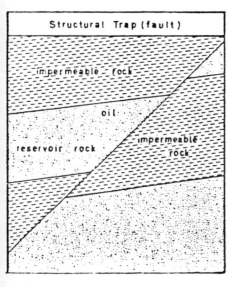

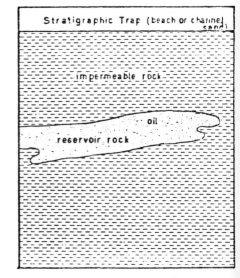

Figure 3.4. Annual crude oil production, North Dakota, 1951-1981

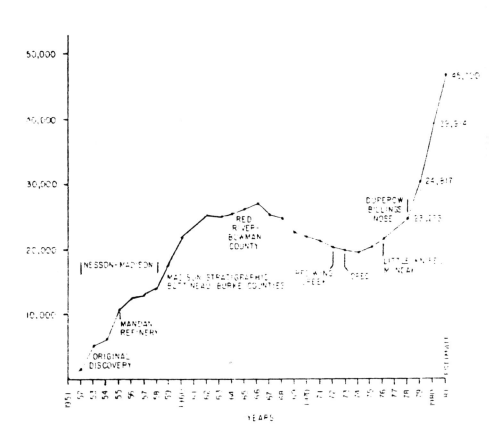

Figure 3.5.   Total number of wells drilled annually, North
               Dakota, 1951-1981

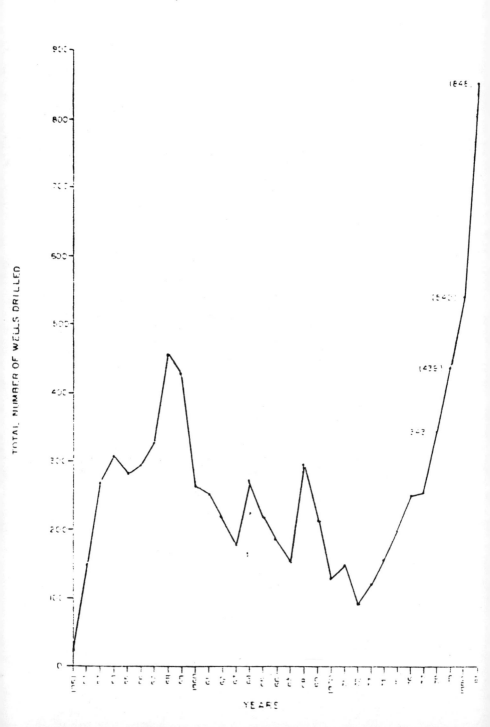

Figure 3.6.   North Dakota oil fields through 1980 with new
               discoveries made during 1981

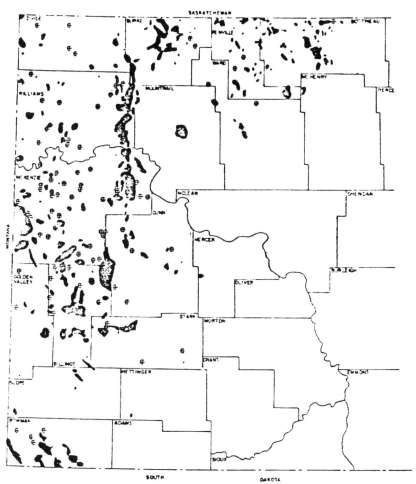

⊕ - NEW FIELD DISCOVERIES - 1981

Figure 3.7. Major structural features of the Williston Basin in western North Dakota and South Dakota, eastern Montana, and northeastern Wyoming

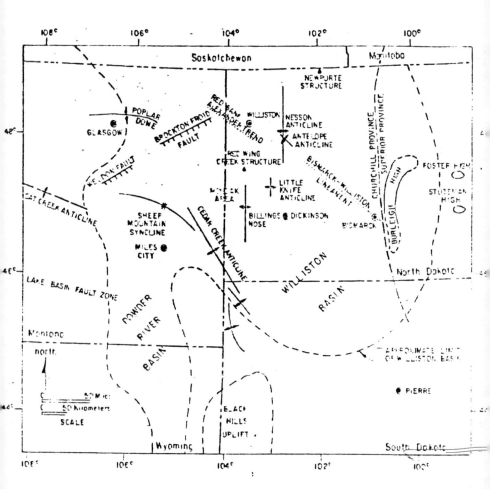

Figure 4.1.   Protective lease stipulations, Theodore Roosevelt
National Park, lease sale of 18 November 1974

THEODORE ROOSEVELT NATIONAL MEMORIAL PARK LANDS

Billings County, North Dakota

SPECIAL STIPULATIONS

As a condition precedent to issuance of a PROTECTIVE OIL AND GAS
LEASE covering lands in the South Unit, Theodore Roosevelt
National Memorial Park, I hereby agree to the following Special
Stipulations to be made a part of the lease:

(1)   No occupancy of the surface is authorized under the
      lease. Lessee may, however, explore for oil and gas by
      directional drilling from lands outside of the Park
      providing such drilling will not result in any
      pollution or adverse environmental impact on the area
      under lease or on surrounding Park administered lands.

(2)   The Superintendent, Theodore Roosevelt National
      Memorial Park, or his designee, shall be afforded the
      opportunity to inspect the location(s) of drill sites
      proposed under lease prior to any surface related
      disturbances. Drill sites and production related phase
      improvements shall be located so as to minimize adverse
      visual impacts from lands included within the boundary
      of the Theodore Roosevelt National Memorial Park.

(3)   Lessee is required to screen from public view and/or
      paint all aboveground [sic] production related
      improvements associated with the lease if such proposed
      facilities, in the opinion of the Superintendent,
      Theodore Roosevelt National Memorial Park, or his
      designee, would impair the scenic and aesthetic values
      of lands under lease or surrounding park lands. If
      facilities are painted, an appropriate color will be
      selected which will harmonize with the surrounding
      environment. The cost of the screening and/or painting
      shall be borne by the lessee.

(4)   Lessee shall employ measures during drilling and
      subsequent production phases of lease which will
      minimize noise and prevent degradation of air quality.

It is understood that these special stipulations will be
additions to stipulations and restrictions contained in
Protective Lease Form 3120-1 [the standard lease form].

Figure 4.2. Slant drilling at Theodore Roosevelt National Park

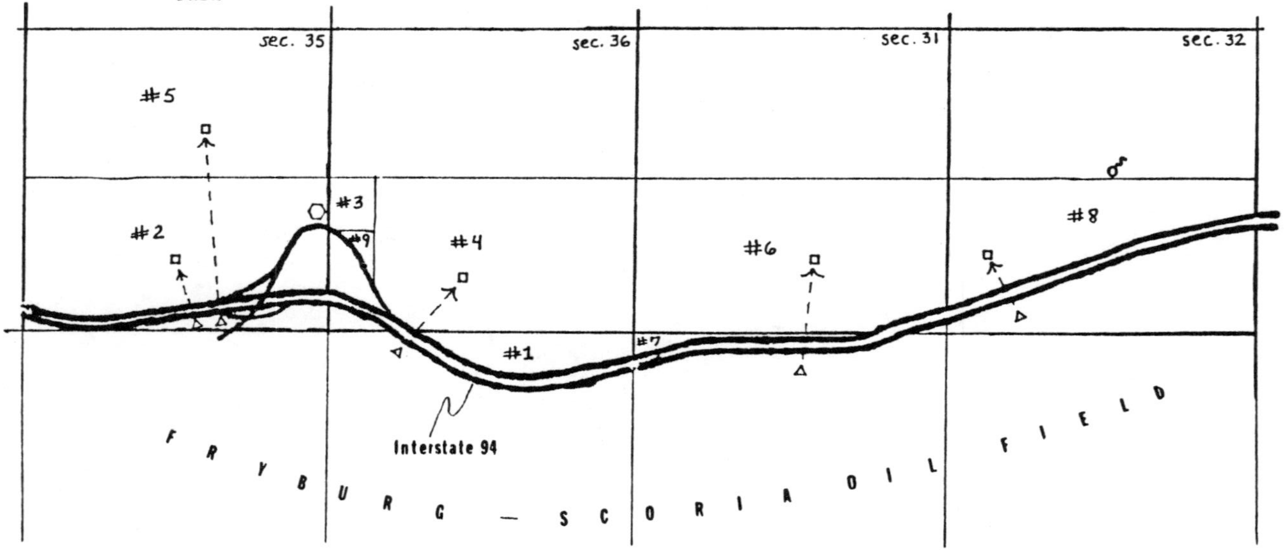

Key

□ producing parcels
△ wellheads
⬡ Painted Canyon Visitor Center
♂ Flowing spring
↙-- approximate direction of drilling

Parcel Number	Size in Acres
1	28.02
2	220.23
3	27.80
4	223.89
5	320.00
6	318.21
7	6.27
8	133.26
9	0.31
TOTAL	1287.99

Table 5.1. Integral vistas associated with Theodore Roosevelt National Park

Observation Point	View Angle	Key Feature	Also Viewed From
Badlands Overlook (South Unit)	353°-7°	badlands terrain	Johnson's Plateau, Painted Canyon, Ridgeline Nature Trail, Buck Hill
Bentonitic Clay (North Unit)	64°-94°	Long X Divide, Killdeer Mountains	Shelter Overlook
Boicourt--South (South Unit)	185°-248°	Bullion Butte, Square Butte	Buck Hill, Ridgeline Nature Trail, Johnson's Plateau
Boicourt--West (South Unit)	267°-298°	Camel's Hump, Twin Buttes	Ridgeline Nature Trail, Buck Hill
Buck Hill (South Unit)	0°-360°	Sentinel Butte, Square Butte, Camel's Hump, Twin Buttes	Painted Canyon, Ridgeline Nature Trail, Johnson's Plateau, Badlands Overlook, Boicourt Ridge
Elkhorn Ranch Site (Elkhorn Unit)	-------	View of surrounding hills	
Johnson's Plateau-- North (South Unit)	358°-54°	North Dakota badlands	Badlands Overlook, Ridgeline Nature Trail, Buck Hill, Painted Canyon
Johnson's Plateau-- South (South Unit)	117°-261°	Chateau de Mores, Bullion Butte, Square Butte, Sentinel Butte	Buck Hill, Ridgeline Nature Trail, Boicourt Ridge
Little Missouri (North Unit)	78°-110°	Custer National Grassland Plateau	Shelter Overlook
Man and Grass (North Unit)	226°-14°	Stocke Butte, Little Missouri National Grasslands	
Medora Overlook (South Unit)	149°-250°	Maltese Cross Cabin, Chateau de Mores, Little Missouri town site	
Oxbow Overlook (North Unit)	65°-224°	Killdeer Mountains, Achenbach Hills, Sperati Point	
Painted Canyon (South Unit)	303°-0°	Buck Hill, Little Missouri National Grasslands	Ridgeline Nature Trail, Boicourt Ridge, Badlands Overlook
Ridgeline Nature Trail (South Unit)	0°-360°	Bullion Butte, Square Butte, Sentinel Butte, Camel's Hump, Twin Buttes	Johnson's Plateau, Buck Hill, Painted Canyon, Boicourt Ridge

Table 6.1. Consumption of Class I sulfur dioxide PSD
            increment, Theodore Roosevelt National Park

Order in Which Application Received	Name of Plant (Owner)	Emission of Sulfur Dioxide in $\mu g/m^3$	Cumulative Percentage of Increment Consumed
1	Coal Creek (UPA/CPA)	1.4	28%
2	Coyote #1 (Montana-Dakota Utilities)	0.7	42%
3	ANG (American Natural Gas)	1.6	74%
4	Antelope Valley #1 (Basin Electric Power Cooperative)	2.0	114%
5	Antelope Valley #2 (Basin Electric Power Cooperative)	2.0	154%

Figure 6.1. Relationship of sulfur-dioxide increment-consuming
sources to Theodore Roosevelt National Park
("Smokestack Triangle")

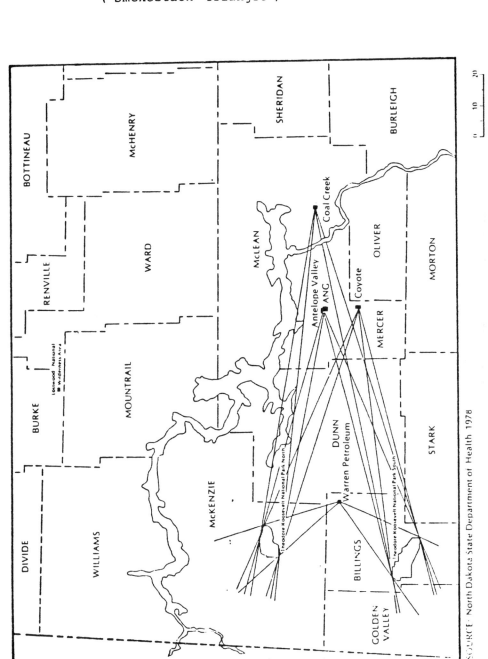

SOURCE: North Dakota State Department of Health 1978

Figure 6.2. Fort Union Coal Region study area and tract locations

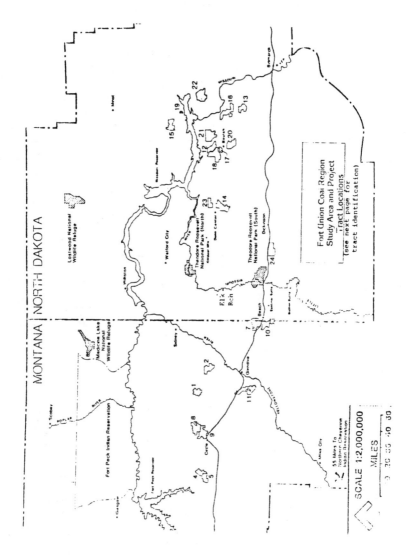

Figure 6.2 (cont'd). Tract identification, Fort Union Coal Region

	Tract	Distance to nearest unit of Theodore Roosevelt National Park in miles (kilometers)
1.	Bloomfield	76 (122)
2.	Burns Creek	57 (92)
3.	Central Bloomfield	n/a
4.	Circle West I	118 (190)
5.	Circle West II	125 (201)
6.	Circle West III	n/a
7.	North Wibaux-Beach	22 (35)
8.	Redwater I	95 (153)
9.	Redwater II	100 (161)
10.	South Wibaux-Beach	24 (39)
11.	Southwest Glendive	63 (101)
12.	Antelope	75 (121)
13.	Center	104 (167)
14.	Dunn Center	43 (69)
15.	Garrison	89 (143)
16.	Glenharold	100 (161)
17.	North Beulah	74 (119)
18.	Renner	66 (106)
19.	Sakakawea	93 (150)
20.	Schoolhouse	79 (127)
21.	Truax	83 (134)
22.	Underwood	107 (172)
23.	Werner	40 (64)
24.	Zenith	10 (16)

n/a--not available

SOURCE: Air Quality Information Supplemental to the Fort Union EIS

Table 9.1. Buffalo round-ups, Theodore Roosevelt National Park, 1962-1985

Year	Number	Destination
1962	20	transfer to North Unit
1963	25	Badlands NM (SD)
1964	25	Badlands NM (SD)
	12	Grand Teton NP (WY)
1965	20	Fort Lathrop State Park (CO)
1966	21	Fort Hall IR (ID)
1967	20*	Fort Wingate (NM)
	1*	Fort Yates -- Standing Rock IR (ND)
1968	22	Fort Lathrop State Park (CO)
	2	Williston (ND) Zoo
	10*	Colorado State Parks Dept., Denver
	4**	Fort Berthold IR (ND)
1969	20	Land Between the Lakes State Park (KY)
	1**	Standing Rock IR (ND/SD)
	3**	Bureau of Indian Affairs
	3**	Mandaree tribe, Fort Berthold IR (ND)
1970	25	Pine Ridge IR (SD)
	18	Standing Rock IR (ND/SD)
	30	Colorado State Park System
	5**	Fort Berthold IR (ND)
	7**	Bureau of Indian Affairs
1972	70	Crow Agency, Crow IR (MT)
1973	25	Crow Agency, Crow IR (MT)
	25	Pine Ridge IR (SD)
1975	18*	Crow Agency, Crow IR (MT)
	9*	Standing Rock IR (ND/SD)
	17*	Rosebud Sioux tribe (SD)
	20	Cheyenne-Arapahoe tribe
	10	Kalispell tribe (MT)
	10	Round Valley tribe
	12	Kaw tribe (OK)
	18	Cheyenne River Sioux tribe (SD)
	15	Oglala Sioux tribe (SD)
	12	Sisseton-Wahpeton Sioux tribe (ND/SD)
	20	Otoe-Missouria tribe (OK)

able 9.1 (cont'd)

Year	Number	Location
1977	26*	Fort Hall IR (ID)
	12*	Fort Belknap IR (MT)
	20*	Keweenaw Bay tribe, L'Anse IR (MI)
	13*	Rocky Boys IR (MT)
	1*	Williston (ND) zoo
1980	57	Cheyenne Agency (SD)
	31	Horton Agency (KS)
	27	North Cheyenne IR (MT)
	27	Crow Agency, Crow IR (MT)
	27	Flathead IR (MT)
	27	Blackfeet IR (MT)
	23*	Rocky Boys IR (MT)
	23*	Jicarilla Apache IR (NM)
1985	56*	Fort Berthold IR (ND)

* = from North Unit
** = animals killed upon request

estinations:

    Indian entities -- 758
    states and state parks -- 102
    Zoos -- 3
    other NPS areas -- 62
    intra-park transfers -- 20

)TAL -- 945

Table 10.1. List of Classified Structures, Theodore Roosevelt National Park

Name, Location, Date Built	Description	Ultimate Level of Treatment
old east entrance station, South Unit (1938)	separate office/ station, privy, & extended walls (stone)	adaptive use with preservation
main ranch house, Peaceful Valley Ranch, South Unit (1885, main house)	frame clapboard house with log & timber additions (wood)	adaptive use of interior with preservation
bunkhouse, Peaceful Valley Ranch, South Unit (1925, bunkhouse)	pine walls with frame addition & scoria roof (pine log)	adaptive use of interior with preservation
barn and equestrian center, Peaceful Valley Ranch, South Unit (1904, barn)	pine log & timber walls with new corral and and paddock (pine log)	adaptive use with preservation
Maltese Cross cabin, South Unit (1884, restored 1960-61, 1978)	hand-hewn railroad ties (pine)	adaptive use with preservation
Civilian Conservation Corps camp tender's cabin, North Unit (1938, remodeled as residence 1953)	board & batten (wood)	removal
picnic shelters (2), North Unit (1938)	scoria foundation, pole uprights, open wall, fireplace (scoria, sandstone, log)	continued use
overlook shelter, North Unit (ca. 1935-38)	low stone walls, tapered piers supporting log roof (sandstone, log)	continued use
entrance signs (3), North Unit (2) and South Unit (1) (1938)	stone with wrought- iron lettering and artwork (ashlar sandstone)	continued use

SOURCES: Richard A. Strait (Assoc. Reg. Dir., RMRO) to Superintendents of region, memorandum, 12 May 1983 (Medora: THRO-A); and "CRM Plan," 46-47.

List current to May 1983.

Table 11.1. Visitation, Theodore Roosevelt National Park,
            1948-1984

1948 --	23,513
1949 --	81,965
1950 --	71,000
1951 --	81,860
1952 --	127,238
1953 --	120,804
1954 --	133,570
1955 --	125,112
1956 --	154,694
1957 --	128,975
1958 --	172,017
1959 --	192,317
1960 --	235,251
1961 --	250,479
1962 --	266,084
1963 --	257,904
1964 --	282,970
1965 --	260,848
1966 --	500,338
1967 --	537,258
1968 --	562,378
1969 --	658,654
1970 --	679,980
1971 --	710,289
1972 --	1,001,957
1973 --	852,829
1974 --	701,696
1975 --	803,993
1976 --	940,721
1977 --	822,495
1978 --	833,306
1979 --	599,122
1980 --	603,210
1981 --	710,349
1982 --	684,490
1983 --	422,594
1984 --	368,615

SOURCES: Strand, 58-59; 1980 North Dakota State Comprehensive
          Outdoor Recreation Plan (Bismarck: North Dakota
          Parks and Recreation Dept., 1980); National Park
          Service Statistical Abstract, 1982 (Washington, DC:
          NPS, 1983); Hellickson to author, 18 October 1985.